JEAN-LUC MARION

Jean-Luc Marion is one of the leading Catholic thinkers of our times: a formidable authority on Descartes and a major scholar in the philosophy of religion.

This book presents a concise, accessible, and engaging introduction to the theology of Jean-Luc Marion. Described as one of the leading thinkers of his generation, Marion's take on the postmodern is richly enhanced by his expertise in patristic and mystical theology, phenomenology, and modern philosophy. In this first introduction to Marion's thought, Robyn Horner provides the essential background to Marion's work, as well as analysing the most significant themes for contemporary theology. This book serves as an ideal starting point for students of theology and philosophy, as well as for non-specialists seeking to further their knowledge of cutting-edge thinking in contemporary theology.

To B and E

Jean-Luc Marion

A *Theo*-logical Introduction

ROBYN HORNER

ASHGATE

Excerpts from: *Jean-Luc Marion, Prolegomena to Charity*, trans. Stephen Lewis, copyright © 1991, Éditions de la Différence, English translation © 2002 Fordham University Press; *Jean-Luc Marion, Being Given: Toward a Phenomenology of Givenness*, copyright © 1997, Presses Universitaires de France, English translation © 2002 by the Board of Trustees of the Leland Stanford Jr. University; *Jean-Luc Marion, In Excess: Studies of Saturated Phenomena*, trans. Robyn Horner and Vincent Berrand, copyright © 2001, Presses Universitaire de France, English translation © 2002 Fordham University Press.

Published by
Ashgate Publishing Limited
Gower House
Croft Road
Aldershot
Hants GU11 3HR
England

Ashgate Publishing Company
Suite 420
101 Cherry Street
Burlington
VT 05401-4405
USA

Ashgate website: http://www.ashgate.com

British Library Cataloguing in Publication Data
Horner, Robyn
    Jean-Luc Marion: A Theo-logical Introduction.
    1. Marion, Jean-Luc, 1946–. 2. Theology.
    I. Title.
    230'.092

Library of Congress Cataloging-in-Publication Data
Horner, Robyn
    Jean-Luc Marion: A Theo-logical Introduction /
    Robyn Horner.
        p.   cm.
    Includes bibliographical references and index.
    1. Marion, Jean-Luc, 1946–. I. Title
    BX4705.M3987H67   2005
    194–dc22

                                                                            2004024413

    ISBN 0 7546 3660 7 (hbk)
    ISBN 0 7546 3661 5 (pbk)

Typeset by IML Typogrpahers, Birkenhead, Merseyside
Printed and bound in Great Britain by MPG Books Ltd. Bodmin

Contents

Acknowledgements

This work has been enabled by the encouragement of Kevin Hart, Gary Bouma, and John Caputo, and the support of grants from the Faculty of Arts at Monash University in 1999 and 2001, the Australian Research Council in 2000, and Australian Catholic University in 2002 and 2003. It has been assisted by the generous engagement of Jean-Luc Marion, conversations with international colleagues, especially Stijn Van den Bossche, and those closer to home, particularly Stephen Curkpatrick. In its final stages, it has been shaped by Stephen's insightful criticism, as well as by the very helpful comments of Shane Mackinlay. It bears the traces of those who have contributed as occasional research assistants to the project, Mark Manolopoulos and Glenn Morrison, and those who assisted with editing, including Margaret Blakeney. But this work has ultimately been made possible by the extraordinary love of my family and friends, including Bosco and Julie, whose support in all manner of ways is what gives me the freedom to travel for research, and the space, time, and confidence to write. In these last months, it has been newly inspired by our own saturated phenomenon, whose heart I first saw beat like a tiny star, and whose face we await with indescribable joy.

Robyn Horner
April 2004

Introduction

How is Christian theology to have a place in twenty-first-century thought? Having reconciled itself—at times uneasily—to the modern, how is it to deal with the questions raised by the postmodern? These questions emerge from a cluster of philosophical issues concerning the possible signification of pure transcendence or alterity, the failure of presentation (including absence as a mode of presentation), the construction of reality in and through language, the collapse of the self-certain subject, the relativisation of authority, and, more recently in particular, the apparent cultural disintegration of many Christian symbols. In the face of issues such as these, how does it remain possible to speak about God? It seems that the simple reassertion of theological assurance is no longer enough, neither in the form of a hyper-theological guarantee of reason, nor in the form of a fideistic claim to be able to override human reason or to function in spite of it. For these issues go to the heart of the basic presupposition of all theology—natural, as well as revealed—that its object (who can never be made an object) can somehow be known (meant or contextualised) *as such*. They put in question, in other words, the commitment of theology to a fundamentally realist ontology.

Jean-Luc Marion is one contemporary thinker who is uniquely qualified to respond to this problem. As a philosopher, he has an encyclopaedic knowledge of the modern, framed both by a thorough understanding of its relationship to the past and an acute awareness of the ways in which it is pushed to its limits in the postmodern. Yet he can also be considered a theologian, not only given his more strictly theological writings, but to the extent that theological themes frequently emerge in counterpoint to philosophical ones in his major works, and clearly mark out for him much higher limits for the possibility of meaning. Marion is an important thinker not because he has all the answers, but because of his profound understanding of the questions. He is significant for theology because he can traverse the terrain of the postmodern without caricature, while having a stake in the question of faith. Marion is most valuable because he comes back, again and again, to the question of the relationship between philosophy and theology, to the possibility of a thought of God that can serve as an adequate context for that which he also accepts unconditionally as primary and known only because revealed. In fine, Marion's work represents a serious starting-point for those who recognise the depth of the challenges raised by the postmodern and seek to think theology *otherwise*.

The present text has two main aims. First, it is designed to introduce Marion's work and the contexts from which it has emerged. There is no doubt that appropriating Marion's thought has been made a complex task by a number of factors. Until recently, very little of his work was available in English. It draws in large part upon debates that have a history in continental philosophy and that are conceptually quite difficult. Without appreciating the background, language, progress, and status of these debates, relevant texts are sometimes too readily dismissed by Anglophones with claims that they make use of "jargon" or are impenetrable (and therefore "nonsensical"). Further, Marion's writing style is particularly taxing. It is very classical, a feature that is difficult to remove in translation while attempting to remain faithful to his text, and tends to progress in spiral rather than linear fashion, which means that it is sometimes initially difficult to distinguish between his exposition of others' ideas and his own, frequently contrasting, views. His brilliance as a philosopher is witnessed in his ability to call upon extremely fine detail from the arguments of others; this brilliance, however, also makes for hard work on the part of the reader, who needs to be able to fill in the conceptual gaps, so to speak. Without diluting the force or originality of his thought, in the present work I hope to give enough of a sense of it in its various contexts to encourage the reader to take it on for her or himself.

A second aim for this text is to suggest a way of understanding what Marion is trying to achieve, when his work is considered as a whole. This is particularly difficult to do while a thinker is still living. But while his different strands of specialisation can be seen to stand independently (theology, Descartes, phenomenology, the history of philosophy), they also seem to converge to form the fabric of a much larger project. It is my argument that Marion ultimately seeks to show that there is a way forward for thought beyond metaphysics. Initially, he maintains that it is theology that best offers that way forward. Nevertheless, the leap from metaphysics to a (non-metaphysical) theology appears too much like the sheer imposition of dogma—and the consequent repetition of metaphysics at a new level. In a second phase of writing, Marion uses phenomenology to push the boundaries of metaphysics, and is then able better to contextualise theology as a non-metaphysical possibility. The two phases remain interconnected, which is why his non-theological critics generally remain suspicious about the extent to which dogma actually drives Marion's philosophical agenda, and why it is difficult to assess the ultimate success of his project. At the same time, however, in observing the process we learn a great deal about the problems of metaphysics, and why theology is not well served by a naïve dismissal of the concerns of the postmodern (or even those of the modern, with reference to so-called "radical orthodoxy"). As a result of Marion's characterisation of the possibility of theology there are momentous implications for the thinking of fundamental theological issues such as revelation and religious experience. A theology that takes postmodern questions seriously will find itself newly confronted by hermeneutics and faith, no longer able to settle secure with absolutes, with more questions than answers, and signed up for a pilgrimage without confirmed destination.

In order to facilitate the achievement of my two aims the book is structured in four parts. Part I begins with a brief introduction to Marion's career and major works. Then follow three chapters designed to situate Marion in relation to the postmodern, which means, inevitably, also sketching the basic lines of the argument with regard to metaphysics, and outlining phenomenology as a response to metaphysics. Part II gives an overview of Marion's attempts to overcome metaphysics with theology. In Chapters 5 and 6, I explore four ways in which Marion generally attempts to think God otherwise than metaphysically, as distance, icon, love, and gift. Chapters 7 and 8 take the form of detailed studies of two of Marion's most important works: *On Descartes' Metaphysical Prism* and *God Without Being*. Using Descartes to illustrate the potential in the modern to resist metaphysics, and Heidegger to show another possibility for non-metaphysical thought, Marion nevertheless concludes each of these books with the claim that theology renders metaphysics more completely destitute than either of these approaches. With the transition to Part III, however, it becomes clear that the destitution of metaphysics by theology has been imposed upon thought rather than argued. In Part III, with which my argument is completed, I move to consider Marion's renewal of phenomenology. With his saturated phenomenon he attempts to show the possibilities within phenomenology to open onto thought that is excessive, which gives theology a new philosophical context. I then look at his examination of love, which reintegrates his theological response to metaphysics with the phenomenological. The appendices of the text contain as complete a primary and secondary bibliography of Marion as I have been able to collect, which constitutes an invitation to the reader to go deeper with Marion than an introductory text will allow. A number of short extracts from Marion's texts are then included to initiate that process. Throughout this volume, existing translations have been used except as otherwise noted in the footnotes. All emphases in quotations are original unless otherwise indicated.

This work will serve different readers in very different ways. For those unfamiliar with some of the issues taken up in continental philosophy, Part I provides signposts that will at least make it possible to situate some of the ideas described in subsequent parts of the book. Part I will not be necessary reading, however, for those already well versed in phenomenology and poststructuralist theory. Parts II and III unfold in demonstration of my argument that Marion first tries to overcome metaphysics with theology, but subsequently attempts to do this by way of a phenomenology that is nevertheless open to the theological. Yet these chapters also have a different function. In keeping with the introductory nature of the text, each chapter serves to summarise Marion's thinking on particular themes, paying close attention to his works. For this reason, these chapters are frequently very dense in texture, and in many ways each stands on its own as a reference with regard to his sources and to the chronological development of his ideas. Additionally, quite apart from the argument—often left playing in the margins— about the extent to which Marion overcomes or simply repeats metaphysics, Part II could be accessed as a guide to his theology, and Part III as a guide to his phenomenology. The need for an introductory volume in this style arises from the sheer difficulty, quantity, and diversity of Marion's work, which has not previously been brought together in any systematic way, and especially not with a view to exploring the theological implications of the full range of his thought. At the same time, however, that very difficulty, quantity, and diversity contribute to an introductory text that is often highly concentrated and can function only within a complex web of associations. For this, I apologise to the reader in advance. It must finally be noted that while Jean-Luc Marion has been very helpful to me in the preparation of this text by making himself available for consultation, any errors in it are mine, not his. I freely admit that I cannot hope to do him justice, for which I beg his forgiveness.

PART I
SITUATING MARION

Chapter 1

Contexts

Jean-Luc Marion was born in Meudon, on the outskirts of Paris, in 1946. The son of an engineer and a teacher, Marion initially pursued undergraduate studies in the humanities at what was then the University of Nanterre, and subsequently at the Sorbonne, before deciding to become a professional philosopher. This choice eventually led to his being accepted at the highly exclusive École Normale Supérieure in the Rue d'Ulm in Paris, where entry is based on competitive examination, and where he was taught by several of the intellectual giants of the day, including Louis Althusser, Gilles Deleuze, and a young Jacques Derrida. At the same time, Marion's deep interest in theology was privately cultivated under the personal influence of theologians such as Louis Bouyer, Jean Daniélou, Henri de Lubac and Hans Urs von Balthasar, and he read widely in this area. Marion's life as a student coincided with a vigorous political climate in France. In 1968, he, like so many others, was caught up in the student riots, and continues to mark those years as some of the most important and formative in his life.[1]

In 1970, Marion married a school-teacher, Corinne Nicolas, and their two sons were born in 1973 and 1975 respectively. From 1972 until 1980, he prepared his *Agrégé de Philosophie, Doctorat d'État* on the early thought of Descartes, while working as an assistant lecturer at the Sorbonne, and contributing as a member of *L'équipe Descartes*.[2] During that time, Marion published what he describes as a first triptych on Descartes: *Sur l'ontologie grise de Descartes* (1975); the *Index des 'Regulae ad Directionem Ingenii' de René Descartes*, with Jean-Robert Armogathe (1976); and an annotated translation: *René Descartes. Règles utiles et claires pour la direction de l'esprit en la recherche de la vérité* (1977).[3] At the same time,

---

[1] See the preface to the English edition in Jean-Luc Marion, *God Without Being* (Chicago: University of Chicago Press, 1991) xix–xxv, xix. The French original of *God Without Being* to which I will refer throughout the present text is *Dieu sans l'être. Hors-texte*, Rev. ed. (1982. Paris: Presses Universitaires de France, 1991). A new edition by Presses Universitaires de France was released in 2002.

[2] The *Équipe Descartes*, founded in 1973 under Pierre Costabel, is a group of scholars working in conjunction with the *Centre National de la Recherche Scientifique* who analyse published research on Descartes.

[3] Daniel Garber notes that *grise* is to be translated as "hidden," rather than "grey," in his Foreword to Marion's *Cartesian Questions: Method and Metaphysics* (Chicago: University of Chicago Press, 1999) ix–xiii, ix. Jean-Luc Marion, *Sur l'ontologie grise de Descartes. Science cartésienne et savoir aristotélicien dans les 'Regulae'*, 3rd ed. (Paris: J. Vrin, 1993); Jean-Luc Marion and J.-R. Armogathe, eds., *Index des 'Regulae ad directionem ingenii' de René Descartes* (Rome: Edizioni dell'Ateneo, 1976); Jean-Luc Marion and Pierre Costabel, eds., *René Descartes. Règles utiles et claires pour la direction de l'esprit en la recherche de la vérité* (La Haye: Martinus Nijhoff, 1977).

however, Marion was also developing a name for himself as a theologian, having published his first articles in *Résurrection* in 1968. *Résurrection* was later to be incorporated into the *Révue catholique internationale Communio*, the French edition of which Marion was to be one of the founding editors, at the behest of none other than the prominent Swiss theologian, Balthasar. This association is not without significance, since it has been argued that *Communio* epitomises neo-conservative Catholicism, and that Marion represents a conservative push within the Church. Jean-Louis Schlegel, for example, observes of the journal:

> Despite the denials of *Communio*, the review has no doubt been founded as a counterpoint to another, more critical, international theological review, *Concilium*. *Communio* is dedicated to making an intellectual (and unconditional) defence of "roman" or "official" catholicism in its diverse aspects (dogmatics, moral theology, ecclesiology, discipline …).[4]

Schlegel's comment is made in the context of an examination of Marion's later work, *Dieu sans l'être* [*God Without Being*], and some years after, David Tracy responds to accusations of theological conservatism by Marion in the Foreword to the English edition of the same:

> In this book, Marion has moved the discussion of the proper model for contemporary theology and philosophy beyond the usual conservative-liberal impasse (for example, in Catholic terms in France and elsewhere, the Concilium-Communio differences). On some ecclesial issues (witness Marion's intriguing reflections here on bishops as theologians), his sympathies are clearly with the Catholic journal *Communio* and not (as are mine) with *Concilium*. What is stunning and heartening in this text, however, is the absence of any inner-ecclesial polemics…[5]

With the contributions both to *Résurrection* and to a number of other journals through the 1970s, Marion indicates the breadth of his theological and philosophical interests. There are articles on revelation, incarnation, and eucharist; examinations of aspects of Augustine, Maximus the Confessor, and Denys the Areopagite (hereafter Denys); studies of hermeneutics, iconography, the "death of God," and, of course, Descartes. Analyses of patristic texts reflect Marion's involvement with the renewal in France during the twentieth century of interest in this area, and his acknowledged indebtedness not only to de Lubac and Daniélou, but also to Jacques Maritain and Étienne Gilson. Serving to bring many of Marion's diverse interests together is his first full-scale theological work, *L'idole et la distance: cinq études* [*The Idol and Distance: Five Studies*], published by Grasset in 1977.[6] It remains a groundbreaking book; ambitious in scope, it represents a serious

---

[4] Jean-Louis Schlegel, "*Dieu sans l'être*. À propos de J.-L. Marion," *Esprit.* (1984): 26–36, 26n1.

[5] Tracy, "Foreword," *God Without Being* ix–xv, xv. Tracy is a member of the editorial board of *Concilium*.

[6] Jean-Luc Marion, *L'idole et la distance: cinq études* (Paris: B. Grasset, 1977); *The Idol and Distance: Five Studies*, trans. Thomas A. Carlson, Perspectives in Continental Philosophy, ed. John D. Caputo (New York: Fordham University Press, 2001).

attempt to think theologically in the wake of Friedrich Nietzsche and Martin Heidegger, with an eye to contemporary directions in the works of Derrida and Emmanuel Lévinas, but with reference to theological classics, including the works of Denys and Gregory of Nyssa. Such a genuine engagement of theology with the full spectrum of European philosophy is rare. This marks a particular contribution of Marion to the development of theology: his extraordinary knowledge of the history of philosophy, including, in particular, its twentieth-century manifestations, means that his dialogue with Christian tradition is extraordinarily rich. Of *The Idol and Distance*, Stanislas Breton comments: "I see here for my part the highest 'figure' of a certain medium of thought, where what one calls 'philosophy' and 'theology' exchange their 'idioms' with neither confusion nor separation ...".[7]

Having received his doctorate in 1980, Marion's first subsequent posting was at the University of Poitiers, some distance to the south-west of Paris, to which he commuted weekly. One of Europe's older universities (it was founded in 1431), Poitiers has the distinction of being the *alma mater* of Descartes himself.[8] But there is a further connection with Poitiers that deepens the significance of Marion's appointment: Lévinas taught there between 1963 and 1967, and remarkably, from this point on Marion has followed in Lévinas' footsteps, at least in an institutional sense. It was in this context that Marion completed his next volume on Descartes, this time with a theological focus: *Sur la théologie blanche de Descartes*.[9] Shortly after the appearance of this work, the French edition of *God Without Being* also hit the shelves, and Marion's controversial place in the history of theology was assured.[10]

By that time Marion already had something of an international reputation, having been invited to speak in several European countries as well as in South America. In Europe he was a recognised Cartesian scholar, and his work on Heidegger had been tested in a forum that involved dialogue with those beyond the French-speaking world.[11] But it was in the early to middle 1980s that Marion's career really began to flourish in every respect, that is to say, not only because of *God Without Being*, but in terms of a number of his intellectual interests: in this case, Descartes, the history of philosophy, and the intersections of philosophy with theology. It was at this point

---

[7] Stanislas Breton, *Archives de Philosophie* 43 (1980): 152–57, 152.

[8] Marion notes the discovery by Jean-Robert Armogathe and Vincent Carraud of Descartes' doctoral thesis, defended in 1616 at Poitiers. Jean-Luc Marion, *On Descartes' Metaphysical Prism: The Constitution and the Limits of Onto-theo-logy in Cartesian Thought*, trans. Jeffrey L. Kosky (Chicago: University of Chicago Press, 1999) xvii. This is the translation of *Sur le prisme métaphysique de Descartes. Constitution et limites de l'onto-théo-logie dans la pensée cartésienne* (Paris: Presses Universitaires de France, 1986).

[9] Jean-Luc Marion, *Sur la théologie blanche de Descartes. Analogie, création des vérités éternelles et fondement*, Rev. ed. (Paris: Presses Universitaires de France, 1991). Daniel Garber translates *blanche* as "blank" rather than "white," in contrast to Jeffrey L. Kosky. See Marion, *On Descartes' Metaphysical Prism* 5.

[10] Responses to *Dieu sans l'être* are found not only in academic journals but also in French national newspapers and in popular ecclesiastical sources.

[11] I refer to the conference that resulted in Richard Kearney and Joseph S. O'Leary, eds., *Heidegger et la question de Dieu* (Paris: Grasset, 1980). Marion's chapter, "La double idolâtrie," later forms part of the text of *Dieu sans l'être*.

that he began to break into the consciousness of North American scholars. As might be expected, Marion had a role to play in Francophone Canada, but more significantly for English speakers, he began giving academic papers in the United States at this time, initially in his role as a Cartesian specialist. It was in 1983 that Marion first addressed a seminar at Columbia University in New York City. This marked the beginning of Marion's relationship with Daniel Garber, now Professor of Philosophy at the University of Chicago. Garber's unrestrained enthusiasm for Marion's work is readily apparent from the opening lines of his Foreword to the English edition of the first volume of *Cartesian Questions*: "Jean-Luc Marion is one of the most important of the younger generation of philosophers working in France today, and one of the three or four most important living historians of modern philosophy."[12] Clearly, many others have either shared this opinion or have been keen to test its validity. Marion's speaking engagements multiplied extraordinarily in the mid-1980s, and since that time have taken him not only to major academic centres in France and in Europe more generally, but also to Canada, to Tunisia, Israel, and Japan, and repeatedly to prestigious institutions in the United States.

The mid-1980s was not only a time when Marion began to travel extensively, but it continued to be a fruitful period for writing. In 1983 and 1984 two collaborative ventures were realised: first, a volume dedicated to Marion's teacher, Ferdinand Alquié, and second, a collection of essays on phenomenology and metaphysics.[13] This latter volume marked the beginning for Marion, in print at least, of the development of a new research focus on Husserlian phenomenology, a focus that has proven to be a highly significant part of his work and a useful tool in his readings of Heidegger. In 1986, the final part of Marion's double triptych on Descartes was published, *Sur le prisme métaphysique de Descartes. Constitution et limites de l'onto-théo-logie dans la pensée cartésienne* [*On Descartes' Metaphysical Prism: The Constitution and the Limits of Onto-theo-logy in Cartesian Thought*], having been completed at Poitiers.[14] The theological work, *Prolégomènes à la charité* [*Prolegomena to Charity*] appeared in the same year, along with a tribute to Jean-François Lacalmontie.[15] Meanwhile, responses to *God Without Being* were emerging with increased momentum. Illustrating the most extreme end theologically is the pamphlet by Roger Verneaux: in the *Étude critique*

---

[12] Garber, "Foreword," Jean-Luc Marion, *Cartesian Questions: Method and Metaphysics* ix–xiii, ix.

[13] Jean-Luc Marion and J. Deprun, *La passion de la raison. Hommage à Ferdinand Alquié* (Paris: Presses Universitaires de France, 1983); Jean-Luc Marion and G. Planty-Bonjour, eds., *Phénoménologie et métaphysique* (Paris: Presses Universitaires de France, 1984).

[14] As noted earlier, the first triptych consists of *Sur l'ontologie grise de Descartes*; the *Index des 'Regulae ad Directionem Ingenii' de René Descartes*; and *René Descartes. Règles utiles et claires pour la direction de l'esprit en la recherche de la vérité*. The second again begins with *Sur l'ontologie grise de Descartes* (hence it is a double triptych) but is completed with *Sur la théologie blanche de Descartes* and *Sur le prisme métaphysique de Descartes*. So Marion is able to write in the Preface to the last work that "we here offer up the conclusion of a double Cartesian triptych." Marion, *On Descartes' Metaphysical Prism* xv.

[15] Jean-Luc Marion, *'Ce que cela donne.' Jean-François Lacalmontie* (Paris: Éditions de la Différence, 1986); *Prolégomènes à la charité*, 2nd ed. (1986. Paris: Éditions de la Différence, 1991).

du livre "Dieu sans l'être" he accuses Marion of ignoring the doctrine of the Trinity and the teaching of Christ, charging Thomas Aquinas with blasphemy, and asserting that the Church is simply wrong.[16] This, and some of the other responses, has had something of the effect of pushing Marion out of theological conservatism and into the realm of the radical.

In 1989 an important new volume appeared with Presses Universitaires de France: *Réduction et donation: recherches sur Husserl, Heidegger et la phénoménologie* [*Reduction and Givenness: Investigations of Husserl, Heidegger and Phenomenology*].[17] Picking up his earlier studies of Heidegger, and setting out for the first time in detail his position on Husserl, in this work Marion quite deliberately moves away from specifically theological questions. Nevertheless, that was not the way the work was received. Controversy over the ensuing years with respect to Marion has rested largely on the very question of the extent to which he is able to separate his theological interests from his philosophical ones.[18] Graham Ward plainly speaks of the tension between Marion's engagement with contemporary theory and his "credal commitment," or elsewhere of his "uncritical dogmatism."[19] By the time *Reduction and Givenness* was published, Marion had made the move from Poitiers to become Director of Philosophy at the University of Paris X at Nanterre, where Lévinas had been from 1967 until 1973, and which had also been home to Paul Ricoeur during the tumultuous times of the late 1960s.[20] He also took up the position of *professeur invité* in the faculty of philosophy at the Institut Catholique de Paris in 1991. The accusations that Marion's phenomenology is a covert theology were possibly reinforced by the publication in that same year of *La croisée du visible*, which looks at the very contemporary question of images—so central to the work of thinkers like Jean Baudrillard—situated in the context of a study of idols and icons and culminating in a consideration of the Cross.[21] *La croisée du visible* is a careful drawing together of phenomenology, Marion's extensive appreciation of fine art, and religion. Its conclusions about reverse intentionality (where the I is constituted by the

---

[16] Roger Verneaux, *Étude critique du livre "Dieu sans l'être"* (Paris: Téqui, 1986).

[17] Jean-Luc Marion, *Réduction et donation: recherches sur Husserl, Heidegger et la phénoménologie* (Paris: Presses Universitaires de France, 1989); *Reduction and Givenness: Investigations of Husserl, Heidegger and Phenomenology*, trans. Thomas A. Carlson (Evanston: Northwestern University Press, 1998).

[18] See the special editions of the *Revue de métaphysique et de morale* 96.1 (1991) and *Transversalités: Revue de l'Institut Catholique de Paris* 70 (Avril–Juin 1999), devoted to Marion, as well as Jacques Derrida, *Donner le temps. I. La fausse monnaie* (Paris: Galilée, 1991); Dominique Janicaud, *Le tournant théologique de la phénoménologie française* (Combas: Éditions de l'Éclat, 1991) and *La phénoménologie éclatée* (Combas: Éditions de l'éclat, 1998).

[19] Graham Ward, "Introducing Jean-Luc Marion," *New Blackfriars* 76.895 (1995): 317–24, 317; "The Theological Project of Jean-Luc Marion," *Post-Secular Philosophy: Between Philosophy and Theology*, ed. Philip Blond (London: Routledge, 1998) 67–106, 229.

[20] For a description of Ricoeur's unfortunate time here, see Edith Kurzweil, *The Age of Structuralism* (New York: Colombia, 1980).

[21] Jean-Luc Marion, *La croisée du visible*, Rev. ed. (1991. Paris: Éditions de la Différence, 1996).

look of the other, through the icon) were drawn out as Marion developed his thinking of *le phénomène saturé* (the saturated phenomenon) in a colloquium with Ricoeur, Jean-Louis Chrétien, and Michel Henry in May 1992. When the proceedings of that conference were published as *Phénoménologie et Théologie* later that year, there was no doubt in the minds of his critics that Marion was using phenomenology to sustain a theological agenda.[22] Marion continues to dispute the claim vehemently; whether the one can be reduced to the other is still a question of debate. Nevertheless, 1992 was also the year in which he was awarded the prestigious *Grand Prix de Philosophie de l'Académie Française.*

All the while, more work on Descartes was being produced. The first volume of *Questions cartésiennes: Méthode et métaphysique* [*Cartesian Questions: Method and Metaphysics*] was launched in 1991, a collection of seven essays on Descartes' method.[23] *Descartes: objecter et répondre*, produced with Jean-Marie Beyssade, appeared in 1994 in the wake of a conference at the Sorbonne and the École Normale Supérieure on that theme.[24] And Marion was part of a group to produce a new French translation of Husserl's *Cartesian Meditations* in the same year.[25] Several of his interests were also brought together in his accepting an invitation from the University of Chicago to be Visiting Professor for three months, teaching on Descartes, Husserl, and Heidegger. This marked the beginning of Marion's long association with that institution, where he now teaches annually in the Divinity School, once again in the wake of Paul Ricoeur.

While Marion's career had long progressed beyond *God Without Being*, the appearance of its translation in 1991 brought him most sharply to the attention of the English-speaking theological world. The work of translation was completed by Thomas A. Carlson, at that time a student of Marion's in Chicago. As I have already noted, while its reception in France had not been entirely uncontroversial, it had at least been contextualised by the earlier appearance of *The Idol and Distance*, and grew fairly naturally out of a particular French philosophical climate. Marion himself describes that first reception in the preface to the English edition: "At the

---

[22] Jocelyn Benoist, "Vingt ans de phénoménologie française," *Philosophie Contemporaine en France* (Paris: Ministère des Affaires Étrangères, 1994) 46–47. The chapter appears in Jean-François Courtine, Jean-Louis Chrétien, Jean-Luc Marion and Paul Ricoeur, *Phénoménologie et théologie* (Paris: Critérion, 1992). Its translation, along with a translation of other material by Janicaud, is included in Dominique Janicaud, Jean-François Courtine, Jean-Louis Chrétien, Jean-Luc Marion, Michel Henry and Paul Ricoeur, *Phenomenology and the 'Theological Turn': The French Debate*, Perspectives in Continental Philosophy, ed. John D. Caputo (New York: Fordham University Press, 2001). For the contextualising of the debate, see Robyn Horner, *Rethinking God as Gift* (New York: Fordham University Press, 2001). See also the excellent introduction by Thomas A. Carlson in Marion, *The Idol and Distance*.

[23] Jean-Luc Marion, *Questions cartésiennes I: Méthode et métaphysique* (Paris: Presses Universitaires de France, 1991); *Cartesian Questions*, trans. Jeffrey L. Kosky, J. Cottingham, and Stephen Voss (Chicago: University of Chicago Press, 1999).

[24] Jean-Marie Beyssade and Jean-Luc Marion, eds., *Descartes: objecter et répondre* (Paris: Presses Universitaires de France, 1994).

[25] Edmund Husserl, *Méditations cartésiennes*, trans. M. B. de Launay, Jean-Luc Marion and others (Paris: Presses Universitaires de France, 1994).

time of its first publication, *God Without Being* provoked some fairly animated debates, in France and elsewhere. Curiously, its theses were better received by the philosophers and academics than by the theologians and believers."[26] Responding to the appearance of the English version, John McCarthy observes:

> Books such as this risk incurring the wrath of both the philosophers and the theologians, with the former appealing to the justice of their objections, the latter to the justice of their replies. It is likely that Marion's dependence upon Heidegger and his destruction of all "metaphysics" has prevented Marion from rendering to each his own. Still, the author's willingness to court odium affords reason enough to applaud his work. After all, we were warned long ago that the truth about such matters could be known rationally only "by a few, and that after a long time, and with the admixture of many errors."[27]

For its English-speaking audience, *God Without Being* was always going to be demanding, for any number of reasons. Fergus Kerr laments, "the hardest thing, for philosophers of religion in the English-speaking context, is ... to cope with talk of 'Being'. The word, at least nowadays, simply does not have the metaphysical aura that it seems to have in French."[28] More concerned with the ready misconceptions that the title is likely to bring about, John Macquarrie writes: "it is very important not to misunderstand the title of Marion's book ... one might think that it denies any independent reality to God and reduces deity to an idea in the human consciousness. But not so."[29] While Macquarrie's sensitivity to the complexity of the implications that might be drawn from the title is important, his review highlights one of the chief difficulties for readers unfamiliar with other (that is, non-Heideggerian) contexts for Marion's work. His reference to the "eccentricities and obscurities of his [Marion's] sentence construction" is not unfounded, since Marion's style is frequently difficult, but Macquarrie's choice of example illustrates the fact that, difficulty aside, what the reader really needs to know is not only Heidegger, but Lévinas.

From a theological perspective, Macquarrie targets the same issues that many reviewers identify in *God Without Being*, that Marion has overstated the case in opposing love to being, and that he appears to have assumed that being is always used univocally.[30] Macquarrie's approach to these issues is nuanced by his deep knowledge of Heidegger, but it is a Heidegger whose work then becomes transformed through a Christian lens, such that a quasi-Heideggerian "Being" becomes the same goal of human desire and self-transcendence as the Christian God, and hence it becomes unthinkable to relinquish the necessity of an ontological framework.[31] Other critics will make similar points, but framed in the context of

---

[26] Jean-Luc Marion, *God Without Being* xix.

[27] John C. McCarthy, *Review of Metaphysics* 46.3 (1993): 627–29, 629.

[28] Fergus Kerr, "Aquinas After Marion," *New Blackfriars* 76.895 (1995): 354–64, 363.

[29] John Macquarrie, "Review of *God Without Being*," *The Journal of Religion* 73.1 (1992): 99–101, 100.

[30] Macquarrie, "Review of *God Without Being*" 100.

[31] Macquarrie is never unaware of the danger of "christianising" Heidegger, and adverts in the review to Heidegger's own warnings in this regard, but in his own work, Macquarrie develops Heidegger's ideas in a Christian framework.

Thomas Aquinas. Brian Shanley's later assertion of a reversal from Marion summarises the debate:

> It is not surprising that the *Revue thomiste* would produce a collection of papers defending Thomas Aquinas from the Heideggerian indictment of Western metaphysics as onto-theology. What is surprising, however, is that the most significant vindication in the collection is authored by none other than Jean-Luc Marion. The reason for the surprise is, of course, that Marion's earlier and influential *Dieu sans l'être* (1982) had contained a damning indictment of Aquinas as the principal progenitor of onto-theology. There Marion had argued that by reversing the Pseudo-Dionysian priority of the good over being in his doctrine of the divine names, Aquinas had moved fatally away from the God of revelation and faith, who is fundamentally Love....[32]

Marion had already, in fact, softened the blow for scholars of Aquinas with the preface to the English edition, rereading Thomas in such a way that he is implicated neither in "chaining" God to "Being" nor in simply perpetuating a metaphysical concept of God. This accords with some of the reconstructive work that forms part of the response from the Thomist side: when Thomas talks about God as "Being," he does so in such a way that there is no simple transference to God of a human concept.[33] But Marion still claims that even if it is freed from its metaphysical overlay, "Being" is not the most appropriate name for God.[34]

Aside from its difficulty, the knowledge of not only Heidegger but Lévinas and others that it demands, and the challenge it presents to traditional readings of Thomas, *God Without Being* is possibly most often remembered for the position it contains on the authority of the bishop. In a chapter titled "On the Eucharistic Site of Theology," Marion argues: "... *only the bishop merits, in the full sense, the title of theologian.*"[35] Originally written in the context of a papal visit to France, this chapter has caused the most controversy over Marion's politics, and in some ways, it is a piece he regrets for the misunderstandings it has provoked. His argument in the most narrow sense is that theology is fundamentally a hermeneutic of the eucharist. As such, only the bishop or the bishop's delegate, acting *in persona Christi*, can do theology.[36] This has many implications, but the roles of lay people,

---

[32] Brian J. Shanley, "Saint Thomas, Onto-theology, and Marion," *The Thomist* 60.4 (1996): 617–25, 617. For Marion's paper see Jean-Luc Marion, "Saint Thomas d'Aquin et l'onto-théo-logie," *Revue Thomiste* XCV (1995): 31–66. This is now reproduced in the 2nd edition (Presses Universitaires de France, 2002) of *Dieu sans l'être* .

[33] See, for example, John Martis, "Thomistic *Esse*—Idol or Icon? Jean-Luc Marion's God Without Being," *Pacifica: Journal of the Melbourne College of Divinity* 9.1 (1996): 55–68; Anthony Kelly, "The 'Horrible Wrappers' of Aquinas' God," *Pacifica: Journal of the Melbourne College of Divinity* 9.2 (1996): 185–203. From a different perspective, more Heideggerian in orientation but sympathetic to Thomas, see John D. Caputo, *Heidegger and Aquinas: An Essay on Overcoming Metaphysics* (New York: Fordham University Press, 1982) 140ff.

[34] Jean-Luc Marion, *God Without Being* xx.

[35] Marion, *Dieu sans l'être* 215; *God Without Being* 153.

[36] See the comments by Caputo, "How to Avoid Speaking of God: The Violence of Natural Theology," 145–46.

including women, in particular, are at issue most pointedly. The broader reading of his argument is that only those in tune with the teaching authority of the Church can legitimately undertake this hermeneutical task. A softer approach, and surely more likely in terms of his own intention (since Marion is not himself ordained), the question would remain about what being in tune with such authority means. Given the recent debate in the United States about the *mandatum* to teach theology, it is still possible to read Marion very conservatively.

In 1996, not only was Marion appointed Director of Philosophy at the Sorbonne (Paris IV), but he also gained the directorships of both the Centre d'Études Cartésiennes, and the "Épiméthée" collection at Presses Universitaires de France. In spite of the doubts that had been raised about the theological focus of his work, Marion had at this point well and truly won the recognition of his philosophical peers. And it is perhaps for this reason that he consistently reasserted his integrity as a philosopher: the move back to the heart of the Latin Quarter in Paris was paralleled by attempts to engage in more strictly philosophical concerns, and this at least for the sake of the separation, necessarily strict in post-revolutionary France, between Church and State. This did not exclude, none the less, an examination of the theology of Descartes, which appeared in the next volume of *Questions cartésiennes.*[37] But the shift in focus was clearly underlined in the responses to his critics that are found throughout *Étant donné. Essai d'une phénoménologie de la donation* (1997) [*Being Given: Toward a Phenomenology of Givenness*].[38] Strangely enough, however, it is this book perhaps more than any other which reinforces the ambiguity of Marion's attempts to limit himself to philosophy, for in it he deals again with the philosophical possibility of phenomena of revelation.

Just prior to the publication of *Being Given*, the argument over the extent to which theological commitments predetermine Marion's philosophical outcomes, and more particularly, shadow his renewal and application of phenomenological method, erupted in Villanova in 1997. John Caputo and Michael Scanlon had invited Marion and Derrida to be keynote speakers for the inaugural "Religion and Postmodernism" conference in September of that year. The papers of Marion and Derrida and their subsequent public debate, cast in terms of the question of the gift, reveal a great deal about questions relating to theology and phenomenology, but also about the state of play between them as two high-profile thinkers, as well as about future directions in French philosophy. In this debate, the student finally confronted the teacher head-on: it seems that this was a debate as much about overcoming as it was about meeting as minds.[39]

---

[37] Jean-Luc Marion, *Questions cartésiennes II: Sur l'égo et sur Dieu* (Paris: Presses Universitaires de France, 1996).

[38] Jean-Luc Marion, *Étant donné. Essai d'une phénoménologie de la donation* (Paris: Presses Universitaires de France, 1997). *Being Given: Toward a Phenomenology of Givenness*, trans. Jeffrey L. Kosky (Stanford: Stanford University Press, 2002).

[39] The text of the papers presented at this conference, and the debate, are reproduced in John D. Caputo and Michael Scanlon, eds., *God, the Gift, and Postmodernism* (Bloomington: Indiana University Press, 1999).

Being Given consolidated Marion's phenomenological work, and is a major contribution to the field. It reflects in many ways the influence of Lévinas, whose passing late in 1995 was to serve as something of a catalyst for many colloquia and new studies about his thought. In 1998 Marion's tribute to him was published as "La voix sans nom. Hommage—à partir—de Lévinas," and in 2000 a major collection of essays by and about Lévinas, *Emmanuel Lévinas: Positivité et transcendance* was released by Presses Universitaires de France under Marion's direction.[40] His own essay in that collection, "D'autrui à l'individu" ["From the Other to the Individual"], focuses his dialogue with Lévinas on the question of subjectivity.[41] In 2001 Lévinas appears as one of the protagonists in a volume dedicated entirely to the saturated phenomenon: *De surcroît: études sur les phénomènes saturés* [*In Excess: Studies of Saturated Phenomena*].[42] This book completes, according to Marion, the triptych of phenomenological works begun with *Reduction and Givenness* and *Being Given*. It represents a significant exploration not only of phenomenological possibilities but also of the role of hermeneutics in phenomenology. The latter is important in terms of earlier criticisms of Marion's work, and especially in terms of the shift between phenomenology and hermeneutics that a developed theology might seem to require.[43] Ironically, it is with a revised version of "In the Name: How to Avoid Speaking of 'Negative Theology' " (which Marion had presented at Villanova) that he chooses to conclude *In Excess*, and so theological questions again come into play. At the time of writing, Marion's most recent work is *Le phénomène érotique*, a study of love which continues the work begun in *The Idol and Distance* and *Prolegomena to Charity*, and so is unquestionably at once philosophical, phenomenological, and theological.[44]

In this very brief account of Marion's career, it has been possible to glimpse a few of the areas in which he has become a controversial figure, to identify his intense theological interests, to observe the prolific nature of his writing, and to gain something of a sense of his international academic success. Yet the complex nature of his thought has also begun to become evident, and this is problematic for those unfamiliar with the worlds in which he moves. It will only be through having some sense of these worlds that his real significance for contemporary theology will be able to be explored.

[40] Jean-Luc Marion, "La voix sans nom," *Rue Descartes: Emmanuel Lévinas* (Paris: Collège International de Philosophie, 1998) 11–26; *Emmanuel Lévinas: Positivité et transcendence*, ed. Jean-Luc Marion (Paris: Presses Universitaires de France, 1999).

[41] Marion, "D'Autrui à L'Individu," *Emmanuel Lévinas: Positivité et transcendence* 287–308; "From the Other to the Individual," trans. Robyn Horner, *Transcendence*, ed. Regina Schwartz (New York: Routledge, 2004) 43–59.

[42] Jean-Luc Marion, *De surcroît: études sur les phénomènes saturés* (Paris: Presses Universitaires de France, 2001); *In Excess: Studies of Saturated Phenomena*, trans. Robyn Horner and Vincent Berraud (New York: Fordham University Press, 2002).

[43] Horner, *Rethinking God as Gift*.

[44] Jean-Luc Marion, *Le phénomène érotique: Six méditations* (Paris: Grasset, 2003).

Chapter 2

Philosophical Perspectives[*]

Introduction

From the brief overview of Marion's intellectual influences and output given in the previous chapter, it will be evident that any attempt to understand his work from a theological perspective will also demand close attention to his philosophical concerns. In this chapter and the two immediately following, I will introduce some of the issues in contemporary continental philosophy that provide a setting for Marion's work. Beginning with the idea that Marion can be situated as a "postmodern" thinker, it will then be necessary to explore what might be meant by the postmodern, and how that relates to poststructuralist trends in philosophy. Yet the use of both these terms—postmodern and poststructuralist—will require an understanding of that to which they predominantly respond, which is metaphysics. Marion's understanding of three important moments in the historical unfolding of metaphysics will provide a basis, in this chapter, for the examination of two significant critiques of metaphysics, those of Nietzsche and Heidegger, in Chapter 4. In between this sketch of metaphysics and an examination of its problems, however, it will be necessary to consider the emergence of Husserlian phenomenology, which can be seen either as a perpetuation of metaphysics or as part of its overcoming. Since Heidegger places Husserl's phenomenology in the former camp, and Marion places it to some extent in the latter, Chapter 3 will provide an overview of it in order to pave the way for references to this debate. Chapter 4 will then provide an introduction to another important trajectory in twentieth-century thought: hermeneutics. Finally, an account of the ways in which Derrida contributes to understandings of metaphysics, phenomenology, and hermeneutics will establish the final part of a platform from which Marion's work with modern, phenomenological, theological, and poststructuralist ideas can be examined in the remainder of the book.

Marion and the Postmodern

In the preface to the English edition of *God Without Being*, Marion claims both that his enterprise "remains 'postmodern'," and yet that it "does not remain

---

[*] An earlier version of parts of this text appeared in Robyn Horner, "The Eucharist and the Postmodern," *Eucharist: Experience and Testimony*, ed. Tom Knowles (Ringwood, Vic.: David Lovell, 2001) 3–24.

'postmodern' all the way through."[1] One of the reasons that Marion's work is valuable is because it arises at a time when the postmodern, and the implications that this has for theology, is an issue. But what is the postmodern, and why is it so significant? In a well-known text from 1990, *The Condition of Postmodernity*, geographer David Harvey makes the following points in drawing some preliminary conclusions about "postmodernism":

> Postmodernist philosophers tell us not only to accept but even to revel in the fragmentations and the cacophony of voices through which the dilemmas of the modern world are understood. Obsessed with deconstructing and delegitimating every form of argument they encounter, they can end only in condemning their own validity claims to the point where nothing remains of any basis for reasoned action. Postmodernism has us accepting the reifications and partitionings, actually celebrating the activity of masking and cover-up, all the fetishisms of locality, place, or social grouping, while denying that kind of meta-theory which can grasp the political-economic processes ... that are becoming ever more universalizing in their depth, intensity, reach and power over daily life.[2]

If we accept what Harvey has to say, it would seem that the postmodern is an approach to thought and culture that has to do with the assertion of meaninglessness, and that it would thereby pose an enormous threat to any theological claim. And yet Marion, both philosopher and theologian, is prepared to say that his work remains postmodern, even if it is not thoroughly postmodern. This does not seem to square with Harvey's reading that postmodern philosophers, "obsessed with deconstructing and delegitimating every form of argument they encounter, ... can end only in condemning their own validity claims to the point where nothing remains of any basis for reasoned action." Whether or not Harvey is right remains to be judged.

Before proceeding any further, it is evident that some clarification of the term "postmodern" is necessary, for this word and related words—postmodernism and postmodernity—are often used interchangeably, but can have very different implications. This is complicated by the fact that different authors may use the same word to mean quite different states of affairs. And the problem of definition is made even more acute because of the way in which "postmodern" and its cognates have become buzzwords, used either to impress or condemn, with little reference to the theoretical contexts out of which they have emerged. Several very useful attempts have been made, however, to trace the usage and interrelationship of the three terms, and I will sketch some of the more relevant points here.

In general, many authors distinguish between postmodernism (or the postmodern) and postmodernity. Postmodernism is often used to refer to a philosophical approach that is critical of modernism.[3] Graham Ward argues that

---

[1] Marion, *God Without Being* xxi.

[2] David Harvey, *The Condition of Postmodernity: An Enquiry into the Origins of Cultural Change* (Cambridge, MA: Blackwell, 1990) 116–17.

[3] Graham Ward, "Introduction," *The Postmodern God*, ed. Graham Ward (Oxford: Blackwell, 1997) xv–xlvii, xxiv.

postmodernity, in contrast, refers to what he calls "certain cultural conditions pertaining to developed countries in the 1970s and 1980s."[4] Postmodernity thus suggests a period following modernity, even though it is not consistently used in this sense. Because of its link with modernism, the term "postmodernism" can also have connotations of an historical period. Postmodernism can be used to describe responses to modernist movements in art, literature, and architecture.[5] Ward uses "postmodern" to name these aesthetic responses, but then he also maintains that "postmodern" used in a different sense describes a type of philosophising. Bringing all these senses together, he speaks of a period of postmodernity as a kind of culmination of postmodern sensibilities. So he might say that the kinds of crises in authority that have characterised recent cultural, social, and intellectual life are a manifestation of the climaxing of postmodern concerns. He would also see that period as passing or having passed.

We are reminded by Lawrence Cahoone that "postmodernism," since the 1980s in particular, has been used to refer to that movement in French philosophy known as poststructuralism, the context in which Marion emerges as a thinker. Yet while poststructuralism is the site of many postmodern concerns, and is in many senses a critical reaction to the modern, especially Enlightenment, project, it does not restrict itself to critique of the modern. Poststructuralism also has the age-old habits of metaphysics in its sights. In spite of the fact that metaphysics is not exclusively a modern preoccupation, Ward lists it as one of the two major concerns of postmodernism: "I have suggested ... two tasks that postmodern philosophical thinking undertakes. First is the overcoming of metaphysics as conceived in modernity as the correlation of Being and reasoning (the thinking through and therefore intelligibility of all that is). Second is the thinking of difference ...."[6] This understanding would be in accord with the partial definition proposed from a theological perspective by Marion himself, where modernity represents metaphysics at its zenith: "if we understand by modernity the completed and therefore terminal figure of metaphysics, such as it develops from Descartes to Nietzsche, then 'postmodernity' begins when, among other things, the metaphysical determination of God is called into question."[7] What Ward means by postmodernity as a period seems to equate to a time of dominance by poststructuralist thought. And it seems to me that what he means by postmodernism is a current of issues emerging in response to metaphysics that is focused in a particular way by poststructuralism.

From this description it might appear that the postmodern is both part of the modern and after the modern. The precise relationship of the modern to the postmodern is an issue, however, that needs further explanation. The debate is easiest exemplified in the positions of two of its main protagonists: Jean-François Lyotard and Fredric Jameson. In the works of these writers we find that

---

[4] Ward, "Introduction," xv–xlvii, xxiv.

[5] Lawrence Cahoone, "Introduction," *From Modernism to Postmodernism: An Anthology* (Malden, MA: Blackwell, 1996) 1–23, 3.

[6] Ward, "Introduction," xv–xlvii, xxvi.

[7] Marion, *God Without Being* xx.

postmodernism is not so much strictly opposed to but inhabits modernism, although radically differently for each. Lyotard declares that "postmodernism … is not modernism at its end but in its nascent state, and this state is constant."[8] For Lyotard, the postmodern is always a disruptive force in the modern. Jameson, for his part, claims that what Lyotard characterises as postmodernism is nothing more than high modernism, or, more famously, that postmodernism is simply "the cultural logic of late capitalism."[9] According to this view, postmodernism is just another phase of the modern. So, is postmodernism related to modernism by virtue of its constantly unsettling it (according to this view the postmodern would behave like the virus of the modern) or by virtue of its completing it? Lyotard, who would be in favour of the first position, confuses the issue when he uses "postmodernity" and "postmodern" without reference to a time period, and "postmodernism" to refer to what apparently progresses in linear fashion in history.[10]

It is clear that there is no single, uncontroversial way of using any of the three terms under consideration, but from these perspectives I will try to clarify the sense in which they are used here. "The postmodern" will refer, somewhat along the lines of Lyotard, to that which inhabits and disrupts modernity. It is my view that the postmodern is less a distinct, new, or surpassable period than the modern, in various ways, coming up against its limits. "The modern" will be used to indicate those particular ways of seeing or understanding that are triumphant in a more or less discernible historical period. But by "the modern" will also be meant that which cannot end, so long as modernity is a way of living that emphasises "the just now," "the latest," or "the up-to-date." It is the modern as a way of life that is emphasised by Lyotard where he says: "modernity is not an epoch but a mode (the word's Latin origin) within thought, speech, and sensibility."[11] For that reason it is important to be cautious about trying to tie down the borders of the modern too absolutely. It is just possible, for example, that like the postmodern, the modern also surfaces other than as an era. The term "postmodernity" will be avoided where practicable, because of the implication that it is a period in time coming after modernity, although Ward is correct in observing that in the last twenty or thirty years there has been a particular focus on postmodern issues. "Postmodernism" will also be avoided, to lessen the link with modernism, but mainly so as not to give too strong a sense of a single, unified movement, that might be suggested by the addition of the "-ism." In fine, the postmodern will here be understood as a collection of philosophical concerns, that have emerged at many points, but especially as they are articulated in the context of poststructuralism. Those concerns include the nature and limits of metaphysics, and questions about hermeneutics, subjectivity, alterity

---

[8] Jean-François Lyotard, *The Postmodern Condition: A Report on Knowledge*, trans. Geoffrey Bennington and Brian Massumi (Minneapolis: University of Minnesota Press, 1984) 79.

[9] See Fredric Jameson, "Foreword," *The Postmodern Condition: A Report on Knowledge* vii–xxi, xvi; and *Postmodernism, Or, the Cultural Logic of Late Capitalism* (Durham: Duke University Press, 1991).

[10] Jean-François Lyotard, *The Postmodern Explained*, trans. Don Barry et al. (Minneapolis: University of Minnesota Press, 1993) 76.

[11] Lyotard, *The Postmodern Explained* 24.

(otherness), relationships, and responsibility. It seems to me that Marion would agree with at least part of this approach, and that he can be well situated within it.

Structuralism and Poststructuralism

What, then, is poststructuralism? By this name are partly characterised those theoretical movements that might be seen as responding to, or coming after, structuralism. If structuralism is broadly defined as an understanding of textual, cultural, or psychological processes that emphasises their deep patterns or structures, poststructuralism could be defined as approaches to these realities that resist their being understood in this way. Structuralism emerges from an analysis of language that emphasises its functioning as a system. Around the turn of the twentieth century, Ferdinand de Saussure focused on language as a system of differences: "cat" is not "cat" because it inevitably refers to a small, furry animal of the feline variety, but because it is not "cot" and not "bat," or "hat," and so on.[12] Anthropologists were among the first to apply the structural insights of linguistics to their field, seeking to understand whole cultures in terms of universal structures of meaning.[13] Literary criticism also adopted structural techniques. To give a very simple example, structuralist analysis of the literary genre of fairytales yields a certain number of functions that are represented by various characters across all fairytales. An analysis of a newly uncovered fairytale would be carried out in terms of those functions. The meaning, what the fairytale was "about," would be determined in accordance with the deep structure that those functions represent. It is possible to see from this example why psychology developed in some ways as a type of structural analysis. Particular human behaviours could be understood in terms of more general, underlying, subconscious structures that would determine them. And it is not difficult to adduce the links between structuralist theory and a Marxist view of the world. One of the advantages of structuralism is that it enables us to think of meaning in terms of relationships, rather than essences. A difficulty with structuralism, however, is that meaning is effectively determined in advance, and can thus seem very restricted.

Structuralism was one of the dominant theoretical approaches taught in the French academy of the 1940s and '50s. But by the time that Marion reached university, poststructuralism was in the ascendancy. It is not without significance that at the École Normale Supérieure he was taught, not only by the Marxist structuralist, Louis Althusser, but also by Derrida and Michel Foucault. Where structuralism emphasises the predetermined, poststructuralism tends to swing the other way, resisting this limitation of meaning by focusing on the irreducibly

---

[12] While Saussure never wrote a book, his lectures were collected and published as Ferdinand de Saussure, *A Course in General Linguistics*, trans. Roy Harris, eds. Charles Bally, Albert Sechehaye, and Albert Reidlinger (London: Duckworth, 1983).

[13] See, for example, the work of Marcel Mauss on the gift: Marcel Mauss, *The Gift: The Form and Reason for Exchange in Archaic Societies*, trans. W. D. Halls (London: Routledge, 1989).

particular, rather than the universal. With that in mind, it is important to observe that poststructuralism is not singular, and further, that it is situated in a broader intellectual current than its suggested identification simply as a response to structuralism would allow. Marion's poststructuralist understandings are, of course, articulated in terms of philosophy. In the twentieth century, so-called "continental" philosophy concerns itself largely with questions based around two approaches: phenomenology and hermeneutics.[14] Poststructuralist philosophy draws from and responds to these approaches as well as reacting to structuralism, questioning the ideological foundations of thought, particularly as these are expressed in metaphysical terms. In this way it reflects the more general poststructuralist or postmodern characteristic of anti-foundationalism.

Metaphysics

Having referred already on several occasions to "metaphysics" and "the metaphysical," it becomes necessary to clarify what is meant by these terms and to try to understand why what they represent has been subject to critique. The easiest way of approaching metaphysics is to see it as an attempt at a systematised understanding of what "is"—metaphysics aims to uncover the ultimate nature of reality. Marion frequently refers to the history of metaphysics and gives very detailed analyses of metaphysics in various modes, but here we basically follow the sketch of three metaphysical moments from the opening chapter of *In Excess*. In any overview of metaphysics it is common to begin with Aristotle, although of course much Greek philosophy prior to Aristotle had concerned itself with the question of the ultimate nature of reality. Yet what is known as Aristotle's "Metaphysics" is, on its own terms, a work on philosophy, and a consideration of the question of which aspect of philosophy is primary. Philosophy for Aristotle is the science of being (*onta*) in so far as it is being (hence, ontology), but in particular, it has to do with knowledge bearing on ultimate and unchanging being—the divine. The title of first philosophy is accorded to this divine science, since it bears on the *ousia akinèntos*, the immutable substance/essence. This double translation of *ousia*, that Marion argues "suffices to render inaccessible what Aristotle had thought indissolubly, if not unitarily," raises difficulties that already hint towards the nature and limits of metaphysics.[15] On the one hand, substance will come to be understood as a permanent substrate to which accidents are added, as subsistence, and ultimately as unknowable in itself. On the other hand, essence, which is used to signify what something is, tends to connote static Platonic form, and is eventually rendered meaningless. Further complicating the situation, Heidegger argues that

---

[14] For a very useful description of the distinction between continental philosophy and analytic or Anglo-American philosophy, see Simon Critchley, "Introduction: What is Continental Philosophy?" *A Companion to Continental Philosophy*, eds. Simon Critchley and William R. Schroeder, Blackwell Companions to Philosophy (Oxford: Blackwell, 1998, 1999) 1–17.

[15] Marion, *De surcroît* 5–6; *In Excess* 5.

ousia itself, because of its close links with *parousia*, comes to mean presence, a point also noted by Marion.[16]

Turning to a second moment in the historical unfolding of metaphysics, Marion uses Thomas Aquinas to exemplify a medieval model, although he is well aware that medieval metaphysics is not singular. In the prologue to his *Commentary on the Metaphysics*, Thomas identifies three meanings of metaphysics drawn from Aristotle, where it is:

> "... called *divine science* or *theology* inasmuch as it considers the aforementioned 'substances'—namely '... those things which are the most separate from matter ... not only rationally, like the mathematical [idealities], but also in Being, as God and the separate intelligences are.' It is called '*metaphysics*,' inasmuch as it considers being and the attributes which naturally accompany being. The transphysical things are discovered by the process of analysis, as the more common are discovered after the less common. And it is called *first philosophy* inasmuch as it considers the first causes of things."[17]

Marion reinforces that for Thomas, metaphysics as the divine science based on a thinking of *ousia* is supplemented by ontology and by the knowledge of causes. Now, the issue over whether or not Thomas thinks God in terms of metaphysics is a delicate one, and as noted in the first chapter, it has been the subject of much debate with regard to Marion's work. A first distinction is readily made between being in so far as being (the being that beings have in common, or common being, *ens*) and the act of being (sheer being, what it means to be, *esse*). As has been pointed out by Thomistic theologians on a number of occasions, and as Marion affirms in his 1991 preface to the English edition of *God Without Being*, metaphysics is the study of the first (which is not to be identified with God) rather than the second (which is Thomas' primary name for God), except where *esse* provides the context for *ens*. Marion again quotes from Thomas: "divine things do not belong to metaphysics as one of its objects; rather, they only intervene in metaphysics indirectly in the capacity of principles for its objects."[18] Similarly, the Thomistic understanding of divine causality does not allow for any simple metaphysical retrieval of God: "...after having reached God following the guiding thread of causality, he (Aquinas) vigorously refused to conceive God according and subject to cause, in rejecting the pertinence of any *causa sui* [cause of itself] and in leaving the divine *esse incausatum* [being uncaused]."[19] At the same time, however, the Heideggerian critique of metaphysics, which will be considered shortly, and which, in its

---

[16] On *parousia*, see Michael Inwood, *A Heidegger Dictionary*, The Blackwell Philosopher Dictionaries (Oxford: Blackwell, 1999) 174. Marion, *De surcroît* 7; *In Excess* 6.

[17] This quote is a helpful compilation of sections of the Prologue, taken from Marion, *On Descartes' Metaphysical Prism* 55–56, where it is given in amplified form and in the context of a fuller discussion of metaphysics rather than first philosophy. See Thomas Aquinas, *Commentary on the Metaphysics of Aristotle*, trans. John P. Rowan, vol. I, II vols. (Chicago: Henry Regnery Company, 1961).

[18] Marion, *God Without Being* xxiii. On the relationship of *esse* and *ens*, see Martis, "Thomistic *Esse*—Idol or Icon?" and Kelly, "The 'Horrible Wrappers' of Aquinas' God."

[19] Marion, *De surcroît* 9–10; *In Excess* 8.

medieval component, refers to Francisco Suarez rather than to Thomas, retains a certain degree of pertinence. God has frequently been thought as the foundation of being, or as the highest being. And even if one responds to Heidegger by maintaining the mysteriousness and indefinability of the *esse* or the cause, or rejecting the identification of God as "highest being," one risks—precisely by persisting with the reference to the foundation—reintegrating God into the metaphysical circuit. The founding of meaning through reference to a point beyond meaning, as we will see, involves what Derrida calls the use of a "transcendental signifier." And while a theologian might argue that this reference can be legitimately invoked, the process of invocation is constantly to be called into question, since it often implies a fundamentally realist ontology.

Returning momentarily to Thomas' conception of metaphysics, however, emphasis on the knowledge of causes is an important moment in the shift to a third historical articulation. Metaphysics as it emerges in modernity relates to the priority of epistemology, that is, to dependence on the thinking subject and its capacity to found knowledge of what is.[20] Being becomes being-known. René Descartes and Immanuel Kant are important protagonists in this third articulation. The former famously uses methodological doubt to establish the certainty of the *ego*—which he thinks substantially—even if he still uses God to guarantee the existence of the world.[21] It is important to recognise, none the less, and again in spite of Heidegger's critique, that while these strategies illustrate Descartes' enmeshment in metaphysics, his thinking of the *ego* and of God is not entirely constrained in this regard.[22] Kant circumscribes the power of knowledge even further as he enshrines its structure: we do not know things as they are in themselves, but only as they appear to us by way of the faculties of the mind. But even Kant can be pressed to think in excess of the system, as his work on the sublime illustrates.[23]

In a comparatively brief sketch, several important themes have already emerged. Metaphysics is the attempt to found knowledge of what is, and this foundation is thought in various and related ways: unchanging *ousia* (which in Latin and related languages comes to be translated by both substance and essence), being in so far as being, the divine, first cause, and knowing subject. Western philosophy is metaphysics in any number of guises. As it becomes more and more aware of its epistemological limits, however, and as regional sciences take over so much of the ground once considered to be its domain, philosophy enters a new phase of crisis. After Kant, and in its Anglo-American or analytic trajectory—a path not followed here—philosophy becomes a focus on logic and language (if we cannot affirm knowledge of "reality" in and of itself, how do we use language meaningfully or pragmatically?). In its continental trajectory, and having passed through the Hegelian climax of dialectic, which affirms the ultimate identity of being and knowing, philosophy becomes phenomenology and hermeneutics (if we cannot

---

[20] See Marion, *On Descartes' Metaphysical Prism* 57.
[21] See René Descartes, *Meditations on First Philosophy*, trans. John Cottingham (Cambridge: Cambridge University Press, 1986).
[22] For an accessible summary, see Marion, *On Descartes' Metaphysical Prism* 277.
[23] See part one of Kant's *Critique of Judgment*.

affirm knowledge of "reality" in and of itself, we can nevertheless describe what appears or presents itself to consciousness and how it is interpreted). Before undertaking an analysis of the possible problems of metaphysics, we turn to consider, at some length, aspects of this latter path.

Chapter 3

Introducing Phenomenology

Development

The term "phenomenology" can be traced back to the eighteenth century, but as a movement, phenomenology has its origins in the work in descriptive psychology of Franz Brentano, as it is taken up and radically transformed by Edmund Husserl in the late nineteenth and early twentieth centuries.[1] Given the apparently unquestioned ascendancy of the empirical sciences, Husserl asserts the primacy of transcendental philosophy in the hierarchy of knowledge and aims to develop a philosophical method to serve as a scientific basis for all knowing.[2] The process of that development is complex, with many revisions and shifts of emphasis in method at various stages in Husserl's career. Some of these shifts have only become apparent with the posthumous publication of much of his work. To complicate the process even further, several of Husserl's students eventually emerge with quite distinctive phenomenological perspectives—Heidegger is a famous example. Paul Ricoeur observes:

> ... phenomenology is a vast project whose expression is not restricted to one work or to any specific group of works. It is less a doctrine than a method capable of many exemplifications of which Husserl exploited only a few ... In Husserl himself the method was mixed with an idealistic interpretation ... As for the parts of his work where the method is actually applied ... they do not constitute one homogeneous body of work with a single direction of orientation. Husserl abandoned along the way as many routes as he took. This is the case to such a degree that in a broad sense phenomenology is both the sum of Husserl's work and the heresies issuing from it.[3]

As a consequence, it is difficult for scholars to reach agreement about the phases in Husserl's research, or about which phase represents Husserlian phenomenology

---

[1] For a concise history of the term, see Dermot Moran, *Introduction to Phenomenology* (London: Routledge, 2000) 6–7.

[2] See Edmund Husserl, *The Idea of Phenomenology*, trans. William P. Alston and George Nakhnikian (The Hague: Martinus Nijhoff, 1964) Lecture I, pp. 20–21. See also Edmund Husserl, *Ideas: General Introduction to Pure Phenomenology*, trans. W. R. Boyce Gibson, vol. 1 (London: Allen and Unwin, 1972) §§18–26. Husserl's mature position on the relationship between philosophy and science, and a crisis in knowledge, can be best observed in Edmund Husserl, *The Crisis of European Sciences and Transcendental Phenomenology*, trans. David Carr (Evanston, IL: Northwestern University Press, 1970).

[3] Paul Ricoeur, *Husserl: An Analysis of his Phenomenology*, trans. Edward G. Ballard and Lester E. Embree (Evanston, IL: Northwestern University Press, 1967) 4. Trans. modified.

most definitively.[4] Rudolf Bernet describes four stages: an early stage bound up in psychologism and represented by Husserl's *Philosophy of Arithmetic*, which is worked through by the time of the *Logical Investigations*; the stage represented by the first volume of *Ideas Pertaining to a Pure Phenomenology (Ideas I)*, where the focus is on a static transcendental phenomenology; a third stage, which shifts into a genetic transcendental phenomenology, best represented by the *Cartesian Meditations*; and a final stage, where the phenomenology of history becomes significant, explored in *The Crisis of European Sciences*.[5] With this complex development in mind, there are nevertheless some important, fundamental concepts emerging from Husserlian phenomenology that will assist in our later appreciation of how it is recovered by Marion. Since a detailed examination of phenomenology is beyond the scope of this study, the discussion that follows will draw largely, although not exclusively, from three of Husserl's main works: *The Idea of Phenomenology, Ideas I*, and the *Cartesian Meditations*.[6]

Overcoming the Dichotomy Between Subject and Object

In Husserl's view, the world cannot be accounted for comprehensively by a naturalist approach. Richard Cohen explains that this is because it "… [substitutes] for the whole of reality a part of reality—object reality, objects of empirical experience—while the whole must include consciousness and the data of consciousness, even though they are not, Husserl insists, reducible to objects or objects of sense experience."[7] Proceeding from a naturalist view, and claiming to be "objective," science neglects the constructive role of subjectivity in giving this world to be studied: "Only a radical inquiry back into subjectivity—and specifically the subjectivity which *ultimately* brings about all world-validity, with its content and in all its prescientific and scientific modes, and into the 'what' and the 'how' of the rational accomplishments—can make objective truth comprehensible and arrive at the ultimate ontic meaning of the world."[8]

While this view may appear at first to support a form of philosophical idealism (and phenomenology is frequently described—by Husserl, too—as "transcendental

---

[4] See, for example, the comments by Joseph J. Kockelmans, *A First Introduction to Husserl's Phenomenology* (Louvain: Duquesne University Press/Editions E. Nauwelaerts, 1967) xx–xxi, 315ff.

[5] Rudolf Bernet, "Husserl," trans. Lilian Alweiss and Steven Kupfer, *A Companion to Continental Philosophy*, eds. Simon Critchley and William R. Schroeder, Blackwell Companions to Philosophy (Malden, MA; Oxford: Blackwell, 1998) 198–207, 201–206.

[6] Here I am taking my lead from Eugen Fink's comments about Husserl's four starting-points for phenomenology. These texts represent an approach by way of Descartes, which provides a neat overlay with Marion, even if Marion's analyses of Husserl are not limited to the Cartesian texts. See Kockelmans, *A First Introduction* xxii–xxiii and xxiiin.6.

[7] Richard A. Cohen, "Foreword to the Second Edition," *Emmanuel Lévinas. The Theory of Intuition in Husserl's Phenomenology*, 2nd ed. (Evanston, IL: Northwestern University Press, 1995) ix–xxxi, xv–xvi.

[8] Husserl, *The Crisis of European Sciences* 69.

idealism"), phenomenology does not deny the empirically real. In a particular sense, phenomenology can be seen to overcome the dichotomy of realist and idealist perspectives, since it is a systematic focus on the nexus of consciousness and world.[9] Husserl recognises that the very positing of subjective and objective poles of reality already depends on their pre-given unity in lived experience (*erlebnis*). Lived experience is the experience of consciousness, and within consciousness, the world is given as my lived experience. Using the medieval concept of intentionality, which simply means that all consciousness is "consciousness of something," Husserl is able to articulate this fundamental relatedness of world and consciousness.[10] In Cartesian terms, I am related to the world as *cogito* to *cogitationes*:

> Anything belonging to the world, any spatio-temporal being, exists for me ... in that I experience it, perceive it, remember it, think of it somehow, judge about it, value it, desire it, or the like ... The world is for me absolutely nothing else but the world existing for and accepted by me in such a conscious *cogito*. It gets its whole sense, universal and specific, and its acceptance as existing, exclusively from such *cogitationes*. In these my whole world-life goes on, including my scientifically inquiring and grounding life.[11]

As an intentional being, I am constantly directed towards life's content, which unfolds as my lived experience of the world. To effectively study the world, I must take into account the way that it appears in my lived experience. This does not mean that the reality of the world is denied, since it remains simultaneously both that within consciousness and that which transcends consciousness.[12] However, the crucial role of consciousness—both in knowing the world and as a constituent part of that reality—is recognised. Ricoeur describes the phenomenological turn as a conversion of intentionality itself: "... the spiritual discipline of phenomenology is a true conversion of the sense of intentionality, which is first the forgetting of consciousness, and then its discovery of itself as given."[13]

---

[9] Nevertheless, Dermot Moran notes: "sometimes ... phenomenology's emphasis on the mutual belonging of the notions of subjectivity and objectivity is expressed as an overcoming of the subject-object divide. But this overcoming, at least in Husserl, is really a retrieval of the essential radicality of the Cartesian project ... We have overcome the subject–object divide only by finding a deeper meaning within subjectivity itself. There is, therefore, a central paradox in Husserl's thought which sought to overcome a certain crude kind of Cartesianism by a radical rethinking of the Cartesian project itself." Moran, *Introduction to Phenomenology* 16.

[10] "... it belongs as a general feature to the essence of every actual *cogito* to be a consciousness *of* something." Husserl, *Ideas: General Introduction* §36, p.119.

[11] Edmund Husserl, *Cartesian Meditations: An Introduction to Phenomenology*, trans. Dorion Cairns (The Hague: Martinus Nijhoff, 1960) §8, p.21.

[12] "From a strictly descriptive point of view, intentionality avoids the alternatives of realism and idealism. Insofar as it appears to a consciousness, one can say that the object *transcends* that consciousness and likewise that the object is *in* that consciousness; but it is there specifically by virtue of being intentional and not by virtue of being a really inherent part of consciousness." Ricoeur, *Husserl* 8.

[13] Ricoeur, *Husserl* 10.

Psychic Elements Versus Essences

It was noted above that the real includes "consciousness and the data of consciousness." Nevertheless, it is important to distinguish Husserl from his teacher, Brentano, when it comes to a consideration of what this means. Husserl does not want to explain the data of consciousness in terms of psychic elements, that is, in terms of individual psychological events in the mind of the thinker. That position is what he rejects as psychologism, which is a type of empiricism.[14] Husserl is instead interested in intentionality in its transcendental phase.[15] He focuses on meanings as distinct from things (or "facts"), considering the universal (as essence) rather than the particular: "As over against this psychological 'phenomenology,' *pure or transcendental phenomenology will be established not as a science of facts, but as a science of essential Being* (as *'eidetic'* Science); a science which aims exclusively at establishing 'knowledge of essences' and *absolutely no 'facts'.*"[16] Husserl defines an essence as the "what" of something, and his emphasis on essences rather than facts initially seems to suggest, once again, that he will discount the empirical in favour of the ideal. However, this is not the case, since he does not discriminate against the empirical as data but only as discrete and passing instances of what he prefers to understand more universally: "At first 'essence' indicated that which in the intimate self-being of an individual discloses to us *'what'* it is. But every such What can be 'set out as Idea'. *Empirical or individual intuition* can be transformed into *essential insight* …"[17] This is the process that Husserl terms "ideation."

The Phenomenological Reduction

To proceed phenomenologically, it is necessary to examine rigorously the essential content of consciousness, and on that basis, to proceed to sure knowledge. Such a

---

[14] See the Prolegomena in Edmund Husserl, *Logical Investigations*, trans. J. N. Findlay, vol. 1, 2 vols. (London: Routledge and Kegan Paul, 1970). As Bernet explains: " … [it is a matter] of understanding how there can be a science of consciousness if consciousness is a collection of multifarious psychic lived experiences which ceaselessly appear and disappear … [T]his is possible only if these acts are described in respect of their invariant or 'essential' structure. Phenomenology will henceforth differentiate itself from empirical psychology by becoming an 'eidetic' science … of acts of consciousness, or 'pure psychology.' … Husserl saw this as a real 'breakthrough' which enabled him to deal with the correlation between lived experiences of consciousness and the ideal objects of logic without falling prey to the contradiction of making the subject-matter of logic, the 'truths of reason,' dependent upon the 'factual truths' which are the subject-matter of empirical psychology." Bernet, "Husserl," 199.

[15] This is in spite of the fact that we are speaking of specific acts of consciousness, and Husserl will devote an enormous amount of energy to their examination. As Paul Ricoeur notes in his study of Husserl: "Here 'consciousness' signifies not the individual unity of a 'flux of subjective processes' but rather each distinct cogitatio turned towards a distinct cogitatum." Ricoeur, *Husserl* 8.

[16] Husserl, *Ideas: General Introduction*, Introduction, p.44. The emphasis is Husserl's unless otherwise noted.

[17] Husserl, *Ideas: General Introduction* §3, p.54.

rigorous examination involves making what Husserl calls the "phenomenological reduction," or εποχή (*epoché*). The phenomenological reduction is the bracketing of the natural attitude or standpoint, the attitude that assumes that "[t]he World is the totality of objects that can be known in terms of experience (*Erfahrung*), known in terms of orderly theoretical thought on the basis of direct present (*aktueller*) experience."[18] Husserl relates the natural attitude to that type of experience designated in German by *Erfahrung*—a traversal, a trial, an undertaking. This is distinct from another word that is also translated into English as "experience," *Erlebnis*, which is significant for phenomenology as it connotes lived or inner experience.[19] With the bracketing of the natural attitude, we have the disconnection of the assumption of the real:

> *We put out of action the general thesis which belongs to the essence of the natural standpoint*, we place in brackets whatever it includes respecting the nature of Being: *this entire natural world therefore* which is continually "there for us", "present to our hand", and will ever remain there, is a "fact world" of which we continue to be conscious, even though it pleases us to put it in brackets.
>
> If I do this ... I do *not* then *deny* this "world", as though I were a sophist, *I do not doubt that it is there* as though I were a sceptic; but I use the "phenomenological" εποχή, which *completely bars* me *from using any judgement that concerns spatio-temporal existence (Dasein)*.[20]

In phenomenology, the question of whether or not we can know that something exists is suspended in favour of asking what gives itself to and is constituted by consciousness.[21] The phrase, "what gives itself to consciousness" is significant, since one of the contentious points in contemporary debate about phenomenology is whether the emphasis is placed on what gives itself or its constitution—and even further its interpretation—by consciousness.[22] This has to do with questions about the extent to which phenomenology is either a perpetuation of metaphysics or a potential means to overcome it.

Intentionality

Consciousness is structured by two features. The first of these, intentionality, has already been basically defined, although a few of its features remain to be noted.

---

[18] Husserl, *Ideas: General Introduction* §I, p.52.

[19] See Kevin Hart, "The Experience of Poetry," *Boxkite: A Journal of Poetry and Poetics* (2/1998): 285–304, 293.

[20] Husserl, *Ideas: General Introduction* §32, p.110.

[21] Moran defines constitution for Husserl as "... the manner in which objects of consciousness come to have the kinds of 'sense and being' that they do, the manner in which subjectivity carries out its function of giving sense," which "... should perhaps be thought as a kind of setting out or 'positing' (*Setzung*), as a giving of sense, 'sense-bestowing' (*Sinngebung*)." Moran, *Introduction to Phenomenology* 164–65.

[22] In the context of a discussion of self-givenness, Husserl observes both that: "Absolute givenness is an ultimate" (p.49) and "Thus as little interpretation as possible (*intuitio sine comprehensione*)." (p.50) Husserl, *The Idea of Phenomenology* Lecture IV.

Intentional experiences are "lived experiences" (*Erlebnisse*), but not every *Erlebnis* is an intentional one, since intentionality is further specified by its being a *directed* movement, or an *aim*: "If an intentional experience is actual, carried out, that is, after the manner of the *cogito*, the subject 'directs' itself within it towards the intentional object. To the *cogito* itself belongs an immanent 'glancing-towards' the object, a directedness which from another side springs forth from the 'Ego', which can therefore never be absent."[23] Nevertheless, it is possible to be explicitly directed towards one phenomenon while catching up other phenomena unthematically in the intentional movement.[24] Husserl also points out that the directedness of intentionality is not always equivalent to the apprehension of an object: "… [I]n the act of valuation we are turned towards values, in acts of joy to the enjoyed, in acts of love to the beloved, in acting to the action, and *without* apprehending all this."[25] In other words, intentionality is not only theoretical, even if, as Lévinas will argue, Husserl ultimately promotes theoretical consciousness as primary.[26]

Intuition, Evidence, and Presence

Intentionality is ordered towards intuition (*Anschauung*), which in Husserl's work is basically about seeing, bringing to light, knowing, understanding, or grasping meaning. In the process of meaning-making, intentionality has a double structure: on the one hand, there is the noema (the givenness of what appears, the content of consciousness, the meant object, the perceived, the appearance), and on the other, the noesis ("the act of consciousness correlative to the noema," the givenness of appearing, meaning, or perceiving).[27] The given phenomenon appears in being constituted in the act of knowledge; this intuition of the phenomenon may be more or less adequate depending on the degree to which it presents itself with evidence. In perfect intuition an intentional object is given or made present "in person," which means that what is intentionally meant coincides either with the actual presence of the transcendent object, or the immanent presence of an object of insight (such as a mathematical truth). As Husserl observes in the *Prolegomena to the Logical Investigations*: "*The experience of the agreement* between the meaning and what is itself present, meant, between the actual *sense of an assertion* and the self-given *state of affairs*, is inward evidence; the *Idea* of this agreement is truth, whose ideality is also its objectivity."[28] This presence in intuition underlies what is called Husserl's phenomenological "principle of principles": "*Every primordial dator Intuition* is *a source of authority* (*Rechtsquelle*) *for knowledge, that whatever*

---

[23] Husserl, *Ideas: General Introduction* §37, p.121.

[24] Husserl, *Ideas: General Introduction* §35, p.117.

[25] Husserl, *Ideas: General Introduction* §37, p.122. In fact, apprehension is a second movement.

[26] Emmanuel Lévinas, *The Theory of Intuition in Husserl's Phenomenology*, trans. André Orianne, 2nd ed. (Evanston, IL: Northwestern University Press, 1995) 53.

[27] Kockelmans, *A First Introduction* 126n.33.

[28] Edmund Husserl, *Prolegomena to the Logical Investigations*, §51, trans. Moran, in *Introduction to Phenomenology* 129.

presents itself in 'intuition in primordial form (as it were in its bodily reality), *is simply to be accepted as it gives itself out to be,* though *only within the limits in which it then presents itself."*[29] The principle of principles encapsulates the conditions for Husserl's concept of evidence (*Evidenz*), which is the "mental seeing of something itself."[30] Ricoeur explains: "Evidence, according to Husserl, is the presence of the thing itself in the original (in contrast to the presentation, memory, portrait, image, symbol, sign, concept, word); one would be tempted to say presence in flesh and blood. This is the self-givenness (*Selbstgegebenheit*) which Husserl calls 'originary'."[31] In Ricoeur's comment we see embedded one of the difficulties with Husserl's work. If Husserl values most highly the presence of the thing itself, more especially the presence of mental objects as a result of insight, he is not taking into account that this presence can never be the presence of anything more than a sign. In other words, Husserl does not acknowledge that ideas are signs, which are re-presentations rather than presentations.

What role does presence play in Husserlian phenomenology, and what is the relationship of presence to evidence? Husserl recognises that the presence of a sense object (in contrast to an object of categorial intuition) will always be imperfect, that is, subject to a succession of intuitions that are only partial and that therefore might affect the quality of evidence. As Ricoeur points out in his discussion of the *Cartesian Meditations*, this suggests that the focus of phenomenology may in fact be on the object rather than its noematic correlate.[32] This is an important feature in any consideration of the extent to which phenomenology overcomes the division between realism and idealism. At the same time, however, Ricoeur argues that this tension is ultimately resolved in favour of transcendental consciousness.[33] The present may pass, but consciousness has in that instant taken hold of its object, and in being able to return to it, constitutes it with evidence. This means that "present presence" yields to the constituting power of the *ego*, self-presence.[34] Any presumption of access to pure presence or self-presence

---

[29] Husserl, *Ideas: General Introduction* §24, p.92. See also the translation from p.43 of the Husserliana edition: "*... every originary presentive intuition is a legitimising source of cognition,* that *everything originarily* (so to speak in its 'personal' actuality *offered* to us *in 'intuition' is to be accepted simply as what it is presented as being,* but also *only within the limits in which it is presented there.*"

[30] Husserl, *Cartesian Meditations* §4, p.10.

[31] Ricoeur, *Husserl* 101.

[32] Ricoeur, *Husserl* 102. "Now, if the object is constituted by 'touches,' 'adumbrations,' 'sketches,' 'perspectives,' what is the originary? How can the unity of the object be anything other than a claimed unity? Is the originary, the adumbration, presented at each instant? The notion of presence in flesh and blood seems to introduce a Self (*Selbst*) of the object (be this object a thing, a value, a state of relation), which 'fulfills' a void, keeps a promise. The thing is present itself."

[33] And this would be supported by passages such as the following: "It is only in cognition that the essence of objectivity can be studied at all, with respect to all its basic forms; only in cognition is it truly given, is it evidently 'seen.' This *evident 'seeing'* itself is truly *cognition in the fullest sense* ... But in givenness we see *that the object is constituted in cognition ...*" Husserl, *The Idea of Phenomenology* 59.

[34] Ricoeur, *Husserl* 101–105.

will, of course, become an issue for those who argue that phenomenology repeats
the presuppositions of metaphysics. Yet Bernet maintains: "… it is a mistake to
characterize Husserl's phenomenology of transcendental consciousness as a
'metaphysics of presence' (as Derrida does, following Heidegger) .…"[35] Marion,
too, is reluctant to overemphasise presence in Husserl's work, pointing out that
signification exceeds presence, and this is a crucial point in Marion's rehabilitation
of Husserl.[36] He emphasises Husserl's recognition that object constitution is never
complete or perfectly achieved, for example, and this is actually one of Derrida's
points. But Marion also wants to speak of saturating intuition, where what is given
defies the capacity of the recipient to present it as any *thing*.

Time-Consciousness

The second overall structural feature of consciousness is the consciousness of time.
Husserl's analysis of this question is set out in lectures he delivered in 1905; these
are published, along with supplementary notes dating up to 1910, in *The
Phenomenology of Internal Time-Consciousness*, although his observations are
developed in later works.[37] One of the important distinctions Husserl makes is
between phenomenologically reduced time and time from the vantage point of the
natural attitude ("objective" time): "We must carefully note the difference between
this *phenomenological time*, this unitary form of all experiences within a *single*
stream of experience (that of *one* pure Ego), and '*objective*', i.e., '*cosmic*' time."[38]
Phenomenological time cannot be measured. While, like cosmic time, it has
different phases (before, now, after), phenomenological time is essentially
characterised by the unity of duration: "The essential property which the term
'temporality' expresses in relation to experiences generally indicates not only
something that belongs in a general way to every single experience, but *a necessary
form binding experiences with experiences*."[39] In the intentional analysis of an
object it is necessary to show that while it is being constituted now, and effectively
in a potentially infinite series of now-points, these points cohere to the extent that
the same object remains under consideration. Within the flux of time, Husserl
identifies the primal impression as that which brings forth the intentional object:
"Primal impressions are absolutely unmodified, the primal source of all further
consciousness and being. Primal impressions have for content what is signified by
the word *now* .…"[40] Nevertheless, under the impetus of temporality, as one primal
impression (the originary impression) is relinquished for a completely new primal

---

[35] Bernet, "Husserl," 203. Yet cf. also the discussion in Leonard Lawlor, *Derrida and
Husserl: The Basic Problem of Phenomenology* (Bloomington: Indiana University Press,
2002) 160–61.

[36] See Chapter 5 of Marion, *De surcroît*; *In Excess*.

[37] Edmund Husserl, *The Phenomenology of Internal Time-Consciousness*, trans. James S.
Churchill (The Hague: Martinus Nijhoff, 1964).

[38] Husserl, *Ideas: General Introduction* §81, p.234.

[39] Husserl, *Ideas: General Introduction* §81, p.236.

[40] Husserl, *The Phenomenology of Internal Time-Consciousness* 92.

impression, it takes on a difference from it only in the mode of its givenness, which becomes past. Using the example of tone in music, Husserl explains: "in the flux of modifications of the past, therefore, a continuous, tone-filled segment of time ... is present, but in such a way that only a point of this segment is given by means of the primal impression, and from that point on, temporal positions continuously appear in a modified gradation going back into the past."[41] Each primal impression is punctual and new, but united with the others in duration.

Static and Genetic Phenomenology; Active and Passive Genesis

Two of the particular problems that emerge for explication by Husserl are how the *ego* constitutes itself, and how another person is constituted in experience. The first of these problems can be better understood in light both of the comments just made on time-consciousness, and of a brief introduction to the concepts of static and genetic phenomenology, and active and passive genesis. Static phenomenology refers to the basic intentional analyses carried out by phenomenology, where what is under examination is considered relatively simply in terms of its manifestation and authentication.[42] Genetic phenomenology, on the other hand, involves the recognition that constitution itself has a history. Under the general heading of genetic phenomenology, Husserl has in mind two forms of genesis, active and passive. He clarifies the meaning of these terms in *Cartesian Meditations*: "In active genesis the Ego functions as productively constitutive, by means of subjective processes that are specifically acts of the Ego."[43] By way of contrast:

> ... anything built by activity necessarily presupposes, as the lowest level, a passivity that gives something beforehand; and, when we trace anything built actively, we run into constitution by passive generation. The "ready-made" object that confronts us in life as an existent mere physical thing ... is given, with the originality of the "it itself", in the synthesis of a passive experience.[44]

---

[41] Husserl, *The Phenomenology of Internal Time-Consciousness* 93. See Bernet et al. for a fuller exploration of this continuity: Rudolf Bernet, Iso Kern, and Eduard Marbach, *An Introduction to Husserlian Phenomenology* (Evanston, IL: Northwestern University Press, 1993) 102ff.

[42] In the context of discussing the complex and slow evolution of Husserl's concept of genetic phenomenology, Bernet et al. neatly define static phenomenology in contrast: "Static phenomenology begins from species of stable objects, both real objects (for example, natural things) and ideal objects (for example, mathematical propositions), and proceeds both noetically and noematically to investigate the complexes of immanent experiences in which these species of objects attain teleologically to givenness. In the course of such an investigation, and within the 'phenomenological reduction,' these objects are regarded purely as the objective correlates of modes of consciousness. The intention in thus regarding them is to clarify the sense and validity of these objects by means of regressing to their systems of manifestation ... and authentication ... within the consciousness by which they are primordially given...." Bernet, Kern, and Marbach, *Introduction to Husserlian Phenomenology* 196.

[43] Husserl, *Cartesian Meditations* §38, p.77.

[44] Husserl, *Cartesian Meditations* §38, p.78.

In other words, passive genesis involves a recognition of the givenness of the object and the ultimate constitutive weakness of the *ego*.

Self-Constitution

It is now possible to return to the question of how the *ego* constitutes itself. The *ego* who is the bearer of intentional experiences can be considered in one sense as merely transcendental, since it is included in the phenomenological reduction and thereby loses its factical specificity as this or that *ego*. Yet Husserl nevertheless maintains the importance of being able to identify the *ego* in its unity, and being able to distinguish it from other *egos*. The first way in which we are able to identify the unity of the *ego* is in its being the identical pole of experiences, and in its simultaneous and continuous self-constitution: "The ego is itself *existent for itself* in continuous evidence; thus, in itself, it is *continuously constituting itself as existing*."[45] But we see this unity more specifically in the enduring nature of the *ego*'s decisions that, while they might change over time, relate to an enduring personal quality, such that "I" am the one who has chosen X and continues to stand by that decision or continues to be that same one in repudiating it: "Since, by its *own active generating*, the Ego constitutes itself as *identical substrate of Ego-properties*, it constitutes itself also as a 'fixed and abiding' *personal Ego* ...."[46] Yet Husserl takes a further step, seeking to identify the *ego* not only as the identical pole of experiences and as the "substrate of habitualities," but also in its "full concreteness" as what he will call the Monad.[47] The concreteness of the *ego* depends on its particular comportments towards its intentional objects and the sense it makes of them as the world: "The Ego can be concrete only in the flowing multiformity of its intentional life, along with the objects meant—and in some cases constituted as existent for it—in that life."[48] While static phenomenological analysis will yield a universal or pure I from every example of a *de facto* I, genetic analysis shows that each *ego* is shaped by what Husserl calls "the form of a motivation." This means that of all the possibilities open to an I as universal, only particular possibilities and their consequences can be chosen or assumed by any concrete I. The universal genesis of an *ego* "is such that past, present, and future, become unitarily constituted over and over again, in a certain noetic-noematic formal structure of flowing modes of givenness."[49] "But," Husserl goes on to say, "within this form, life goes on as a motivated course of particular motivations and motivational systems, which, according to *universal laws of genesis*, produce a unity of *universal genesis of the ego*. The ego constitutes itself for itself in, so to speak, the unity of a 'history'."[50] This history, which marks the concreteness of the

---

45 Husserl, *Cartesian Meditations* §31, p.66. Trans. modified.
46 Husserl, *Cartesian Meditations* §32, p.67. Trans. modified.
47 Husserl, *Cartesian Meditations* §33, pp.67–68.
48 Husserl, *Cartesian Meditations* §33, p.68. Trans. modified.
49 Husserl, *Cartesian Meditations* §37, p.75.
50 Husserl, *Cartesian Meditations* §37, p.75. Trans. modified.

monad, is both actively and passively constituted, or as Marion will maintain, the I actually finds itself in some measure always and already given to itself.[51]

Intersubjective Constitution

It remains to examine all too briefly the question of intersubjectivity; again, we find a response to this problem in the *Cartesian Meditations*, where it is worked out in relation to the problem of the constitution of a shared, objective world.[52] The intersubjective difficulty lies in working out how the other person can be constituted as another subject, rather than as an object. Husserl's approach here is to carry out not only a first, but a second reduction: where the first is the bracketing of the natural attitude, the second is the reduction to the sphere of "ownness."[53] In the bracketing of the natural attitude, what is put in question is the actual existence of another person, and what remains are my own constitutional experiences of others. The reduction to the sphere of ownness involves bracketing even these experiences, so that I am left with nothing more than experience which is exclusively my own, including experience of myself as belonging to nature through having a body.[54] Yet Husserl observes that even when both these reductions have been carried out with the utmost strictness, the psychical *ego* remaining still has what he calls a "mundanizing apperception."[55] This means that the psychical *ego* necessarily possesses a consciousness of ownness and otherness, of other *egos*. It is these other monads who actually make the experience of an objective world possible.[56] A further question is nevertheless raised at this point: how exactly do we experience others as other *egos*? Husserl argues that we never directly experience the other as another *ego*. Instead, we have a direct intentional experience of the other as another body, and only an appresentation, or indirect assimilation, of the other as another

---

[51] Husserl, *Cartesian Meditations* §38, pp.77ff. See Chapter 9 of the present text for a discussion of Marion on this point.

[52] Bernet et al. point out that this is still a limited attempt, and refer to the yet to be translated *Zur Phänomenologie der Intersubjektivität* (*Concerning the Phenomenology of Intersubjectivity*), which appears in volumes XIII, XIV, and XV of the *Husserliana*. Bernet, Kern, and Marbach, *Introduction to Husserlian Phenomenology* 155.

[53] Husserl, *Cartesian Meditations* §44, pp.92ff.

[54] "*What is specifically peculiar to me as ego, my concrete being as a monad*, purely in myself and for myself *with an exclusive ownness*, includes <my> every intentionality and therefore, in particular, the intentionality directed to what is other; but, for reasons of method, the synthetic effect of such intentionality (the actuality for me of what is other) shall at first remain excluded from the theme." Husserl, *Cartesian Meditations* §44, p.94.

[55] "In that I, this ego, have constituted and am continually further constituting as a phenomenon (as a correlate) the world that exists for me, I have carried out a *mundanizing apperception* ... By virtue of this mundanization everything included in the ownness belonging to me transcendentally (as this ultimate ego) enters, as something *psychic*, into 'my psyche'." Husserl, *Cartesian Meditations* §45, pp.99–100.

[56] Husserl, *Cartesian Meditations* §49, pp.107ff. For an exploration of the contradiction within the *Cartesian Meditations* relating to Husserl's idea of ownness, see Bernet, Kern, and Marbach, *Introduction to Husserlian Phenomenology* 158ff.

ego like me.[57] While appresentations normally accompany presentations in constitution, in this case, consciousness of the other as *alter ego* is given in a type of passive synthesis known as "pairing." Wherever the *ego* is given to consciousness, the *alter ego* is also given. In addition, the *alter ego* is recognised as such in conjunction with the experience of the other as a body that does not coincide with mine *here* but coexists with it *over there*.[58] While there are difficulties remaining for phenomenologists concerning the success or otherwise of his attempt to arrive at a phenomenological description of the experience of the other person, it is ultimately Husserl's reliance on the constitution of the other as an *alter ego* that is an issue for thinkers such as Lévinas, and following him, Marion. How Marion deals with this and other problems in phenomenology will be observed in later chapters. In this very introductory sketch, however, it has at least been possible to indicate some of the areas of Husserlian phenomenology that have either shown promise or raised new difficulties for later philosophers.

---

[57] "... neither the Ego itself, nor its subjective processes or its appearances themselves, nor anything else belonging to its own essence, becomes given in our experience originally ... *A certain mediacy of intentionality* must be present here, going out from the substratum, 'primordial world' ... and making present a 'there too', which nevertheless is not itself there and can never become an 'itself-there'. We have here, accordingly, a kind of *making 'co-present'*, a kind of *'appresentation'*." Husserl, *Cartesian Meditations* §50, p.109. Trans. modified.

[58] Husserl, *Cartesian Meditations* §53, pp.112–17.

Chapter 4

Postmodern Imperatives[*]

The End of Metaphysics?

> A virtue has to be *our* invention, *our* most personal defence and necessity: in any other sense it is merely a danger. What does not condition our life *harms* it: a virtue merely from a feeling of respect for the concept "virtue", as Kant desired it, is harmful. "Virtue", "duty", "good in itself", impersonal and universal—phantoms, expressions of decline, of the final exhaustion of life ....[1]

> Men of conviction simply do not come into consideration where the fundamentals of value and disvalue are concerned. Convictions are prisons. They [men of conviction] do not see far enough, they do not see things *beneath* them: but to be permitted to speak about value and disvalue one must see five hundred convictions *beneath* one—and *behind* one.[2]

> Skepticism regarding morality is what is decisive. The end of the moral interpretation of the world, which no longer has any sanction after it has tried to escape into some beyond, leads to nihilism. "Everything lacks meaning" (the untenability of one interpretation of the world, upon which a tremendous amount of energy has been lavished, awakens the suspicion that all interpretations of the world are false).[3]

One of the thinkers bringing the problems of a metaphysical tradition most violently to philosophical attention at the end of the nineteenth century is Friedrich Nietzsche. In the brief examples from his work given above we find three important and characteristic themes suggested: the arbitrary nature of the attribution of grounds; the abyss underlying the presumption of one's being able to occupy an absolute standpoint; and the issue of relative truth, as a result. Metaphysics fails because the framework for ultimate reality that it provides can be shown to be nothing more than a construction, a construction in which we have heavily invested. For Nietzsche there is no certainty other than the certainty of one's own will to decide. The attempts of philosophy or religion to give meaning to life are, for Nietzsche, entirely empty, futile expressions emerging from fear in the face of an indifferent universe. What Nietzsche brings to light will haunt the twentieth century: whether one agrees with him or not about the value of one's own

---

[*] An earlier version of parts of this text appeared in Robyn Horner, "The Eucharist and the Postmodern."

[1] See Chapter 11 of Friedrich Nietzsche, *The Anti-Christ*, trans. R. J. Hollingdale (Harmondsworth, Middlesex: Penguin, 1968) 121–22.

[2] See Chapter 54 of Nietzsche, *The Anti-Christ* 172.

[3] See Book One, 1.3 of Friedrich Nietzsche, *The Will to Power*, trans. Walter Kaufman and R. J. Hollingdale (New York: Vintage Books, 1967) 7.

valuations, the point is that they remain valuations—judgements or beliefs about what is absolute, right, or meaningful. To a metaphysical cosmos ordered by truth, the real, and a reasoned moral framework, Nietzsche brings the chaos of judgement and perspective, chaos that at times threatens to be overwhelming, given the vitriolic style with which it emerges in his work. Yet while Nietzsche is a crucial figure in the erosion of confidence in the brilliance of modernity, it is in the work of Heidegger that the issues of a deficient metaphysics are most rigorously addressed. Heidegger will, in fact, judge Nietzsche to be the culminating figure of a certain type of metaphysics, since even Nietzsche espouses a value, that of the will to power.[4] It is Heidegger who relentlessly uncovers the fragility and inadequacy of a metaphysical thinking of being as substance, as cause, and as presence. It is he who (admittedly, in the name of being) protests the thinking of God as highest being— most substantial, *causa sui*, most present, ultimate ground. The philosophy against which Heidegger writes asserts the dominance of an apparently objective, theoretical understanding; the potency but isolation of the subject; and the hardening of things and relationships into what can be manipulated and controlled. The phenomenological method that he inherits and then develops seeks to take into account what it means, instead, to be situated always and already as part of the world. For Heidegger, to be human is to be caught up in a network of relationships that is without beginning or foundation, and whose end lies beyond the realm of experience. And while we may judge that Heidegger does not escape metaphysics entirely, his way of thinking opens up in many respects the space for questions that might be called postmodern.

In the work of the early Heidegger, it is not metaphysics as such but the way that metaphysics has been undertaken, and particularly its epistemological dimension, that comes under attack.[5] In *Being and Time* and *The Basic Problems of Phenomenology*, Heidegger takes as his point of departure the question of being,

---

[4] See Martin Heidegger, "The Word of Nietzsche 'God is Dead'," trans. William Lovett, *The Question Concerning Technology and Other Essays* (New York: Garland, 1977).

[5] As Michael Inwood explains: "Heidegger regards 'metaphysics' as equivalent to 'ontology'... But owing to its association with God, which persists beyond Aristotle down to Hegel, he often calls it 'ontotheology'... Heidegger initially approved of 'metaphysics.' Like 'ontology,' it contrasts with 'epistemology' ... to which he is invariably hostile, and with science, which studies beings, but not being (or the nothing). It is equivalent to '(good) philosophy,' what Heidegger himself does." Michael Inwood, *A Heidegger Dictionary* 126. Nevertheless, Inwood also indicates that after 1935, Heidegger is progressively more critical of metaphysics: "'Metaphysics' has a new meaning that depends on Heidegger's sharpening of the ontological difference. Metaphysics, i.e. traditional philosophy since Aristotle, askes [sic] the 'guiding-question,' What are beings as such? but not the 'basic question,' What is (the truth of) being? Metaphysics goes 'beyond' beings to beings as a whole ... interpreting them variously as spirit, matter and force, becoming and life, representation, will, substance, subject, *energeia* (Aristotle) or eternal recurrence of the same (Nietzsche) ... Often it postulates a transcendent, supersensible world.... Metaphysics addresses four main questions: 1. the nature of man; 2. the being of beings; 3. the essence of the truth of beings; 4. how man takes and gives the 'measure [Mass]' for the truth of beings, e.g. whether ... what is depends solely on what man can be certain of ... But it does not go so far beyond as to ask about being ...." Inwood, *A Heidegger Dictionary* 127.

and his whole purpose is to elaborate a thinking of being that is otherwise than according to traditional metaphysics.[6] So we learn that the principal failure of philosophy has been its inability to think the "ontological difference," the difference between being (*das Sein*) and beings (*das Seiende*).[7] In obscuring this difference, metaphysics has thought being only as the ground or cause of beings, or as Marion suggests, as the "beingness" of beings. Marion continues: "Beingness thus transforms the question of Being … into a question of the *ens supremum*, itself understood and posited starting from this requirement, decisive for being, of the foundation."[8] Metaphysics is *onto-theo-logy*, which, appropriating a phrase from John D. Caputo, "is a search for grounds (logic) in the highest ground (theo-logic) and in the most general ground (onto-logic)."[9]

One of the chief targets of Heidegger's criticism is Descartes (and on the basis of Descartes, Kant), whom he locates in the tradition of the metaphysics of Suarez. In *Being and Time*, Heidegger observes:

> With the peculiar character which the Scholastics gave it, Greek ontology has, in its essentials, travelled the path that leads through the *Disputationes metaphysicae* of Suarez to the "metaphysics" and transcendental philosophy of modern times, determining even the foundations and the aims of Hegel's "logic". In the course of this history certain distinctive domains of Being have come into view and have served as the primary guides for subsequent problematics: the *ego cogito* of Descartes, the subject, the "I", reason, spirit, person. But all these remain uninterrogated as to their Being and its structure, in accordance with the thoroughgoing way in which the question of Being has been neglected.[10]

The modern is the culmination of a metaphysical tradition, which does not think the meaning of being, but only foundations and causes (*ego cogito*, the subject, the "I", reason, spirit, person). It is exemplified in the work of Descartes:

---

[6] Martin Heidegger, *Being and Time*, trans. John Macquarrie and Edward Robinson (London: Blackwell, 1962). See also the newer translation by Joan Stambaugh (Albany, NY: State University of New York Press, 1997). My references are to the Macquarrie and Robinson translation unless otherwise noted.

[7] Martin Heidegger, *The Basic Problems of Phenomenology*, trans. Albert Hofstadter, Rev. ed. (Bloomington: Indiana University Press/Midland, 1988) 120. Most translators struggle to make a distinction in English between *sein* (the infinitive, to be, sometimes translated with the gerund, being), (*das*) *Sein* (the substantive, being, sometimes but not always translated as Being), *das Seiende* (that which is, being, often translated as beings or entities), and *seiend* (the present participle, be-ing). See Inwood, *A Heidegger Dictionary* 26–28, as well as the notes on pages 19 and 22 of the Macquarrie and Robinson translation of *Being and Time*. Hofstadter does not distinguish *Sein* by using a capital. Any quotations included in this text will follow the style of the source. Other references will utilise only the lower case.

[8] Marion, *God Without Being* 34.

[9] John D. Caputo, *Heidegger and Aquinas: An Essay on Overcoming Metaphysics* (New York: Fordham University Press, 1982) 150. The phrase originally refers to Hegel, but Caputo goes on to say: "All metaphysics, as this paradigm case makes plain, understands Being in terms of ground and beings in terms of the grounded, and it thinks the difference between Being and beings as the difference between ground and grounded. God Himself, therefore, enters metaphysics as the highest ground, the first cause, the *causa prima* and *ultima ratio* of beings."

[10] Heidegger, *Being and Time* 43–44.

With the *"cogito sum"* Descartes had claimed that he was putting philosophy on a new and firm footing. But what he left undetermined when he began in this "radical" way, was the kind of Being which belongs to the *res cogitans*, or—more precisely—the *meaning of the Being of the* "sum" ... He [Descartes] defined the *res cogitans* ontologically as an *ens*; and in the medieval ontology the meaning of Being for such an *ens* had been fixed by understanding it as an *ens creatum* ... But createdness in the widest sense of something's being produced, was an essential item in the structure of the ancient conception of Being. The seemingly new beginning which Descartes proposed for philosophizing has revealed itself as the implantation of a baleful prejudice, which has kept later generations from making any thematic ontological analytic of the "mind" such as would take the question of Being as a clue and would at the same time come to grips critically with the traditional ancient ontology.[11]

Heidegger observes at least four problems with Cartesian metaphysics. The first concerns the thinking of being as substance, or substantial. Descartes maintains that there are three kinds of substance, each defined by its attributes: the two finite substances are *res extensa*, extended things, and *res cogitans*, thinking things; infinite substance is God.[12] One of the difficulties with this understanding is that it does not clarify, for example, the distinction between the type of being of the finite and that of the infinite, which suggests that God is thought in the manner of a thing.[13] Next there is the problem that being is conceived as presence (*Anwesenheit*). According to Heidegger's approach, this conception does justice neither to being nor to the dynamic of time, but means that being is thought as what can be grasped, manipulated, or made present by consciousness, and time is fixed as a sequence of present instants or "nows."[14] The third problem concerns the difficulty alluded to in the quotation above, that being is thought as what is caused or produced, or in the case of God, as the producer (*causa sui*). [15] If we put these problems together with a fourth, that being is thought on the basis of the *logos*, that what founds is in turn founded by the reasoning subject (whose being yet remains unclarified), we begin to have a sense of why Heidegger finds a metaphysical thinking of being deficient.[16]

In his attempt to overcome the problems of metaphysics, or better, in his attempt to think being anew, Heidegger begins with phenomenology. Nevertheless, this is a phenomenology very different from that of his teacher, Husserl. Heidegger claims that Husserlian phenomenology is too focused on the ontic (in terms of the essence

---

[11] Heidegger, *Being and Time* 46.

[12] Heidegger, *Being and Time* 126, 23. Marion's analysis of Descartes on this point reveals a radical modification of the concept of substance, but he argues that it is insufficient to avoid the conclusion that Heidegger reaches. See Marion, *Sur le prism métaphysique* 235–38; *On Descartes' Metaphysical Prism* 223–26.

[13] Heidegger, *Being and Time* 126. On the impropriety of referring to God as substance see Marion, *Sur le prisme métaphysique* 230–35; *On Descartes' Metaphysical Prism* 218–22.

[14] Heidegger, *Being and Time* 48, 47.

[15] Heidegger, *Being and Time* 122ff., especially at 25.

[16] See Heidegger, *Basic Problems* 126ff. On Heidegger and the *logos*, see Heidegger, *Being and Time* 55. See Marion's discussion in "Descartes and Onto-theology," *Post-Secular Philosophy: Between Philosophy and Theology*, ed. Philip Blond (London: Routledge, 1998) 67–106, 75.

of the object, objectness) instead of the ontological (being as being). For Heidegger, the whole point of phenomenology is its bringing to manifestation of what "lies *hidden*," "the *Being* of entities," that which presents entities without being present itself.[17] This "*Being* of entities" he understands not in relation to any being in particular, which would be a type of essentialism, but in relation to being as a whole: "Being ... is no class or genus of entities; yet it pertains to every entity. Its 'universality' is to be sought higher up. Being and the structure of Being lie beyond every entity and every possible character which an entity may possess."[18] In so far as it investigates being in this way, phenomenology is authentic ontology.[19] Heidegger's entire project is an attempt to gain access to this sense of being: first, by way of thinking the being of the being for whom its being is an issue, *Dasein* ("there-being," not strictly human being, but a modified subject, thought non-essentially, and only in terms of the meaning of its existence); and later, by way of the nothing.[20] While it is ultimately the event of being [*Ereignis*] that allows beings to come forth or be manifest, being is finite, does not serve as a cause, and itself has no ground, or reason.[21] It is this abyssal thinking that perhaps marks the greatest contribution of Heidegger to a disturbance—rather than an overcoming—of metaphysics. (In the work of Derrida and Marion there are lingering doubts about whether Heidegger has overcome metaphysics, and in Derrida, even doubts about whether it is at all possible to overcome metaphysics entirely.)

Returning momentarily to Husserl, it must be noted that while to some extent he sets out to overcome one of the leading problems emergent from metaphysics, that is, the question of whether or not things "really exist" (which he puts to one side in the reduction, asking instead how they are known to us), Heidegger judges that in many ways Husserl remains within a metaphysical framework. It was already noted above that Heidegger considers Husserl to focus too much on the object, which, according to Heidegger's reading, is always a present object. If we compare the two thinkers in broad terms, Husserl is interested—at the micro-level—in ideational essences, or the ways in which meanings are presented, whereas Heidegger is interested in meaning-structures, and only to the extent that they point towards the macro-level of meaning as a whole. To claim that Husserl is still involved in a metaphysical enterprise is to say that he is still searching for *what* is (as essence, even if not substance, and on the basis of an intending and constituting subject). In contrast, Heidegger is often engrossed with the question of *that*—what does it mean *that* it is? And in his response he resists attempting to answer *why*, which is one of

---

17 Heidegger, *Being and Time* 59.
18 Heidegger, *Being and Time* 62.
19 Heidegger, *Being and Time* 60.
20 See Heidegger, *Being and Time*; "Postscript to 'What is Metaphysics?'", trans. Walter Kaufman, *Existentialism from Dostoyevsky to Sartre*, ed. Walter Kaufman (New York: Penguin, 1975); "The Way Back into the Ground of Metaphysics," trans. Walter Kaufman, *Existentialism from Dostoyevsky to Sartre*; "What is Metaphysics?", trans. Walter Kaufman, *Existentialism from Dostoyevsky to Sartre*.
21 Martin Heidegger, *The Essence of Reasons*, trans. Terrence Malick (Evanston, IL: Northwestern University Press, 1969). On the finitude of being, see Inwood, *A Heidegger Dictionary* 69–71; on *Ereignis*, 54–57.

the means by which he avoids making any theological claims. Of course, while he resists any theological explication, he nevertheless situates theology as a regional study less fundamental than ontology, and famously introduces in his later philosophy the idea of the "fourfold" with all its attendant mythology. I do no more than observe here that these aspects of Heidegger's thought have significant theological implications.[22]

It is of note that Lévinas is a careful reader of both Heidegger and Husserl. His criticisms of the latter relate broadly to two areas: the ways in which signification sometimes actually overruns our ability to contain it, that is, he argues that not everything can be reduced to what can be understood (love, goodness, or the infinite, for example); and the ways in which otherness, and particularly the otherness of the other person, is absolute, and so cannot be thought in terms of the *alter ego.* With respect to Heidegger, Lévinas again has two main areas to put in question. This time he fears that the reduction to being has been made absolute, with a consequent lack of attention to what resists or exceeds being, most particularly the other person. Further, he maintains that this overlooking of the other person shows Heidegger's inexcusable lack of interest in ethics.[23] While Lévinas sees himself within a phenomenological trajectory, picking up what remains unexplored in Husserl, he also goes beyond phenomenology and develops—perhaps confusingly—what he calls a "metaphysics."[24] It is not, however, a metaphysics characterised by the same features as a traditional metaphysics. By using this title he both situates himself in opposition to Heidegger and what he sees as the suffocating theme of ontology, and places an emphasis on that part of the word that simply means "beyond" [*meta-*]. Lévinas' post-phenomenological style is exemplified in the means he uses to write about the other person, for example, where the other is not phenomenalised *as such* but addresses me (from a "height") and calls me to responsibility.[25] It is further exemplified in the way in which, for Lévinas, the subject (I or *ego*) is always subsequent to a more basic "me," who is

---

[22] I refer the reader to studies such as George Kovacs, *The Question of God in Heidegger's Phenomenology* (Evanston, IL: Northwestern University Press, 1990).

[23] See Emmanuel Lévinas, *The Theory of Intuition in Husserl's Phenomenology*; *En découvrant l'existence avec Husserl et Heidegger*, 5th ed. (Paris: Vrin, 1994), parts of which are translated as *Discovering Existence with Husserl*, trans. Richard A. Cohen and Michael B. Smith (Evanston, IL: Northwestern University Press, 1998); and Lévinas' two major works, *Totality and Infinity: an Essay on Exteriority*, trans. Alphonso Lingis (The Hague: Martinus Nijhoff, 1979) 45–48, for example, and *Otherwise than Being or Beyond Essence*, trans. Alphonso Lingis (The Hague: Martinus Nijhoff, 1981) Chapter I, or Chapter V, Part I, for example.

[24] See his comments in Richard Kearney, *Dialogues with Contemporary Continental Thinkers* (Manchester: Manchester University Press, 1984) 50.

[25] On questions to do with the extent of Lévinas' phenomenalisation of the face, see Jacques Derrida, "Violence and Metaphysics," trans. Alan Bass, *Writing and Difference* (London: Routledge, 1978) 79–153; Robyn Horner, *Rethinking God as Gift* 66–67; Jean-Luc Marion, "D'Autrui à L'Individu"; "From the Other to the Individual"; "The Face: An Endless Hermeneutics," *Harvard Divinity Bulletin* 28.2–3 (1999), 9–10; *De Surcroît*; *In Excess* Chapter 5, Part 3; John Milbank, "Only Theology Overcomes Metaphysics," *New Blackfriars* 76.895 (1995): 325–42.

constituted by the call of the other rather than self-constituting. Lévinas' interpretations of Husserl and Heidegger form an important influence on Marion.

At this point it becomes pertinent to reintroduce more explicitly the work of Derrida, whose early writing was devoted to the extensive critical examination of Husserl. For Derrida, there is little doubt that Husserl exhibits many of the tendencies of metaphysical thought. His critique of Husserl has two main thrusts.[26] The first concerns the problem of genesis, and focuses on the fact that having made the phenomenological reduction, Husserl is always left with an irreducible remainder of what is already constituted instead of constituting.[27] Leonard Lawlor summarises the problem in the following terms:

> The irreducible inclusion of retention implies that the constituting is always preceded by a constituted, even though retention issues from the constituting of primal impression. Supposedly first, intentionality is already actual; supposedly original, consciousness is already invested with a sense; supposedly second, sense is already there. The reduction, therefore for Derrida, cannot capture, within temporal lived experience, the absolute constituting source: genesis.[28]

This is a criticism of Husserl with which Lévinas and Ricoeur would be sympathetic.[29] Marion, however, would maintain not only that Husserl is aware of the shortcomings of the constituting consciousness, but that by favouring givenness he actually allows for it.[30] The second thrust of Derrida's critique of Husserl is developed in terms of language, and is worked out in both *Edmund Husserl's 'Origin of Geometry': an Introduction* and *Speech and Phenomena and Other Essays on Husserl's Theory of Signs*.[31] In these works Derrida argues that Husserl

---

[26] These are described in Leonard Lawlor, *Derrida and Husserl*.

[27] See, for example, Jacques Derrida, *Le problème de la genèse dans la philosophie de Husserl* (Paris: Presses Universitaires de France, 1990) 40.

[28] Lawlor, *Derrida and Husserl* 81.

[29] See Paul Ricoeur, *Husserl* 110ff; Lévinas, *Otherwise than Being*, 32–34.

[30] See, for example, *Réduction et Donation*; *Reduction and Givenness* Chapter 1; *De Surcroît*; *In Excess* Chapter 5, Part 1.

[31] Jacques Derrida, *Edmund Husserl's 'Origin of Geometry': an Introduction*, trans. John P. Leavey, Jr. (Lincoln: University of Nebraska Press, 1989); *Speech and Phenomena and Other Essays on Husserl's Theory of Signs*, trans. David B. Allison and Newton Garver (Evanston, IL: Northwestern University Press, 1973). We see both ideas together in the following example from *Edmund Husserl's 'Origin of Geometry'* at p.152: "The discursive and dialectical intersubjectivity of Time with itself in the infinite multiplicity and infinite implication of its absolute origins entitles every other intersubjectivity in general to exist and makes the polemical unity of appearing and disappearing irreducible. Here delay is the philosophical absolute, because the beginning of methodic reflection can only consist in the consciousness of the implication of *another* previous, possible, and absolute origin in general. Since this alterity of the absolute origin structurally appears in *my Living Present* and since it can appear and be recognized only in the primordiality of something like *my Living Present*, this very fact signifies the authenticity of phenomenological delay and limitation. In the lackluster guise of a technique, the Reduction is only pure thought as that delay, pure thought investigating the sense of itself as delay within philosophy."

reflects the metaphysical understanding that objects are present to (a self-present) consciousness rather than mediated through signs. He comments powerfully in *Speech and Phenomena*:

> Do not phenomenological necessity, the rigor and subtlety of Husserl's analysis, the exigencies to which it responds and which we must first recognize, nonetheless conceal a metaphysical presupposition? Do they not harbor a dogmatic or speculative commitment which, to be sure, would not keep the phenomenological critique from being realized, would not be a residue of unperceived naïveté, but would *constitute* phenomenology from within, in its project of criticism and in the instructive value of its own premises? This would be done precisely in what soon comes to be recognized as the source and guarantee of all value, the "principle of principles": i.e. the original and self-giving evidence, the *present* or *presence* of sense to a full and primordial intuition.[32]

It is to the role of signs and the multiple possibilities of their interpretation that we now turn.

Hermeneutics

An important part of Heidegger's work, particularly in his early explorations of the meaning of the being of *Dasein*, lies in his recognition that reality is not "out there," waiting to be discovered and named, but that we only have access to reality as always and already interpreted. This is part of what it means to be "enworlded," that is, always and already part of the world instead of being an observer somehow external to it. According to the hermeneutic circle, the thinker cannot stand apart from the thought, and meaningfulness arises not from a process of naming and analysing hitherto "blank" objects but instead by participation in the world of what has already been pre-understood. To restate the famous example from *Being and Time*, a hammer has meaning for us not as a heavy piece of metal, in a particular shape, attached to a handle, but as that which *hammers* when we take it and use it. If I might offer a contemporary example (despite Heidegger's loathing of technology), the meaning of a computer for the average user is not in the complexity of its internal operations, in the idea or the "how" of its functioning, but in its integration into the production of work—its "that"—when one goes to write. For both the hammer and the computer, not only is my first engagement with the tool non-theoretical (I do not primarily see it in terms of its composition or foundation, its substance or cause), but when I take it up it is already *as* something. This does not mean that there can be no novelty, but that even novelty requires a pre-interpretative context if it is to be appropriated. Hence Heidegger's other very famous example, that of Van Gogh's painting of the peasant woman's shoes. According to Heidegger, the genius of the artist lies in his ability to elicit, in a new

---

[32] Derrida, *Speech and Phenomena* 4–5. On the linguistic critique, see especially *Speech and Phenomena*, Chapter 4, and the seminal essay in the same collection, "Differance" (129–60).

way, the meaning of the woman's life. To appreciate the painting requires not only the ability to recognise shoes as such, but also an understanding of the context of peasant life of the era in which the painting is set. Speaking of the rich symbolic value of the painting, Louis-Marie Chauvet imagines it being observed by Amazonian Indians who at the time "knew nothing of the world of Europeans." "Not only would the picture say nothing to them," he says, "but they would not even 'see' it."[33]

Heidegger's understanding of enworldedness is deepened by an examination of Derrida's appreciation of textuality, that can be approached through his well-known aphorism from *Of Grammatology*, ‹il n'y a pas de hors-texte› [there is nothing outside the text].[34] Yet it is necessary to clarify that for Derrida the word "text" need not be confined to words written on a page. Text refers us to a whole system of meaning. To say that there is nothing outside the text is, therefore, to say that it is not possible for a human being to stand outside the human system of meaning. We are always and already implicated in that system, which is what Heidegger suggests by the hermeneutic circle. But to say that there is nothing outside the text is also to say that we do not have access to reality apart from our engagement in language. There are not first things presented to consciousness, that are then matched up with signs to represent them, but always and only signs that refer to other signs or resonate as symbols in a web of meaning.[35] Reality is not what is present in or behind the signs, but effectively remains constructed by them as text. In other words, reality is always and already mediated: we inhabit a symbolic order.

There are several important implications to be drawn from this understanding of textuality. One of these has to do with finitude and infinitude. It might seem that a statement such as "there is nothing outside the text" is making a claim for the finite nature of human reality. There is nothing "else" beyond this system of language, beyond a pure immanence. But in a strange way, such a statement also opens onto a claim for the infinite nature of meaning. Meaning depends on signs being repeatable, or iterable. The word "cat" is not meaningful if I invent it, use it only once, and subsequently refer to the cat as a bat or a hat. Yet at the same time, the word "cat" is only meaningful because of its consonantal differences from "bat" or "hat." So in a particular sense, the words bat and hat, as well as many others, always linger in the shadows of the word cat to make it what it is. What is different from cat is always implied in it as a trace. I will never be able to separate the word from all the structural differences it implies. Moreover, there are many shades of meaning in

---

[33] Louis-Marie Chauvet, *Symbol and Sacrament: A Sacramental Reinterpretation of Human Existence*, trans. Patrick Madigan and Madeleine Beaumont (Collegeville, MN: Pueblo/The Liturgical Press, 1995) 127.

[34] Jacques Derrida, *Of Grammatology*, trans. Gayatri Chakravorty Spivak (Baltimore, MD: Johns Hopkins University Press, 1976) 158.

[35] This is the thrust of one of Derrida's key points in his critique of Husserl. See Derrida, *Origin of Geometry: An Introduction*; *Speech and Phenomena*. Chauvet quotes Maurice Merleau-Ponty (the reference given is from the French text) as he makes a crucial observation: "Language is not the illustration of a thought already formed, but the taking possession of this thought itself." Chauvet, *Symbol and Sacrament* 146. See Maurice Merleau-Ponty, *Phenomenology of Perception* (London: Routledge and Kegan Paul, 1962).

the word "cat": it might refer to *Felis domestica*, but then it may be used pejoratively of a woman who is spiteful, or it might mean "jazz musician," or it may appear with quite a different meaning in the phrase "it's raining cats and dogs." One cannot always foresee the limits to the ways in which the word "cat" might be used. The meaning of the word will always depend on the context, and since I cannot foresee all contexts in advance, I can never, strictly speaking, fence off all the possible shades of meaning that it might invoke. These characteristics of language—its being structured by difference and by the endless deferral of meaning—are referred to with Derrida's neologism, "*différance.*" Returning to his aphorism, "there is nothing outside the text," what we have in effect is both a statement about finitude (the text is all we have) and a statement about infinitude (textual meaning is potentially infinite). What has happened here is that the borders between finite and infinite, as well as those between present and absent, have broken down, such that each member of the pair cannot be thought outside the other but both have to be thought together. This has fascinating consequences.

Traditionally, metaphysics constructs reality according to series of opposing values: finite versus infinite; inside versus outside; immanent versus transcendent; male versus female, and so on. The terms are mutually exclusive, and in any given context usually one is privileged over and against the other—we are forced to choose between terms. In his work, commonly characterised as "deconstruction," Derrida constantly draws our attention to the points in philosophical history where such choices have been made, and his text, "Plato's Pharmacy," provides a powerful example.[36] Here Derrida examines the ways in which speech is arbitrarily privileged over writing in Plato's text, and supposed presence over absence, as well as the way in which the polysemy of *pharmakon* (remedy, but also recipe, poison, drug, philter) is inevitably betrayed by translation.[37] What Derrida argues is that the binary oppositions of metaphysics are false, because neither of the terms of the opposition is ever absolute but only has meaning in relation to that which it attempts to suppress. The attempt to make male normative and absolute, for example, is always unsettled by the ghost of female which is needed in order for male to be male. A metaphysical thinking of infinite in opposition to finite is always and already contaminated by finitude. Similarly, presence is never the full presence of metaphysical dreams. It is always interrupted by absence, by a withdrawal or removal that forbids us from seizing it and grasping it. Presentation is always *re*-presentation; meaning is never absolute for us, even if it is for God.

A second and related implication to arise from Derrida's understanding of textuality is that it does not allow for a *known* extra-textual space from which to guarantee the meaning of the text—a transcendental signified.[38] If the text can only refer (albeit in an infinite way) to itself, it cannot of itself appeal to a higher authority to ensure its good sense. We cannot use language to argue beyond

---

[36] Jacques Derrida, "Plato's Pharmacy," trans. Barbara Johnson, *Dissemination,* ed. Barbara Johnson (Chicago, IL: University of Chicago Press, 1981) 61–171.

[37] Derrida, "Plato's Pharmacy," 70–71, 96–102.

[38] See Derrida, *Of Grammatology,* 20; *Positions,* trans. Alan Bass (Chicago, IL: University of Chicago Press, 1981) 19.

language (hence the problem with a commitment to a realist ontology, where the beyond can actually only be posited *within* a continuous horizon of being). This is simply another way of saying that any appeal to a ground must remain only that— an appeal. That is not, however, to argue that since meaning is infinite and not guaranteed from beyond, any position is as meaningful as any other. Harvey's claim, noted at the beginning of Chapter 2, that since postmoderns are always "deconstructing and delegitimating every form of argument they encounter, they can end only in condemning their own validity claims to the point where nothing remains of any basis for reasoned action," overestimates the scope of what many "postmodern" thinkers would aim to be doing. Put in the terms of many a student on his or her first encounter with Derrida, why would one write a book to claim that there is no meaning? Unless we are to sink into the most empty cynicism, this would be an absurd gesture to make. On the other hand, if it were to be recognised, not that there is no meaning, and not that there is every meaning, but that making meaning involves judgements, choices, and decisions, then deconstruction could bring us to the point of discerning the ethical and appreciating the nature of faith. Deconstruction would have an ethical dimension in our seeking to uncover choices that had been made, and subsequently, voices that had been repressed. To deconstruct a text would be to seek the infinitely other of the text, as part of a process that would never come to complete closure.

There is nothing outside the text, but the text is constantly exceeded by what cannot be reduced to reason or to measure or to a ground. Does Derrida thereby overcome the problems of metaphysics? There is a particular sense in which this is the wrong question to ask: Derrida uncovers the metaphysical presuppositions of texts while at the same time recognising that in writing (or speaking, or thinking) we never entirely free ourselves from some kind of metaphysical commitment. At the same time, he does try to think the otherness or infinity of the text in such a way that it nevertheless does not hold itself up in yet another opposition. To think that otherness or infinity is constantly to be at risk of exposing it to re-incorporation by metaphysics, unless we proceed by way of the aporia, which is no way at all, but a knot in which we remain stuck, the locus of what Derrida calls "the impossible."[39] An aporia cannot be solved through recourse to reason but only re-solved through recourse to *a kind of faith*. I am quite deliberately cautious in saying "*a kind of faith*," because the religious connotations of the phrase should not limit its meaning in advance. Metaphysics is *interrupted* rather than overcome. It is interrupted by the impossible (which for Derrida does not simply mean "what is impossible," but that which is the source of desire for the absolutely other), interrupted by justice, love, the gift, forgiveness, hospitality, and so on.[40] Deconstruction brings us to the point

---

[39] See Jacques Derrida, "Form and Meaning: A Note on the Phenomenology of Language," *Margins of Philosophy*, trans. Alan Bass (Chicago, IL: University of Chicago Press, 1982) 155–173; *Aporias*, trans. Thomas Dutoit (Stanford, CA: Stanford University Press, 1993).

[40] See Robyn Horner, "Aporia or Excess: Two Strategies for Thinking r/Revelation," *Other Testaments: Derrida and Religion*, eds. Kevin Hart and Yvonne Sherwood (London: Routledge, 2004); *Rethinking God as Gift*.

of appreciating the nature of faith because it uncovers moments of decision, where the knot of what cannot be known has only been undone by a choice. To decide is not to know that one course is better than another but to place one's faith in it. It is to step into the abyss of what is undecidable, on the basis of a judgement or an assent. Deconstructive critique would never offer advice on which choice to make, but neither would it deny that such a choice was often necessary, nor forbid that such a choice be made. It is for this reason that the simple opposition of deconstruction to Christian faith is not very helpful.

Otherness

In light of the above reflections, and in drawing Part I of this text to a close, it may be useful to summarise by suggesting that the flip side of the problem of metaphysics is the question of how to think alterity, or otherness. Metaphysics seeks to found what is by reference to another order, but it actually founds that order with reference to itself, and so finds in its supposed other only the selfsame. In its attempts to think its own ground—usually God or the self—it is confronted by the falseness of its sense of security, since the God it invokes and the self it names can be seen to be nothing more than empty projections of the will. And yet if we look closely, metaphysics is constantly haunted by the other. Its attempts to think God and the self, or similarly the other person, the infinite, death, and so on, are inevitably interrupted by an alterity that metaphysics can neither systematise nor contain, without destroying that very alterity. The problem of how to think otherness without turning it into more of the same is relevant, too, both for phenomenology and for theology, in so far as they can be implicated in metaphysics. To characterise Marion as a postmodern thinker is to situate him in the context of the inadequacy of metaphysics and the desire to find a way for otherness to have a meaning precisely as other. But this desire for the possible signification of the other takes on a particular urgency for Marion, committed as he is, in advance, to a God who can be thought in so far as revealed, and, as we will see, to an other who can reveal her or himself as lover. In the remainder of the present text, we basically follow the strategies Marion employs in order to think alterity.

PART II
THE THEOLOGICAL
DESTITUTION OF
METAPHYSICS

Introduction to Part II

In the first part of this book the focus was on introducing some of the contexts from which Marion's thought has emerged. As we move into the second section, the focus shifts to an examination of Marion's actual engagement with metaphysics and its potential overcoming. More specifically, a preliminary consideration will be made of Marion's fundamental view that it is theology that renders not only metaphysics, but also the thought that "overcomes" metaphysics, destitute. This is a view that characterises Marion's earlier works in particular, although later it is not so much absent as perhaps more cautiously articulated. While it would be possible to give an overview of Marion's theology from other perspectives, such as by way of his preference for mystical theology, for example, it seems to me that the theme of the theological destitution of metaphysics actually offers a far more unifying focus. In this regard, he makes use of four basic theological motifs: distance, the icon, love, and the gift. God enters into thought as distance, gives Godself to contemplation in the icon, is only to be known as and through love, and this more particularly as a gift of love. Each of these motifs is used to characterise a way of thinking that nevertheless "exceeds" thought, apparently going beyond metaphysical recuperation. Whether and how that can happen are significant questions that will constantly trouble the exposition provided here. While it will be important to go on to examine Marion's specific characterisation of metaphysics, particularly as it is set out in *On Descartes' Metaphysical Prism*, it will also be necessary to anticipate that characterisation as each of his theological motifs is being described. If I may partially repeat the summary I gave in Chapter 2, metaphysics is the attempt to found knowledge of what is, and this foundation is thought in various and related ways: unchanging *ousia* (substance or essence), being in so far as being, the divine, first cause, and knowing subject. Drawing from Chapter 4, metaphysics founders because none of these foundations can be absolute for thought, because each relies on the presumption of a presence to consciousness (a coincidence between being and meaning) that cannot ultimately be sustained. This fracturing of presence highlights the way in which the world is constructed or mediated by language, rather than described by it. In looking at each of Marion's theological motifs, then, we will need to bear in mind a crucial question. Remembering that theology is first and foremost determined by a commitment of faith, to what extent does each motif work with that commitment, or does it attempt to absolutise the knowledge that flows from faith? In other words, does the theology that Marion develops repeat the moves of metaphysics or subvert them?

In this part I give an outline of each theological motif as it functions in Marion's early, largely theological works (Chapters 5 and 6), before considering in some detail *On Descartes' Metaphysical Prism* (Chapter 7) and *God Without Being* (Chapter 8). In the first of these texts, Marion determines the character of metaphysics as onto-theo-logy in Cartesian thought, locates Descartes' resistance to metaphysics in his idea of the infinite, and then describes Pascal's destitution of metaphysics by way of charity. The second text illustrates Marion's use of the icon in opposition to metaphysical idolatry, as well as his attempt to overcome Heidegger's "nonmetaphysical" thought of being with a thought of God as love— given as gift.

Chapter 5

A Theology of Distance

With this chapter we begin our examination of the theological motifs used by Marion to "think" God otherwise than by way of metaphysics. Already I am constrained to qualify what Marion means by "think": as will become evident throughout this section of the book, in a particular sense, Marion seeks to overcome not only metaphysics, but thought as such, even if this actually means that he must then characterise theology as a different kind of thought. Distance is the theological motif most consistently used in Marion's work, and, in fact, it is determinative of each of the others, yet because it is employed in very different ways in various contexts, it can be difficult to be sure of its meaning, especially since its very use implies an excess of meaning over any concept. At the most basic level, distance seems to refer to the absolute difference between God and humanity. In other words, distance operates to mark the non-coincidence of God with any concept of God. But because it is a spatial metaphor, this marking does not always work to best effect: it can seem to suggest that God and humanity are at either end of a continuum. Further, when Marion speaks of distance in specific settings, we find that it takes on the characteristics of other ideas he is examining. This is so in the examples that will be considered shortly. Where metaphysics often thinks God as the foundation of being and the guarantee of meaning, Marion uses distance as a figure of the interruption of thought, maintaining that it resists recuperation either as a foundation or as what can be presented or represented in knowledge. At the same time, however, he will often suggest that distance can be recognised, and it frequently comes to be recognised in his work as God. In addition to analysing Marion's usage of the term in some detail, in this chapter I will note at various points the question of whether such recognition works to undermine the excessive quality of the interruption.

Genealogy

The principal origin of the concept of distance in Marion's thought is probably Hans Urs von Balthasar, who develops it in four dimensions, two human and two divine.[1] Balthasar argues that from the human side there is both a natural distance from the divine, and a distance that is the result of sinfulness. The idea of a natural distance—*diastasis*, or difference—is explained by Balthasar as follows: "The basis of the

---

[1] Marion notes the connection with Balthasar, as well as the ambivalence of the concept, in *Sur le prisme métaphysique* 326n30; *On Descartes' Metaphysical Prism:* 307n30. See also *The Idol and Distance* 155.

biblical religion is the *diastasis*, the distance between God and the creature, that is the elementary presupposition that makes it possible for man to understand and appreciate the unity that grace brings about."[2] To underline this distance of the human from the divine is not unusual, and the idea is found in the works of other writers, such as Gregory of Nyssa and John of the Cross.[3] This is a distance, nevertheless, that is not necessarily equivalent to separation, and which is also the precondition for authentic communion: "... the *analogia entis* (the irreducible 'otherness' of created nature) excludes any kind of fusion and confusion" yet at the same time the divine and human come together "in this ever-intensifying reciprocal interpenetration."[4] Sinful distance (a "deeper *diastasis*"), in contrast, is what separates the human unnaturally from God, and is that which Christ overcomes.[5] From the divine side, there is an eternal intra-trinitarian distance of the Son from the Father, which actually forms the condition of possibility for the divine-human *diastasis*.[6] Then there is a distance between the Son and the Father which is a result of Christ's taking on human sinfulness, and which leads to the *hiatus* of the Cross, and to the descent into Hell.[7] Balthasar observes of the eternal intra-trinitarian distance that "the Son's eternal, holy distance from the Father, in the Spirit, forms

---

[2] Hans Urs von Balthasar, *Explorations in Theology*, trans. Brian McNeil, vol. III: Creator Spirit, 4 vols. (San Francisco, CA: Ignatius Press, 1993) 173. Gardner and Moss comment: "*Dia-stasis*, in its etymological constitution, invokes no valorization of an interval, but rather the dynamic movement of that which properly belongs together—a distance which gives unity. For the creature, *diastasis* is simply the fact of creation, the 'magic circle' in which it turns and whose borders are internal to the constitution of its own finitude. The creature does not run up against God as its proper limit, but turns in the horizon of its own presensing [sic]." In their analysis of Balthasar in terms of the question of sexual difference, Gardner and Moss then claim that Balthasar's notion of distance is fixed rather than fluid (86). Lucy Gardner and David Moss, "Something Like Time; Something Like the Sexes—an Essay in Reception," *Balthasar at the End of Modernity*, eds. Lucy Gardner, David Moss, Ben Quash, and Graham Ward (Edinburgh: T & T Clark, 1999) 69–138.

[3] Balthasar traces the idea of *diastasis* as "spacing" to Gregory. See Hans Urs von Balthasar, *Presence and Thought: An Essay on the Religious Philosophy of Gregory of Nyssa*, trans. Marc Sebanc (San Francisco, CA: Ignatius Press/Communio Books, 1995) 27–35, especially 27–28. See also John of the Cross, *The Ascent of Mt Carmel*, trans. E. Allison Peers, 3rd rev. ed. (Garden City, NY: Doubleday-Image, 1958) 117.

[4] Hans Urs von Balthasar, *Theodrama*, trans. Graham Harrison, vol. IV: The Action, 5 vols. (San Francisco, CA: Ignatius Press, 1992) 383. See also Balthasar, *Explorations III* 174. While some commentators stress that distance need not be equivalent to separation, Marion's interpretation of Balthasar is that there is an "obvious sense of a separation (*Abstand*)," referring to the German edition of *The Glory of the Lord*, vol. II, at pp.561 and 579.

[5] Balthasar, *Explorations III* 175. See also Hans Urs von Balthasar, *Mysterium Paschale*, trans. Aidan Nichols, Rev. ed. (Grand Rapids, MI: William B. Eerdmans, 1990) 12–13. Of this distance, Balthasar's commentator, Angelo Scola, comments: "The distance between God and man caused by the godlessness of sin is thus overcome and conquered in the 'yes' of the Son. In the loving obedience that leads the Son to extreme abandonment, the most radical reversal takes place: there is a passage from death to eternal life, from extreme distance to extreme nearness." Angelo Scola, *Hans Urs von Balthasar: A Theological Style* (Grand Rapids, MI: William B. Eerdmans, 1995) 82.

[6] Balthasar, *Mysterium Paschale* 79; *Theodrama IV* 325; *Theodrama V* 81ff.

[7] See Balthasar, *Mysterium Paschale*.

the basis on which the unholy distance of the world's sin can be transposed into it, can be transcended and overcome by it."[8] Scola explains how this eternal distance enables the embracing of the human distance marked by sin: "Jesus can be abandoned ... on the strength of the intra-trinitarian distance (*otherness*) between Father and Son, which is eternally overcome and confirmed by the Spirit. However frightening the alienation contained in the sinful distance of the world from God may be, it can be annulled, and this can take place only in the *difference* of the divine hypostases."[9] Thus there is a constant tension in Balthasar's theology between distance and nearness, a tension that is never ultimately overcome, even as distance is healed of its sinful dimension.[10]

The other writer who may be a source for Marion's understanding of distance is Lévinas, for whom relationships are characterised by an irreducible distance, or difference.[11] This means that while I am in relation to the other (*l'autrui* rather than *l'autre* where a personal other is intended, for Lévinas often translated with "the Other"), I cannot simply reduce that other to the dimensions of my own thought or understanding. So we read that desire for the other as Other:

> … has another intention; it desires beyond everything that can simply complete it. It is like goodness—the Desired does not fulfill it, but deepens it.
>
> It is a generosity nourished by the Desired, and thus a relationship *that is not the disappearance of distance*, but a bringing together, or—to circumscribe more closely the essence of generosity and of goodness—*a relationship whose positivity comes from remoteness, from separation*, for it nourishes itself, one might say, with its hunger.[12]

More strongly, Lévinas writes: "the *sway* [*pouvoir*] of the I will not cross the distance marked by the alterity of the other."[13] Or again: "transcendence designates a relation with a reality infinitely distant from my own reality, yet *without this distance destroying this relation and without this relation destroying this distance*, as would happen with relations within the same...."[14] It is important to note that, for Lévinas, the infinitely Other need not be God. He does, however, describe the relationship with the other as "religion," which hints more at the extent to which he seeks to remove himself from regular philosophical discourse, than at any confessional basis for his work.[15] Marion often uses "distance" in much the same

---

[8] Balthasar, *Theodrama IV* 362.

[9] Scola, *Hans Urs von Balthasar* 80.

[10] See John J. O'Donnell, *Hans Urs von Balthasar* (Collegeville, MN: Liturgical Press, 1992) 108.

[11] See also Ward's discussion in Graham Ward, "Kenosis: Death, Discourse and Resurrection," *Balthasar at the End of Modernity*, eds. Lucy Gardner, David Moss, Ben Quash, and Graham Ward (Edinburgh: T & T Clark, 1999) 15–68, 52ff.

[12] Emmanuel Lévinas, *Totality and Infinity* 34. Emphasis added.

[13] Lévinas, *Totality and Infinity* 38. The use of the lower case here in "other" reflects an attempt by the translator to mark a broader sense of otherness than just the other person.

[14] Lévinas, *Totality and Infinity* 41. Emphasis added.

[15] Lévinas, *Totality and Infinity* 40.

way as Lévinas, trying to think relationship in terms of a distance that protects the infinitude of the other, whether that is God or a human other.

Early Explorations

The idea of distance appears in several seminal articles from the early part of Marion's career.[16] In "Distance et béatitude," which concerns the understanding of *capacitas* in St. Augustine, Marion simply defines distance as "the relationship of the creature to the Creator."[17] Referring to the creature, distance implies being made from nothing, and having a radical dependence on God, yet it is also a "receptivity that is not yet a recipient."[18] This last feature exemplifies the difficulty involved in trying to analyse the concept of distance in Marion's work, because it seems here to have become part of *capacitas* itself. If we continue, we find that the first two features can also be applied to creation more generally, which, being made from nothing and so being radically dependent, exhibits the same distance as humanity from God. Like Balthasar, Marion also refers to the distance that constitutes the trinitarian relations. These points are reinforced in the summary on distance that he later provides in "Les deux volontés du Christ." Here he refers to Balthasar's idea of a "distance that safeguards," going on to clarify:

> I take as understood and distinguished here the concept of distance:
> 1st   Trinitarian distance (see *Résurrection* 38:51) as alterity beyond opposition.
> 2nd   Distance of goodness (see *Résurrection* 38:97–99) as creation.
> 3rd   Distance as (re-)placing in distance and beatitude (see *Résurrection* 29:58).[19]

However, distance is also seen as a necessary feature of all relationships. It is that which puts in place the ability to recognise the other as other, and which allows for a love that, in the setting of contingency, is without ground, as it were: "Distance, which in the Trinity plays in the notion of person, is unfolded in creation with the instability of that which can only find itself in looking for other than itself ...."[20]

---

[16] It is explored in some detail in Jean-Luc Marion, "Distance et béatitude: sur le mot *capacitas* chez Saint Augustin," *Résurrection* 29 (1968): 58–80; "Distance et louange," *Résurrection* 38 (1971): 89–122; "Le verbe et le texte," *Résurrection* 46 (1975): 63–80. It is also mentioned in "Ce mystère qui juge celui qui le juge," *Résurrection* 32 (1969): 54–78; "Généalogie de la 'Mort de Dieu'," *Résurrection* 36 (1971): 30–53; and "Les deux volontés du Christ selon saint Maxime le Confesseur," *Résurrection* 41 (1972): 48–66. Distance is also explored in relation to sexual difference. See "Le présent de l'homme," *Revue Catholique Internationale Communio* 7.4 (1982): 2–9.

[17] Marion, "Distance et béatitude," 59.

[18] Marion, "Distance et béatitude," 62. Note the emphasis in Balthasar's theology on reception, and the linking of reception and distance observed by Lucy Gardner and David Moss: "... it should direct our attention to the very configuration of the *theme of reception* at the heart of Balthasar's theology. A figuration imitative of creaturely existence itself, which is to say the *receptivity* and *ek-stasis* of the creature in its distance (*diastasis*) from God." Gardner and Moss, "Something Like Time," 69.

[19] Marion, "Distance et béatitude," 62; "Les deux volontés du Christ," 53n13.

[20] Marion, "Distance et béatitude," 62.

Love is made possible, according to Marion, because of a distance "which only separates to reunite."[21] In creation, distance is manifested by time. Yet frequently, this distance is misunderstood: time serves to put humanity at a distance from the distance that is the condition of all relations with God. This distancing can only be overcome by God's entry into time.[22] By that entry and reconciliation, true distance is restored as "proximity by alterity."[23] So, in the context of Augustine, distance is a condition of possibility both for the capacity for God (as receptivity) and for participation in God (as loving reception). But it is also that capacity and that participation.

"Distance et louange" is focused on the thought of Denys. Here Marion describes distance as "the place where God gives Godself to him [humanity], where man receives himself from the hands of God."[24] Distance itself cannot be understood, for that would be to compromise what it holds apart. Instead, "the distance of transcendence constitutes the place of Creation's ecstatic disappropriation, where only man in receiving it without understanding it, is conceived as ecstatically in difference, thus also in reference to God...."[25] By preserving incomprehensibility, distance enables the manifestation of the other: "The unthinkable of distance constitutes precisely the seal in it of love ... it is not about admitting distance in spite of the unthinkable, but of carefully drawing together the unthinkable, as sign of the excessive origin of distance. Distance which is love can only be received and never conceived ...."[26] Participation of the created in the Creator does not destroy distance; distance instead provokes participation.[27] In the work of Denys, distance enables denomination (in this case, of God as the Cause of all Goodness) without fixing its terms.[28] Yet distance is also this very Goodness itself.

A third place in which the idea of distance is developed is in the article from 1975, "Le verbe et le texte." Here there is a double sense of distance: the intra-trinitarian distance between Father and Son is reflected in the distance of Christ as Word from the Scriptures: "The hermeneutic distance of Christ to the Scriptures is founded on the exegetical distance of the Word to the Father."[29] In this context, distance performs the function of allowing a reference to be made from one to the other, without enclosing or restricting that other. For example, the Word is in Scripture in the sense that it gives its coherence, but cannot be identified with it.[30] Perhaps there are echoes of Karl Barth here, at least as he is refracted through the prism of Balthasar. An important question to be addressed to Marion, however, will

---

21 Marion, "Distance et béatitude," 63.
22 Marion, "Distance et béatitude," 66–71.
23 Marion, "Distance et béatitude," 71.
24 Marion, "Distance et louange," 97–98.
25 Marion, "Distance et louange," 98.
26 Marion, "Distance et louange," 99.
27 Marion, "Distance et louange," 100–101.
28 Marion, "Distance et louange," 117.
29 Marion, "Le verbe et le texte," 70.
30 Marion, "Le verbe et le texte," 69–70.

be the extent to which his hermeneutics is absolute.[31] How can distance both allow reference but resist absolute reference? (Or, in the terms of "Distance et louange," how can distance allow denomination without fixing its terms?) This is essentially the question that was raised at the beginning of this chapter. A response to the problem does not adequately emerge until many years later, where it is made clearer that the references to God made in mystical theology (the "third way") function pragmatically: they allow prayer to be addressed to God but with an addressing that is always a mis-addressing. In prayer there is a naming of what nevertheless "has no name," a naming which invokes "the name of nobody".[32] "With the third way, not only is it no longer a matter of saying (or denying) something about something, it is also no longer a matter of saying or unsaying, but of referring to the One who is no longer touched by nomination, a matter no longer of saying the referent, but of pragmatically referring the speaker to the inaccessible Referent."[33] In the later work, distance can be seen to function, for hermeneutics, as the guarantee of its infinitude.

Development

The Idol and Distance reflects a consolidation of Marion's understanding of distance, and is a systematic study of the way that distance functions to subvert idolatry. In this work Marion describes God's self-giving "within the distance that he keeps, and where he keeps us."[34] Distance is what enables proximity.[35] Infinite space promotes, at the same time, the greatest intimacy. This provides the setting for a detailed examination of trinitarian relations, where "poverty coincides with super-abundance," and where abandonment translates into glory.[36] Divinity is manifest only in the distance of withdrawal. The Paschal mystery shows Christ's divinity in two such moments: on the Cross, the distance of withdrawal is seen as his complete distinction from the Father; and in the Resurrection, the distance of withdrawal is seen as his complete unity with the Father. What this means for the disciples is that manifestation only ever coincides with disappearance. Disclosure is only ever offered subject to a distance that forbids recuperation.[37]

---

[31] See John D. Caputo, "How to Avoid Speaking of God: The Violence of Natural Theology," *Prospects for Natural Theology*, ed. E. T. Long (Washington, DC: The Catholic University of America Press, 1992) 144ff. See also the problems occasioned by Marion's more recent article and Shane Mackinlay's commentary: Jean-Luc Marion, "They Recognized Him; and He Became Invisible to Them," *Modern Theology* 18.2 (2002): 145–52; Shane Mackinlay, "Eyes Wide Shut: A Response to Jean-Luc Marion's Account of the Journey to Emmaus," *Modern Theology* 20.3 (2004): 447–56.
[32] Jean-Luc Marion, "In the Name: How to Avoid Speaking of 'Negative Theology' (including Derrida's Response to Jean-Luc Marion)," *God, the Gift and Postmodernism*, eds. John D. Caputo and Michael Scanlon (Bloomington: Indiana University Press, 1999) 122–53, 47. This is the paper and subsequent debate at Villanova. The paper is Chapter 6 of *De surcroît*; *In Excess*.
[33] See Marion, *De Sûrcroit* 171; *In Excess* 142.
[34] Marion, *L'idole et la distance* 132; *The Idol and Distance* 103.
[35] Marion, *L'idole et la distance* 133; *The Idol and Distance* 104.
[36] Marion, *L'idole et la distance* 139, 141; *The Idol and Distance* 111, 113.
[37] Marion, *L'idole et la distance* 148; *The Idol and Distance* 118–20.

Once again, our key question must be brought to bear on the text, although here in reverse. Since distance is seen to function only in withdrawal (or interruption), how are we to identify God there at all? Marion himself articulates the complexity of this problem in the following passage:

> Paternal distance offers the sole place for a filiation. Since in it the intimacy of the divine coincides strictly with withdrawal, the paradox can lead to confusion: distance must, in order that we might inhabit it, be identified. It will be identifiable only if we can say it and speak of it. We will be able to speak of it only if we come from it and remain in it. To speak of distance: concerning it, and also starting from it. But what language can be suitable to distance?
>
> It is not a question of speaking the supreme Being within a predication of which it would be the object. Nor is it a question of letting the supreme Being, as absolute subject, state a predication about itself and by itself. It is a question of designating the advent of a withdrawal to us. No being, even supreme, gives itself to be grasped, since the gift surpasses what any being could here give. Doubly unspeakable, this stake is characterised no less by the very conditions of its ineffability. For if, as Denys posits in principle, "it is necessary to understand the divine things divinely," the impossibilities of thinking coincide with the authenticating conditions of that which gives itself to be thought. As a censure and as a condition, distance requires one to think the doubly unthinkable according to excess ... and according to lack ....[38]

The mark of distance is its withdrawal; the impossibility of thinking what is ultimately excessive is the way in which distance is given to thought. But it is this very characteristic of excessiveness that both refers us to God in distance and yet simultaneously forbids absolute reference. Now, in the same way that in other passages distance is not only the spacing in which the divine–human relationship occurs or that which maintains the absolute difference between God and humanity, but becomes identified with receptivity, participation, and with Goodness respectively, here we find that distance "is"—in a very circumscribed sense—God. Not simply subject or object at the other end of a spatial continuum, God might nevertheless be thought excessively as the spacing itself. The spacing not only makes the relationship possible, but "constitutes" God as the "term" of the relationship. In other words, distance is grace. When viewed in this way, some of the features of the earlier articles fall into place more readily. What is given in the divine–human relationship is distance (grace as the possibility of receptivity, grace as our participation in God, grace as Goodness). It exceeds our ability to conceptualise, and though it is the Name, it eludes our naming with its many names. Further on in the chapter on Denys in *The Idol and Distance*, it is not such a surprise, then, to read:

> The distance of the Ab-solute precedes every utterance and every statement by an anteriority that nothing will be able to abolish. Anterior distance escapes every conception. But precisely, must distance be conceived? Anterior distance conceives us because it engenders us. Distance is not given to be understood, since it understands us.

---

[38] Marion, *L'idole et la distance* 178; *The Idol and Distance* 139–40.

Distance is given only in order to be received. Anterior distance demands to be received because it more fundamentally gives us [the chance] to receive ourselves in it. Distance, precisely because it remains the Ab-solute, delivers the space where it becomes possible for us to receive ourselves … We discover ourselves, in distance, delivered to ourselves, or rather delivered for ourselves, given, not abandoned, to ourselves. This means that distance does not separate us from the Ab-solute so much as it prepares for us, with all its anteriority, our identity. It denotes, therefore, the positive movement of the Ab-solute, which, through its being set in distance, is ecstatically disappropriated from Itself in order that man might receive himself ecstatically in difference.[39]

Marion has moved to a more evident personification of distance (as God). He has also shifted ground in a very characteristic way: as we will see in the next chapter, like Balthasar, and in the tradition of the Fathers, Marion frequently reverses the theological perspective so that it is not a question of human meditation on God but of God's meditation on us. In writing of icons, John Damascene makes the same move: "knowing God, or rather being known by Him."[40] In this vein Balthasar observes that it is not a question of grasping God so much as being grasped by God.[41]

In God's being "identified" with distance, an identification that is, nevertheless, only of the mark of the incomprehensible, the unthinkable, and the infinite, it is also possible to see another strongly Patristic theme.[42] Gregory of Nyssa is important in this regard, for example, in moving away from the Platonic understanding that infinity, and therefore incomprehensibility, would be in some way an imperfection.[43] In Gregory's *Life of Moses* we read:

> For leaving behind everything that is observed, not only what sense comprehends but also what the intelligence thinks it sees, it keeps on penetrating deeper until by the intelligence's yearning for understanding it gains access to the invisible and incomprehensible, and there it sees God. This is the true knowledge of what is sought; this is the seeing that consists in not seeing, because that which is sought transcends all knowledge, being separated on all sides by incomprehensibility as by a kind of darkness.[44]

And later:

> This truly is the vision of God: never to be satisfied in the desire to see him. But one must always, by looking at what he can see, rekindle his desire to see more. Thus, no limit would interrupt growth in the ascent to God, since no limit to the Good can be found nor is the increasing of desire for the Good brought to an end because it is satisfied.[45]

---

[39] Marion, *L'idole et la distance* 192; *The Idol and Distance* 153. Translation modified.

[40] St. John of Damascus, *Apologia Against Those Who Decry Holy Images* Part I.

[41] Balthasar, *The Glory of the Lord I* 134.

[42] See Marion's comments on the infinite at Marion, *L'idole et la distance* 186–89; *The Idol and Distance* 148–51.

[43] See Anthony Meredith, *The Cappadocians* (London: Geoffrey Chapman, 1995) 66.

[44] Gregory of Nyssa, *Life of Moses*, s.163, eds. A. J. Malherbe and E. Ferguson, *Gregory of Nyssa. The Life of Moses* (New York: Paulist, 1978).

[45] Gregory of Nyssa, *Life of Moses*, s.239, *Gregory of Nyssa. The Life of Moses.*

Now Marion's understanding of distance can be seen in a broader context: "to claim to comprehend distance, or to lament that it remains incomprehensible betrays a double inconsistency: not only does distance reject absolute knowledge by definition, but it symptomatically reveals the disappropriation of the Ab-solute by itself ...."[46] The reason for the incomprehensibility of distance is not that it puts a space between God and us, but that it *is* the spacing that "is" God. We do not perceive distance, but are held in it and by it. In the light of these reflections, it is, therefore, not so unusual that despite all the definitions of distance, it remains undefined. This is the conclusion reached at the beginning of Section 17 of *The Idol and Distance*: "first, distance has a definition. Second, it remains indefinable by definition."[47]

Distance occurs between people (Marion uses the words "between others" to reinforce the distinction between them), as well as between God and humanity.[48] It is that which makes relationships possible, and the reinforcement of this point serves to make it the baseline of our ongoing interpretation.[49] Distance is "neither subject of discourse nor object of science." It defines us as one of the terms in a relationship, defining the other as indefinable. The poles of the relationship formed by distance are thus asymmetrical, reminding us very much of Lévinas.[50] Distance does not form a third element in the relationship (as that which engenders it), but is the indefinable term.[51] Hence, once again, the play between distance as spacing and distance as God. Distance is the spacing in which relationships occur, but it is also the infinite term of a relationship. It is neither subject, nor object: it is not any *thing*. Marion then goes on to compare distance to ontological difference. He insists that distance precedes difference, a claim that Derrida will make of *différance*, which, like distance, is neither subject nor object, yet makes thought possible.[52] Nevertheless, as much as Derrida would argue that *différance* is not God, Marion argues that distance is not *différance*.[53] Distance instead puts in play a fourth dimension, where not only the difference between being and beings is recognised, but the difference between God and being is broached.[54] The way in which this difference is given echoes the way in which *Ereignis* gives-in-withdrawal for Heidegger.[55] These themes are developed more fully in *God Without Being*.

---

46 Marion, *L'idole et la distance* 193; *The Idol and Distance* 154.

47 Marion, *L'idole et la distance* 247; *The Idol and Distance* 198.

48 Marion, *L'idole et la distance* 247; *The Idol and Distance* 198.

49 In conversation, Marion insists that distance is simply this.

50 See, for example, Lévinas, *Totality and Infinity* 215–16.

51 Marion, *L'idole et la distance* 249; *The Idol and Distance* 199.

52 See the essay "Differance," especially at 30, 34 and 59. See also Derrida, *Given Time* 40.

53 Derrida resists a theological personification of *différance* or *khôra*. See "Faith and Knowledge: the Two Sources of 'Religion' at the Limits of Reason Alone," trans. Samuel Weber, *Religion*, eds. Jacques Derrida and Gianni Vattimo (Stanford, CA: Stanford University Press, 1998) 1–78, 21; *Speech and Phenomena* 134 and 59.

54 Marion, *L'idole et la distance* 294ff.; *The Idol and Distance* 245ff. See also the discussion in Victor Kal, "Being Unable to Speak, Seen As a Period: Difference and Distance in Jean-Luc Marion," *Flight of the Gods: Philosophical Perspectives on Negative Theology*, eds. Ilse N. Bulhof and Laurens ten Kate (New York: Fordham University Press, 2000) 148, 152, 153.

55 Marion, *L'idole et la distance* 295ff.; *The Idol and Distance* 246ff.

Distance: An Approach

Having examined Marion's usage of distance in a number of different settings, it is now possible to try to offer an explanation of his use of the term.[56] Distance primarily refers to a separation or spacing that makes relationships (intra-trinitarian, divine with human, and human with human) possible. But it is also that which protects those relationships from totalisation, that is, it prevents us from reducing the other (divine or human, or even work of art) to our own dimensions. However, distance is used in its strongest sense to mean God, or grace, the self-giving of whom resists comprehension even while pointing towards the origin of such excess. The difficulty with this varied use of the concept (distance as spacing versus distance as God) is that it is not clear exactly how the different terms of the relationships are to be identified. It is pointed out that God's self-giving in and as distance will be unmistakable, but it is not so clear how this can be distinguished from the self-giving of other persons, unless the protective rupture of distance is not total. Yet if that is the case, our key problem again emerges: if distance (absolutely) refers us to God, then the very transcendence it is designed to protect is betrayed. Perhaps a different way of understanding distance would be to say that God gives Godself in and as a spacing in which all other relationships are held, that God "is" the irreducible spacing of relationships. While the meaning of the term opens onto a number of difficulties, its theological function cannot be underestimated in Marion's attempt to think God "otherwise" than according to being. The function of distance is to destitute thought by giving in withdrawal, by interrupting conceptualisation in much the same way that for Lévinas, the "Saying" always exceeds the "Said."[57]

---

[56] Distance is mentioned in a number of later texts, but the basic points have been made. Sections of those texts will be highlighted in later chapters.

[57] See, for example, Lévinas, *Otherwise than Being* 5–9; 34–51; *Totality and Infinity* 195.

Chapter 6

The Icon, Love, and the Gift

The examination of distance in the previous chapter was undertaken in some detail. While each of the other "theological motifs" to be examined here—the icon, love, and the gift—merits at least the same amount of attention, their treatment will be abbreviated to allow for their revision in later chapters, as it becomes necessary. A shift is evident in how Marion conceives the idol and icon, for example, as his work becomes more explicitly phenomenological. While this shift is already underway by the time of *La croisée du visible*—a work to be considered here—it is more fully articulated in the phenomenological trilogy, and particularly with *In Excess*. In exploring idol and icon in this chapter, I will pause at the threshold of that development, since more detail on Marion's approach to phenomenology will be required in order to contextualise their further reconception. Similarly, Marion's thinking on love can only fully be appreciated in light of *Le phénomène érotique* (2003), and his work on the gift provokes substantial debate and development in a phenomenological context. Issues surrounding love and the gift will therefore only be noted in a preliminary way. Here, once again, we will need to consider not only the sources of Marion's thought with regard to each motif, and how he understands the icon, love, and the gift, but also whether or not they function in an absolute manner.

The Idol Versus the Icon[1]

Although he rehearses the concepts in earlier publications, Marion first clearly frames his thinking in terms of the idol and the icon in 1977.[2] *The Idol and Distance* begins with an examination of the idolatrous concept of God that—in Marion's view—dies along with metaphysics; the same work ends with a rethinking of God according to the icon of distance. Similar material sets up the approach in *God Without Being*. In that work Marion defines as idolatrous that which saturates the gaze with visibility and dazzles it, acting as an invisible mirror to the one who gazes upon it. An idol becomes so only because it functions as such in the eye of the beholder, and is there subject to the limitations of that perspective. Idolatry, in other words, does not occur so much because an image has reference to a god, but principally because it makes a

---

[1] Earlier versions of parts of the following text appear in "The Face as Icon," *Australasian Catholic Record* 82.1 (2005).

[2] Jean-Luc Marion, "Distance et louange" 104–12; "Généalogie de la 'Mort de Dieu'," *Résurrection* 36 (1971): 30–53; "Note sur l'athéisme conceptuel," *Résurrection* 38 (1971): 119–20. Prior to *God Without Being*, see "Fragments sur l'idole et l'icone," *Revue de Métaphysique et de Morale* 84.4 (1979): 433–45.

god of the idolater. Ideas also function as idols in this way. Ludwig Feuerbach's observation that people fashion God according to their own images, Nietzsche's condemnation of the moral God, or Heidegger's rejection of the God who is *causa sui*, are examples less of an increased modern tendency towards atheism than of the fact that concepts of God effectively limit God to the measure of the human. Attempts to overcome these idolatries may, in turn, produce their own idols, such as Nietzsche's *Übermensch* with its will to power, and Heidegger's *Sein*, which Marion goes on to interpret as idolatrous in its presumed anteriority to any question of God.[3]

In contrast to the idol, the icon refers not to the viewer, but beyond itself; the icon is a visible reference to the invisible. Nevertheless, Marion argues that in making this reference, the icon does not thereby contain it. The background to his thinking on this issue is found in the work of John Damascene, *Apologia Against Those Who Decry Holy Images*, in which comments by many other patristic writers are also drawn together, including observations by Basil of Caesaria, Gregory of Nazianzus, Gregory of Nyssa, and Denys. Writing in the eighth century against the iconoclasts, and echoing Gregory of Nazianzus and Romans 1:20, John argues that images are important in Christian worship, for "since the creation of the world the invisible things of God are clearly seen by means of images."[4] It is the incarnation of the *Logos* that most powerfully authorises the veneration (*proskinesis*, in contrast to adoration, *latreia*) of icons: "In former times God, who is without form or body, could never be depicted. But now when God is seen in the flesh conversing with men, I make an image of the God whom I see. I do not worship matter; I worship the Creator of matter who became matter for my sake ... Never will I cease honouring the matter which wrought my salvation! I honor it, but not as God."[5] The image is not the same as the prototype to which it refers, but as Basil declares, is honoured so that honour may be transferred to the prototype.[6] What is clear is that the image is not intended to reduce the original to its own dimensions, but allows us to move through its contemplation to the worship of the invisible God.[7] The purpose of the

---

[3] Marion, *Dieu sans l'être* 20–27, 44ff., 104; *God Without Being* 12–6, 29ff., 69.

[4] John Damascene, *On the Divine Images: Three Apologies Against Those Who Attack the Divine Images*, trans. David Anderson (Crestwood, NY: St. Vladimir's Seminary Press, 1980) 20. Another important resource in this regard are the decisions of the (Eastern) Quinisext Council of 692. See Leonid Ouspensky, *Theology of the Icon*, trans. J. Meyendorff (Crestwood, NY: St. Vladimir's Seminary Press, 1978) 113ff.

[5] Damascene, *On the Divine Images* 23. For an explanation of the distinction between *latreia* and *proskinesis*, see David Anderson, "Introduction," *St. John of Damascus: On the Divine Images* 7–12, 8–9.

[6] Damascene, *On the Divine Images* 73–74. At 36 and 91 he quotes from Basil of Caesarea: "The image of the emperor is also called the emperor, and there are not two emperors. Power is not divided, nor is glory separated. Just as He who rules us is one power, so the homage He receives from us is united, not divided, for the honor given to the image is transferred to the prototype. Therefore, the One whom the image materially represents is He who is Son by nature. Just as the likeness of a corresponding form is made by the artists, so also in the divine and unconfused nature, union is accomplished by divine indwelling."

[7] "You see that the law and everything it commanded and all our own practises are meant to sanctify the work of our hands, leading us through matter to the invisible God." Damascene, *On the Divine Images* 67. Cf. Marion, *La croisée* Book IV.

image is to help in this regard: "All images reveal and make perceptible those things which are hidden."[8] In fact, the image is necessary for finite minds:

> Anyone would say that our inability immediately to direct our thoughts to contemplation of higher things makes it necessary that familiar every-day media be utilized to give suitable form to what is formless, and make visible what cannot be depicted, so that we are able to construct understandable analogies. If, therefore, the Word of God, in providing for our every need, always presents to us what is intangible by clothing it with form, does it not accomplish this by making an image using what is common to nature and so bringing within our reach that for which we long but are unable to see? The eloquent Gregory [Nazianzen] says that the mind which is determined to ignore corporeal things will find itself weakened and frustrated.[9]

Marion's many descriptions of the theological significance of icons follow John's teaching closely, as well as that of the Second Council of Nicaea of 787.[10] Icons bring the invisible to visibility, not by representing it *as such*, but by opening onto it.[11] Up to this point, Marion simply reinforces the tradition, but there are further and very important dimensions to his work with icons that mark it as distinctive. First, in the same way that Marion refers to conceptual idols, he also thinks more broadly than the visual by referring to conceptual icons, and this will form the basis of much of his theology. In response to the problem of how to think God without falling into idolatry, Marion maintains that it is possible, not through the traditional metaphysical route that focuses on being, but through the mystical route of love, which is explored in *God Without Being*. Yet there is a second and more profound development in Marion's appropriation of icons to overcome metaphysics. Icons function in orthodox liturgy to mark the participation in that prayer of the whole communion of saints, to affirm the reality of a world already transformed, and the concomitant transformation by *theosis*, or deification, of the worshippers.[12] They function in personal prayer to bring the believer explicitly into that transformed realm and to visually articulate his or her prayer: "… a worshipper approaches an ikon to pray and finds that his prayer is already expressed and translated into the painting."[13] But for Marion, the icon also functions as a locus for a significant reversal. What is made visible in the icon is the gaze of the invisible other, who looks at my gaze, or whose look crosses my gaze.[14] The contemplation of the icon is

---

[8] Damascene, *On the Divine Images* 74.

[9] Damascene, *On the Divine Images* 76–77.

[10] Marion, *La croisée* 122ff.

[11] Marion, *Dieu sans l'être* 16–17; *God Without Being* 8–9.

[12] Ouspensky, *Theology of the Icon* 10, 191ff.; John Stuart, *Ikons* (London: Faber and Faber, 1975) 33. See also Gennadios Limouris, "The Microcosm and Macrocosm of the Icon," ed. Gennadios Limouris, *Icons: Windows on Eternity* (Geneva: WCC Publications, 1990) 93–123.

[13] Vladimir Soloukhin, quoted in Stuart, *Ikons* 29.

[14] Marion, *Dieu sans l'être*, 29–30; *God Without Being* 18; *La croisée* 147ff.; *Prolégomènes à la charité* 100ff.; *Prolegomena to Charity* 80ff. While this might seem to be an obvious understanding, it is rarely expressed in the literature. John Baggley notes: "… the lines of perspective are reversed, to converge not at some distant point in the scene, but in

thus an experience of a type of *kenosis*: where looking at the idol reinforces the identity of the *ego*, coming before the icon empties the *ego* of its ability to control, to understand, to manipulate, to grasp. To come before the icon is to allow oneself to be overcome by the irreducible, inconceivable other who gazes upon me. We see here the source for Marion's philosophical reflections on subjectivity, the other person, and God—reflections that will pick up a number of Lévinasian nuances but that also reinforce Balthasar's fundamental theological view that what is important is not our experience of God, but God's experience of us: "When the word 'experience' (*peira*) finally appears in the writings of the Apostolic Fathers, it is to denote God's experience, not man's: 'We must undergo the *peira* of the living God and be trained in this life so that we may be crowned in the next' (2 Clem 20:2)."[15] This has echoes of Origen: "The one who is seen, does not appear in the same way to those who look at him, but to the extent of their capacity to receive him."[16] For Marion, the icon gives the invisible to thought, not on the basis of the capacities of the metaphysical *ego*, but on its own terms.

There is a relationship between the icon and distance. Distance disrupts the concept ("the icon obliges the concept to welcome the distance of infinite depth"). Further, in the relationship of the believer to the icon, distance means that "union increases in the measure of distinction, and reciprocally." To contemplate the icon is a contemplation in distance, a contemplation, in other words, that does not yield knowledge or comprehension.[17] It is distance, through the icon, which contemplates the believer.[18] Praise, while opening distance, "neither asks nor tolerates that one fill it but that one traverse it, in an infinite praise that feeds on the impossibility or, better, the impropriety of the category." Marion is again speaking of Denys, and when he suggests that distance be traversed, he clearly does not mean "understood," since he immediately goes on to qualify that praise does not deliver a concept of God, but only "the luminous darkness," which again is reminiscent of Gregory of Nyssa.[19]

---

front of the icon in the eyes of the beholder; one is left feeling that the beholder is essential to the completion of the icon. The essence of the exercise has been to establish a communion between the event or persons represented in the icon and those who stand before it, to 'make present' to another person what is presented in the icon ...." John Baggley, *Doors of Perception: Icons and Their Spiritual Significance* (London: Mowbray, 1987) 80–81. Nevertheless, while Baggley goes on to say that the face is in communion with the beholder, he also comments that the eyes of the icon look inward, away from the world (83). Limouris quotes an ancient tradition that comes closer to the idea of the crossing of gazes: "'When you enter your room, bow to the icon and catch the glance of God!'" Limouris, "The Microcosm and Macrocosm of the Icon," Limouris, ed., *Icons* 107–08. My thanks to Lawrence Cross for his insights on the centrality of the eyes for iconographers (and defacing the eyes for the iconoclasts), as well as on the links with Palmyran art.

[15] Hans Urs von Balthasar, *New Elucidations*, trans. Mary Theresilde Skerry (San Francisco, CA: Ignatius Press, 1986) 25.

[16] *Against Celsus*, quoted in Jean-Luc Marion, "Ce mystère qui juge celui qui le juge," *Résurrection* 32 (1969): 54–78, 74.

[17] Marion, *Dieu sans l'être* 36; *God Without Being* 23.

[18] Marion, *Dieu sans l'être* 160; *God Without Being* 111.

[19] Marion, *Dieu sans l'être* 115; *God Without Being* 76.

In *La croisée du visible* Marion analyses the working of the icon extensively, particularly with regard to the ways in which it functions differently to an ordinary work of art. The icon is painted without reference to the viewer's perspective; it does not use invisibility to organise the visual space but only to reveal a look.[20] The painted look serves as the locus of encounter between the invisible gaze of the holy, and the look of the one who prays. In this way, the invisible interrupts or subverts the visible.[21] This is related to the encounter with the face of the other person, where the look is drawn to the place of invisibility *par excellence*, the pupils of the eyes.[22] What is seen here is not an object but the interruption of the visible by an invisible look.[23] In the encounter either with the icon or the face, two interrelated factors are important for Marion. One is that the I who looks is put in question, finding itself not the author of perspective but its object.[24] The other is that the icon and the face provide ways of approaching invisibility. Nevertheless, we need to ask to what extent the reference to invisibility by way of the icon is absolute for Marion: if the icon reduces the invisible to visibility, then we risk thinking it as visible or conceivable. Marion goes some way towards addressing this question in an examination of the functioning of the Cross, which serves both as an icon in its own right (icon of Christ and, in turn, icon of God) and as a measure of all icons.[25] Seeking to protect the distance between the image and the prototype, Marion invokes a hermeneutics: the same visible can provoke so many different interpretations that there can be no ultimate or single reference.[26] Only prayer, he then maintains, can pass from the visible to the invisible.[27] Presumably, however, even prayer can only appeal to the undecidability of the constituting gaze; that the eyes of the beholder do in fact meet a gaze cannot be established in any definitive sense, and it is here precisely that the basis for establishing a theological overcoming of metaphysics can be called into question.

---

[20] Marion, *La croisée* 41–42. Limouris also notes the reversal of perspective, "The Microcosm and Macrocosm of the Icon," *Icons* 104.

[21] Marion, *La croisée* 42–43, 106–107.

[22] There is a natural theological link between the icon and the face, as Limouris observes: "… the icon helps us to decipher every human face as an icon. For every human face is an icon. Beneath all the masks, all the ashes, every human being, however ravaged he or she may be by his or her destiny … carries within him or her the pearl of great price, this hidden face. During the liturgies in an Orthodox church, when the priest censes the people, he censes every individual Christian, and in every individual Christian he censes the possibility, the opportunity, of the icon, in some sense or other, the chance of the ultimate beauty, of true beauty." "The Microcosm and Macrocosm of the Icon," *Icons* 118–19.

[23] Marion, *La croisée* 43, 101–102. This becomes very important for Marion, as we will observe, in his development of the Lévinasian theme of encounter with the face. See Marion, "The Face: An Endless Hermeneutics"; *De surcroît*; *In Excess* Chapter 5.

[24] Marion, *La croisée* 45, 72.

[25] Marion, *La croisée* 122ff. See also my discussion in *Rethinking God as Gift* 168–71. The cross is a difficult example to choose in the context of a discussion of the constituting gaze, since the cross (and even a crucifix) need not function through eyes. Marion argues that the cross is an icon of Christ, and in that way invokes a more focused point of withdrawal to invisibility.

[26] Marion, *La croisée* 129–30.

[27] Marion, *La croisée* 133.

Love

"Love alone is worthy of our faith. The revelation that Christ brings, that 'God is love' (1 John 4:18) shows us not only what we can know [*ce que nous pouvons connaître*], but, moreover, how we can know [*comment nous pouvons connaître*]. Love constitutes the content as well as the advancement of faith ...."[28] Writing in 1970, with these words Marion sets the agenda for his entire life's work: God's first name is love (not being), love is the content of revelation, and revelation is only to be known by loving; this is essentially Marion's complete theological manifesto. One of the most interesting questions to arise from this formulation, however, will be just what is meant by "knowing" in this context. In fact, that is the question of central concern throughout our investigation. If theology overcomes metaphysics, and if—as we will see in the examination of *On Descartes' Metaphysical Prism* and *God Without Being*—it is also seen to overcome even the thought that overcomes metaphysics, then how is theology itself to be thought? What does theology know and how does it know it? In the passage from the 1970 article just quoted, Marion utililises the distinction available in French between knowing personally or being acquainted with (*connaître*), and knowing a fact or a thing (*savoir*). While the same distinction appears elsewhere, it is not something that is explicitly argued to be of significance. Nevertheless, it reinforces Marion's constant association of theological knowing with the will (loving) rather than with reason.[29] A further characteristic of Marion's treatment of loving-as-knowing is his emphasis, very much in line with Balthasar, on knowing as being known.[30] While we need to reflect on how he uses the motif of love, there is little need to speculate on why it is a major theological focus for Marion. To name God as love clearly has biblical foundations and Marion's reflections on love are often set in this context, but he also picks up the resonances of love throughout Christian tradition, particularly as they occur in the works of Augustine, Denys, Bonaventure, and Pascal.

In *The Idol and Distance* we find that love is initially opposed to conceptual knowledge as such. Nevertheless, it still involves a kind of knowing, and since "knowledge presupposes conceptual and, minimally, linguistic mediation," Marion goes on to ask: "can language, including conceptual language, become

---

[28] Jean-Luc Marion, "Amour de Dieu, amour des hommes," *Résurrection* 34 (1970): 89–96, 90.

[29] See, for example, Marion, *Prolégomènes* 77ff.; *Prolegomena* 58ff. The essay from the collection to which these references refer—"L'Évidence et l'éblouissement" ("Evidence and Bedazzlement")—was written in 1978.

[30] In *The Idol and Distance* Marion quotes Paul from 1 Corinthians 8:1–3; note especially v.3: "but if someone loves God, he is known by God." See also Jean-Luc Marion, "De la 'mort de Dieu' aux noms divins. L'itinéraire théologique de la métaphysique," *L'être et Dieu*, ed. D. Bourg (Paris: Cerf, 1986) 116. Balthasar frequently speaks of "being seen" rather than seeing, for example in Hans Urs von Balthasar, *The Glory of the Lord: A Theological Aesthetics*, trans. Brian McNeil, vol. VII: Theology: The New Covenant, 7 vols. (San Francisco, CA: Ignatius Press, 1990) 286–87.

homogeneous with Love?"[31] He then argues that the knowing of love can only take place according to distance:

> Distance offers the sole, unique form of manifestation suitable to Goodness. Because Goodness deepens infinitely within a hyperbole that we will see later refer finally to the Trinity, it remains unthinkable to us. The unthinkability of distance within it constitutes the mark and the seal of love, which "came down [to us] from heaven" (John 6:50). The unthinkable, as the distance of Goodness, gives itself—not to be comprehended but to be received. It is therefore not a question of giving up on comprehending (as if it were a question of comprehending, and not of being comprehended). It is a question of managing to receive that which becomes thinkable, or rather acceptable, only for the one who knows how to receive it. It is not a question of admitting distance despite its unthinkability, but of preciously receiving the unthinkable, as the sign and the seal of the measureless origin of the distance that gives us our measure. If love reveals itself hermetically as distance (which is glossed by *cause* and *goodness*) in order to give itself, only love will be able to welcome it.[32]

The knowledge of love can only be received rather than thought (it is "not to be comprehended but to be received") and in being received, it destitutes thought ("it remains unthinkable to us"). It has to do with being comprehended rather than comprehending. "Love reveals itself hermetically as distance": extraordinarily, it is sealed (with "the seal of the measureless origin of the distance that gives us our measure")—and yet recognised *as* love because welcomed *by* love.

Love has a significant role to play in the unfolding of the two texts we will shortly consider in detail: *On Descartes' Metaphysical Prism* and *God Without Being*. Marion makes use in the former of the work of Pascal, for whom love provides a way beyond metaphysics. For the moment, I will simply note Marion's observations in this text about the relationship between knowing and loving. First, while love appears to go beyond thought for Pascal, it still bears a relationship with thought:

> Not that love dispenses with knowing or requires some sacrifice of intelligibility, but love becomes, instead of and in the place of *intuitus*, the keeper of evidence, the royal road to knowledge: "When speaking of things human, we say that we should know them before loving them—a saying which has become proverbial. Yet the saints, on the contrary, when speaking of things divine, say that we should love them in order to know them, and that we enter into truth only through charity."[33]

Love involves a movement of the heart, or will, and provides access to a new kind of knowing, functioning as a hermeneutic principle that opens onto a new world: "To see the 'order of charity,' one has not so much to know a new object, as to know

---

31 Marion, *L'idole et la distance* 183; *The Idol and Distance* 145. Trans. modified. "Nothing less would be necessary than a linguistic model of the dispossession of meaning in order to begin approaching what is at stake here." (183/144)

32 Marion, *L'idole et la* distance 194; *The Idol and Distance* 155.

33 Marion, *Sur le prisme métaphysique* 324; *On Descartes' Metaphysical Prism* 305.

according to a new condition, loving ....".[34] This contrasts somewhat with the formulation from 1992 in "Christian Philosophy and Charity," where love actually allows new phenomena to be seen: "... new phenomena appear among the things of this world to an eye that is initiated in charity," or later: "... only those who love see the phenomena of love ... The result is that for many observers, perhaps even most, these phenomena remain invisible, or else are reduced to an arbitrary interpretation, one of several possible interpretations ....".[35] (With the latter point—and in the remainder of this article, in fact—we may wonder whether Marion is invoking an absolute hermeneutics, that is, whether he is arguing that the Christian interpretation is not actually an interpretation at all but coincides with what is given in the present as knowledge.) In *God Without Being*, it is love that enables us to go beyond not only metaphysics, but also beyond ontological difference. As we will see, here love is thought of in terms of the gift.

The 1986 article, "De la 'mort de Dieu' aux noms divins ...." offers a very focused consideration of the knowledge that is the knowledge of love. As in *On Descartes' Metaphysical Prism*, love is described as a third order beyond the order of concepts.[36] Marion here speaks of a choice "without reasonable guarantee (without concept, or spectacle ...)," a choice "without conceptually constraining reason," an "insane" choice, for or against God.[37] The rationality of this choice lies not in the mind but in the will:

> Charity allows [us] to know rigorously on the condition, at least, that it is a question of knowing charity itself. The objection that contests the epistemic power of charity does not consider, actually, the exceptional demands that the luminous darkness fixes here on all knowledge [*toute connaissance*] that would wish to be constituted as *theo*logical: to secure knowledge [*un savoir*] without being fixed on an idol, thus to know [*savoir*] without representation of an object.

The choice for love does not mean a choice, however, for "the emptiness of a pure undecideable."[38] Love knows—or recognises—love: ... the one who loves does not see God as an object, but recognises God as the dominant logic of his or her own act of love ... In short, God is recognised as and in the very act by which God makes me love ....".[39] God is known, in other words, by way of the movement of love that the person is enabled to make. This insight prompts Marion to propose two theses: first, what is known is not an object, but love itself, offering to love "the invisible look of love" reminiscent of what is given in the icon; second, love is its own proper mode of knowledge, accomplished as the transgression of idolatry.[40] From this point onwards, Marion repeats and reinforces a number of his arguments from *God*

---

[34] Marion, *Sur le prisme métaphysique* 333, 336; *On Descartes' Metaphysical Prism* 313, 316.

[35] Jean-Luc Marion, "Christian Philosophy and Charity," *Communio* XVII (1992): 465–73, 469, 470.

[36] Marion, "De la 'mort de Dieu'" 117.

[37] Marion, "De la 'mort de Dieu'" 118.

[38] Marion, "De la 'mort de Dieu'" 119.

[39] Marion, "De la 'mort de Dieu'" 120.

[40] Marion, "De la 'mort de Dieu'" 120–21.

Without Being concerning the priority of Love as the divine name, but there is one further comment that is worthy of note. This is the claim—made in response to objections to *God Without Being*—that "to try to think God without being does not imply being condemned to thinking without reason."[41] Marion argues that it is necessary to think according to the logic of the gift that precedes being, that is, according to a different reason, but not without reason altogether.

A final text that demands examination with regard to the question of love is *Prolegomena to Charity*.[42] This work is a collection of essays from as early as 1978; the 2002 edition in English benefits from the additional inclusion of a very pertinent article from 1994, "What Love Knows." Before we turn to this article, however, aspects of two earlier chapters must be considered. "Evidence and Bedazzlement," composed in 1978, concerns the role of evidence in apologetics. Here we find insights from "De la 'mort de Dieu' ...." and *On Descartes' Metaphysical Prism* prefigured: "... faith neither compensates for the lack of evidence nor resolves itself in arguments, but decides by the will for or against the love of Love."[43] In order to know love, the will must abandon itself both to distance and to the gift. But this is not to say, Marion argues, that the will thus abandons itself to irrationality. The obscurity of what is given is not obscure because it is defective or deficient, but because it is excessive. To this extent, it dazzles the beholder.[44] The gaze

> ... finds too much to see there, too much to envisage and look at squarely, and thus, too much to interpret and to allow to interpret us, and so it flees .... Only love, "which bears all" (1 Corinthians 13:7), can bear with its gaze Love's excess. In proportion to our love, our gaze can open, be it only by blinking, to the evidence of Love. In this proportion also, bedazzlements can become evidence ....[45]

As we will observe in later chapters, this will become the basis for Marion's concept of saturated phenomena. In terms of our guiding question of whether what is given is given absolutely, that is, without the need for a hermeneutics, two further comments from Marion are instructive. Shortly after this passage, he equates seeing with interpretation ("... one always begins in apologetics with the weakest evidence possible, which requires a small investment of love to be seen and thus interpreted ..."). Here there is no claim for the absoluteness of the given phenomenon in terms of the capacity of the one who receives. A preliminary investment of love is required in order to see at all, and seeing involves an interpretation. Further, he notes that the "terminal point [for any proof of God] is a leap."[46] This underlines the point just made, and suggests that the assertion that

---

41 Marion, "De la 'mort de Dieu'" 128.

42 Marion uses both love (*l'amour*) and charity (*la charité*) in his writings, sometimes interchangeably, although he is not unaware of the differences in their connotations. See Marion, *Prolegomena* 155. He finally articulates his dislike of the distinction in *Le phénomène érotique* 13–15.

43 Marion, *Prolégomènes* 80; *Prolegomena* 62.

44 Marion, *Prolégomènes* 82–86; *Prolegomena* 64–67.

45 Marion, *Prolégomènes* 85–86; *Prolegomena* 67.

46 Marion, *Prolégomènes* 88; *Prolegomena* 69.

Marion simply overcomes metaphysics with dogma may already have been unsettled in advance.

"The Intentionality of Love" (1983) again foreshadows Marion's phenomenology of the other person and of the decentred subject, but it also picks up aspects of his theology of the icon. Asking how it is that I can experience an other, Marion develops a quasi-Lévinasian intentionality of love that depends, not on seeing the other (and thereby reducing the other to the scope of my own gaze), but on feeling the weight of the other's unsubstitutable gaze as it crosses my intentional aim. This weight is experienced as an always-prior injunction that exposes and obliges me.[47] "To love would thus be defined as seeing the definitively invisible aim of my gaze nonetheless exposed by the aim of another invisible gaze; the two gazes, invisible forever, expose themselves each to the other in the crossing of their reciprocal aims."[48] The interlocking of the two gazes is the point at which the lovers share a common lived experience: "They experience one another in the commonality of the lived experience of their unique tension ...."[49] This can occur, Marion argues, only if each of the lovers is prepared to surrender egoity (in favour of exposure), which ultimately involves the surrender of intentionality.[50] The knowledge of love would therefore again reside in the will, lived out in the act of self-surrender.

We finally turn to the very lucid essay from 1994, "What Love Knows," where this thesis is confirmed and strengthened. Here there is no ambiguity about the status of love as knowing: "... because love has also been distinguished from knowledge, we will attempt to think of love itself as a knowledge—and a preeminent knowledge to boot."[51] Similarly there is no ambiguity about the kind of knowledge it enables: "... love opens up knowledge of the other as such."[52] After considering the Husserlian account of intersubjectivity, and with passing reference to Kant's articulation of the categorical imperative, Marion argues that access to the other person is in fact only possible subsequent to my decision to love him or her: "For when it is a question of knowing (and not merely experiencing) the other, the other *I* who, because just such, will never therefore become for me an available and

---

[47] Marion, *Prolégomènes* 103ff.; *Prolegomena* 83ff. Marion differs from Lévinas, however, in that he tries to argue for the specificity of the other, whereas Lévinas' other has been seen to resist specification. This is further developed by Marion in "D'Autrui à L'Individu." See also the translator's note in Marion, *Prolegomena* 83. Marion also differs from Lévinas in that while the other puts the I in question, the relationship is not entirely asymmetrical as it is in Lévinas. Interestingly enough, Marion further notes that "the injunction does not come from the other toward me ... It actually arises in me ..." (91). Finally, he differs from Lévinas in maintaining that love ultimately exceeds intentionality (98, 100n15).

[48] Marion, *Prolégomènes* 107; *Prolegomena* 87.

[49] Marion, *Prolégomènes* 109; *Prolegomena* 89.

[50] Marion, *Prolégomènes* 117; *Prolegomena* 97–98. Intentionality would inevitably reduce the other to the I; Marion argues that the surrender of intentionality actually confirms the unsubstitutability of this particular other, who must be imposed as this other in order for me to experience the other's gaze.

[51] Marion, *Prolegomena* 160.

[52] Marion, *Prolegomena* 160.

constitutable object—it is necessary to resort to charity. Charity in effect becomes a means of knowledge when our concern is with the other, and no longer with objects ...."[53] The very phenomenality of the other, or the other's gaze, is dependent on my preparedness to accept the other as other. This requires that I give the other "the space in which to appear," my own space.[54] Equally, it requires that I risk being exposed to the other's choice to love me—or not, and thereby to constitute me.[55]

I will leave an examination of *Le phénomène érotique* until the final chapter; however, from the analysis given so far we have the essential features of Marion's thinking on love. These features are intrinsically related to his other theological motifs: distance, the icon, and the gift. While Marion claims that loving is not a type of intentionality, he nevertheless maintains that it is a type of knowing, and while it is a knowing that does not have an object, it involves a certain personal recognition. This is, perhaps, the point at which we might continue to question him. If knowing the other—and knowing God—depends on a decision in advance to recognise the other as other (to admit, basically, that I am seen), which is then confirmed in the act of loving the other, then knowledge of God, at least, is based on nothing more than my will to believe that God gives Godself to me in love. But perhaps this is precisely the issue. The choice for God involves, as Marion admits, a type of madness; while the risk may be subsequently confirmed in an experience of love, it will never be confirmed in any absolute sense, and the aporia remains.

The Gift

We turn now to the last of the four dominant theological motifs in Marion's work, that of the gift. Ironically, while it is a constant in his theology, it remains largely unthematised as such in theological contexts. As early as 1974, Marion is aware of the phenomenological dimensions of an analysis of the gift, which at this stage he dismisses: "... the gift most often becomes pretext to a banally 'phenomenological' analysis...."[56] It is not until 1994 that Marion undertakes his own—far from banal—phenomenological study, which culminates in the analysis presented in 1997 with the French text of *Being Given*.[57] Marion's subsequent claim at Villanova late in the same year is striking: "... right now, at this stage of my work, I have to emphasize that I am not interested in the gift and I am not interested in the religious meaning of the gift."[58] Presumably, this is because by this point Marion is

---

53 Marion, *Prolegomena* 164.
54 Marion, *Prolegomena* 166.
55 Marion, *Prolegomena* 167.
56 Jean-Luc Marion, "Présence et distance: remarques sur l'implication réciproque de la contemplation eucharistique et de la présence réelle," *Résurrection* 43–44 (1974): 31–58, 33.
57 Jean-Luc Marion, "Esquisse d'un concept phénoménologique du don," *Archivio di Filosofia* LXII.1–3 (1994): 75–94; "Sketch of a Phenomenological Concept of the Gift," *Postmodern Philosophy and Christian Thought*, eds. J. Conley and D. Poe (Bloomington: Indiana University Press, 1999).
58 Richard Kearney, Jacques Derrida and Jean-Luc Marion, "On the Gift: A Discussion between Jacques Derrida and Jean-Luc Marion, Moderated by Richard Kearney," *God, the*

constantly having to battle the accusation that his phenomenology is a surreptitious theology. Temporarily putting this argument to one side, however, a consideration of Marion's strictly theological use of the gift motif, without the benefit of his phenomenological framework, will be quite limited.

Marion's early theological articles tend to focus on two interrelated themes: the gift of presence, and the eucharist as gift. In 1969 "the gift of presence" is the understanding he employs to explore the resurrection appearances. Using terms that prefigure his phenomenological work, but that also draw from the biblical texts and from Balthasar, Marion describes how the resurrected Christ "gives himself to be seen."[59] Christ's presence here is superabundant; in revealing God entirely, it can only be seen in being received as absolutely other, that is, according to distance, and with the recognition of faith.[60] Apart from the link between the gift and self-givenness, and its excessive presence, however, we are given no more detail about the gift. In a later article, the gift of eucharist is also understood to deliver Christ's presence. Here the meaning of "gift" is explored a little more: the gift can be understood (phenomenologically) as a term in human commerce, but it can in a different sense come to symbolise the way in which a giver gives him or herself: "… the gift of the giver submerges the material gift, and reinterprets it …."[61] Christ's gift of himself in the eucharist is kenotic, entailing the abandonment of divinity in a "thing," "… manifesting in this way his divinity as such."[62] The emphasis on presence is reoriented in "Le présent et le don" (first published in 1977, it appears in a revised form in *God Without Being* in 1982).[63] It is not the gift that is to be thought according to presence but presence that is to be thought according to the gift; the gift orders temporality. The eucharistic gift orders the present according to both past (memorial) and future (advent), making a gift of each moment according to charity, and dispossessing the primacy of the (metaphysical) here and now.[64]

In *The Idol and Distance*, and at other points in *God Without Being*, the question of the gift is handled more deliberately. Three significant insights are delivered in these texts. First, the gift of God is only given in withdrawal; there is a relationship, in other words, between gift and abandonment ("the two movements of one distance"):[65] "The withdrawal [*repli*] or what seems to us 'in appearance' a withdrawal, deploys the gift in its singularity to the point of giving to the beneficiary the gift of appropriating it to himself. The obvious absence of the giver is not an obstacle to the gift, but a path between the gift, the giver, and the recipient."[66] This

---

Gift and Postmodernism, eds. John D. Caputo and Michael J. Scanlon (Bloomington: Indiana University Press, 1999) 54–78, 56.

[59] Marion, "Ce mystère qui juge" 71.

[60] Marion, "Ce mystère qui juge" 73–74.

[61] Marion, "Présence et distance" 34. Here I am deliberately overlooking the context of this observation, which is an argument about the relative merits of transignification and transubstantiation.

[62] Marion, "Présence et distance" 41, 39.

[63] This process is in fact begun in Marion, "Présence et distance."

[64] Marion, *Dieu sans l'être* 241–249; *God Without Being* 171–76.

[65] Marion, *L'idole et la distance* 141; *The Idol and Distance* 113.

[66] Marion, *L'idole et la distance* 152; *The Idol and Distance* 124. See also 178ff.; 139ff.

giving in withdrawal can in some ways be compared to Heideggerian *Ereignis*.[67] It enables Marion to imagine a giving (of God) that would not be an appropriation. Distance again arises in this context as that which is given without thereby being taken over. A nuanced definition is offered: "Distance: the gap that separates definitively only as much as it unifies, since what distance gives consists in the gap itself." This point is reinforced in "The Gift of a Presence" (1983) where Marion describes Christ giving himself in "taking a distance."[68]

Second, Marion explains that the gift traverses distance only in order that, in withdrawing, the giver can be "read on the gift."[69] Hence the gap (distance) both gives God to be recognised and simultaneously forbids our seizing God: "Distance implies an irreducible gap, specifically, disappropriation. By definition, it totally separates the terms ...."[70] But at the same time, it leads us back to God: "At the heart of *agape*, following its flux as one follows a current that is too violent to go back up, too profound for one to know its source or valley, everything flows along the giving, and, by the wake traced in the water, but without grasping any of it, everything indicates the direction and meaning of distance."[71] In other words, as we saw earlier, while distance protects the divine term it remains possible to risk naming the giver by virtue of the strength of what impedes (or, better, interrupts) knowledge.

A third insight from these texts is that the gift itself is no-thing, that is, no thing other than the capacity to give: "to receive the gift amounts to receiving the giving act, for God gives nothing except the movement of the infinite kenosis of charity ...."[72] This enables Marion to argue—perhaps more problematically—that receiving the gift prompts its return.[73] We might ask not only whether figuring the gift in a cycle of return or exchange does a kind of violence to what might be considered one of its essential characteristics (that it be given freely and not out of obligation), but also whether return of the gift to God is essentially a recuperative movement that annuls distance: "the giving traverses distance by not ceasing to send the given back to a giver ...."[74] Along with identifying God in any definitive sense as giver, these problems remain the nub of the disagreement between Marion and Derrida on the question of the gift.[75] Two arguments may ameliorate Marion's position. In "The Gift of a Presence" he makes clear that Christ's gift of himself to the disciples, in a presence that is interrupted by distance, prompts the disciples' gift to the world.[76] The movement of the gift is therefore not necessarily one of exchange but of relay. Finally, and as I noted in the previous chapter, much later

---

[67] Marion, *L'idole et la distance* 288ff.; *The Idol and Distance* 239ff.; *Dieu sans l'être* 151ff.; *God Without Being* 104ff.

[68] Marion, *Prolégomènes* 162; *Prolegomena* 136ff.

[69] Marion, *Dieu sans l'être* 151; *God Without Being* 104.

[70] Marion, *Dieu sans l'être* 152, see also 238n14; *God Without Being* 105, see also 229n15.

[71] Marion, *Dieu sans l'être* 153; *God Without Being* 106.

[72] Marion, *L'idole et la distance* 205; *The Idol and Distance* 166. See also 215.

[73] Marion, *Dieu sans l'être* 154; *God Without Being* 107.

[74] Marion, *Dieu sans l'être* 151; *God Without Being* 104.

[75] See the discussion in Horner, *Rethinking God as Gift*.

[76] Marion, *Prolégomènes* 173; *Prolegomena* 147.

Marion and Derrida will almost come to agreement on the possibility and impossibility of naming. God will always be named, Marion argues, improperly, with a name that cannot appropriate or present God but that functions only pragmatically in prayer.[77] This might reintroduce at least some element of undecidability into Marion's affirmations.

In this chapter we have examined—in a preliminary way—Marion's use of the icon, love, and the gift, as ways of referring to God. With each of these motifs distance is ultimately invoked as a guarantee of their excessiveness; this places them, more explicitly than we might otherwise observe, within the framework of his attempt to do theology without reinscribing it in metaphysics. Without this use of distance it is questionable as to what degree each motif can function without its reference to God being in some way made absolute. Yet once again, it is sometimes unclear whether or not even distance sufficiently protects God's alterity. This is particularly the case with the motif of the gift, where the capacity to recognise the giver on the gift, the possible return of the gift, and the subsequent "traversal" of distance, act together to weaken the irrecuperability of the "thought" of God. Having made an initial appraisal of these ideas, we now turn to examine two major texts where Marion claims to overcome metaphysics by way of theology.

---

[77] Marion, "In the Name."

Chapter 7

Thinking God: Descartes and the Idea of the Infinite

Introduction

While much of Marion's interest for contemporary theologians will lie in his engagement with phenomenology and poststructuralism, the theological implications of his studies of modern philosophy must also be taken into account. These works—especially the volumes on Descartes—are not only numerous, but highly specialised and incredibly detailed, often taking the form of very close examinations of particular texts. This means that it can be difficult for the non-specialist to enter into the issues that they address. At the same time, however, a number of more general themes emerge from these studies that enable them to be situated in the larger context of Marion's work. Such themes include the extent to which individual thinkers perpetuate and/or overcome metaphysics, and how that relationship to metaphysics affects their thinking of God. In limiting the current treatment of the early modern material to these two questions, for reasons to do with space and clarity, I will also largely limit my consideration to Descartes, and particularly to one of Marion's most important Cartesian texts: *On Descartes' Metaphysical Prism: The Constitution and Limits of Onto-theo-logy in Cartesian Thought* (1986, English translation 1999).[1] It was observed in an earlier chapter that one of the chief targets in Heidegger's critique

---

[1] In emphasising this text, I am cognisant of Marion's comments that his earlier volumes, *Sur l'ontologie grise de Descartes* (1975) and *Sur la théologie blanche de Descartes* (1981), are brought together in the work of 1986. "*Sur l'ontologie grise de Descartes* attempted to draw out, from behind the appearance (and the reality) of the *Regulae*'s anti-Aristotelean epistemology, the counter-ontology that … is deployed in what Descartes set forth. *Sur la théologie blanche de Descartes* attempted to identify the place of the first principle and the ambiguity of (the) primordial being. … Today, we can join these two attempts…" *On Descartes' Metaphysical Prism* 5. Descartes' ontology is described as "hidden" or "grey" because it functions without explicit designation; his theology is "blank" or "white" because it founds the ontology while itself remaining undetermined. Marion notes in the preface to the American edition that appears in the translated volume of *On Descartes' Metaphysical Prism*, that the revised edition of *Sur la théologie blanche de Descartes* (1991) "validates" this text, but also that the two volumes of *Questions cartésiennes* are to be considered "as commentaries, confirmations, and sometimes corrections of the theses advanced in the 1986 work, which I still consider the focus of the interpretation" (xiii). See also later texts confirming Marion's basic theses, such as "The Idea of God," trans. Thomas A. Carlson and Daniel Garber, *The Cambridge History of Seventeenth-Century Philosophy*, eds. Daniel Garber and Michael Ayers, vol. I (Cambridge: Cambridge University Press, 1998) 265–304; and "Le paradigme cartésien de la métaphysique," *Laval Théologique et Philosophique* 53.3 (1997): 785–91.

of metaphysics is Descartes. In *On Descartes' Metaphysical Prism*, Marion seeks to establish whether Heidegger's critique is justified, by clarifying the nature of metaphysics as onto-theo-logy and determining the extent of Descartes' onto-theo-logical engagement. Marion locates in Descartes' work both metaphysical structures and moments of resistance to these structures, the latter principally in the thinking of the freedom of the *ego* and the infinitude of God. He then uses the theology of Pascal to illustrate the possibilities for overcoming Cartesian metaphysics. In terms of the two questions framing this chapter, then, it will be helpful to use *On Descartes' Metaphysical Prism* as a basis for consideration.

Metaphysics as Onto-theo-logy

Observing the shift that seems to occur in the concept of metaphysics with Descartes—that is, the shift away from the scholastic emphasis on metaphysics as the science of being, towards an emphasis on metaphysics as the science of the first principles of knowledge—Marion seeks a model of metaphysical constitution with which he can evaluate Descartes' work. In other words, given that metaphysics comes to be understood in different ways, he seeks a measure of metaphysics that can be applied in spite of these different understandings. Marion finds an appropriate model in Heidegger's reading of metaphysics as onto-theo-logy, although it is a model that he will also call into question at certain points.[2] Onto-theo-logy is the term used to indicate that the *logos* (word or reason) forms the foundation for and links together being as being (the subject of onto-logy) and the highest being (the subject of theo-logy).

> The λόγος which says (and grounds) being in Being also, in a profound and confused unity, says it (and grounds it) in the supreme being ... Onto-theo-logy provides the 'fundamental trait' of all metaphysics, because it marks not only the tension between two dimensions of being (being as such ... and being at its most excellent ...) but also because it marks the foundation that unites them reciprocally and governs them from the ground up ... The being par excellence finds its ground insofar as it accomplishes beings in their Being and exemplifies the way of Being of beings. Reciprocally, beings in their Being can be grounded in their mode of production by the being that excels at accomplishing the Being of all beings.

The foundation may be named with different terms by different thinkers (for example, as "λόγος *ratio, causa,* sufficient reason, concept"), but it can always be identified as "the sole condition of condition itself—logical conditioning."[3] In

---

[2] Marion, *Sur le prisme métaphysique* 2–8, 88–97, 177–184; *On Descartes' Metaphysical Prism* 2–7, 81–90, 167–73.

[3] Marion, *Sur le prisme métaphysique* 93; *On Descartes' Metaphysical Prism* 86. Marion later gives another very cogent definition of onto-theo-logy: "... the Being of beings as such grounds all beings (onto-logy) and, inseparably, the being par excellence grounds and supports the Being of beings (theo-logy). The Being of beings as such maintains a relation of reciprocal grounding with the being par excellence—though, in each case, the modes of grounding differ ... ." (122/115).

terms of the description of metaphysics provided in Chapter Two (metaphysics is the attempt to found knowledge of what is, on the ground of unchanging *ousia*, being in so far as being, the divine, first cause, or knowing subject), and Heidegger's critique of it outlined in Chapter 4 (in metaphysics being is thought as present substance, what is caused as well as the one who causes, and ultimately on the basis of the *logos*), metaphysics is onto-theo-logical in so far as in it being not only bifurcates, but is constantly brought back to the dimensions of conceptual reasoning, with a concomitant emphasis on presence as self-presence (which is to say that knowing and being coincide).

Cartesian Figures of Onto-theo-logy: Onto-theo-logy as "Re-doubled"

Using onto-theo-logy as the measure, to what extent is Descartes' thought metaphysical? Marion observes that one of the difficulties in trying to determine the metaphysical character of Descartes' work is that he so rarely uses the word "metaphysics," preferring instead to use "first philosophy."[4] Further, for Descartes, first philosophy does not concern a first being, but the order in which things are known.[5] In Descartes' texts, " ... metaphysics becomes first philosophy inasmuch as all beings are considered not first as they are, but as known or knowable; accordingly, primacy passes from the supreme being (whichever it might be) to the authority [*instance*] of knowledge (whichever it might be)."[6] This, in turn, means that for Descartes all founding authority with regard to being is granted to the *ego* in its cognition of objects. Marion judges that in this respect Heidegger's reading of Descartes is correct, that is, Descartes' work is onto-theo-logical, because "[a] declaration about the way of Being of beings (onto-logy) and a proposition concerning the singular existence of a being par excellence (theo-logy) [for Descartes in *Meditation II*, the *ego*] thus maintain a reciprocal relationship of grounding."[7] While there may be difficulties with regard to Descartes' use of the terminology of metaphysics, since his thought can be shown to be onto-theo-logical, it is therefore metaphysically constituted.

Nevertheless, Marion's consideration of the onto-theo-logical nature of the Cartesian corpus is far from complete. Given that Descartes seems to regard the "being par excellence" as the *ego*, the question remains about how he thinks God. While it is possible to have an idea of God, which suggests that God, too, is subject to the *ego*, this is an idea that for Descartes must always remain incomprehensible.[8] "This fundamental trait of being [being as being known] leaves out at least one

---

[4] Marion, *Sur le prisme métaphysique* 9; *On Descartes' Metaphysical Prism* 9.

[5] Marion, *Sur le prisme métaphysique* 40–41, 58–59; *On Descartes' Metaphysical Prism* 38, 53–58.

[6] Marion, *Sur le prisme métaphysique* 74; *On Descartes' Metaphysical Prism* 68. Trans. modified.

[7] Marion, *Sur le prisme métaphysique* 102–03; *On Descartes' Metaphysical Prism* 95.

[8] Marion, *Sur le prisme métaphysique* 107–08; *On Descartes' Metaphysical Prism* 99–100.

region of being—not the least but the first: God, bearing the name of the infinite. The infinite, otherwise named *incomprehensible power*, exceeds the onto-theo-logy of the *cogitatio*."[9] Marion is thus able to ask whether or not in Descartes' thought there is something more fundamental than the *cogitatio*. A positive response to this question is prompted by the recognition that Descartes not only thinks being as being known, but also being as being caused. For Descartes, cause is related to a being's very existence, which is why ultimately God, too, must be subject to the requirement for a cause.[10] We are assisted in our understanding of what Descartes means by cause with Marion's adoption of the slightly later terms of Gottfried Leibniz. Cause, for Descartes, is equivalent to what Leibniz means by the principle of sufficient reason:

> We must rise to metaphysics, making use of the *great principle*, commonly but little employed, which holds that nothing takes place without sufficient reason, that is to say nothing happens without its being possible for one who has enough knowledge of things to give a reason sufficient to determine why it is thus and not otherwise.[11]

This is an absolute principle, since it is not grounded in any other principle. Even the *cogitatio* must be understood in terms of being caused, and while the cause of the *cogitatio* can be traced to the *ego*, the *ego* itself must have a cause, which Descartes traces to a new being *par excellence*:[12] "… if the onto-theo-logy of *causa* oversteps that of the *cogitatio*, the corresponding being par excellence must be displaced from the *ego* to God …."[13] Yet how can God be both the being *par excellence* and subject to causality? The answer lies in Descartes' understanding of the being *par excellence*, and therefore of God, as the cause of itself (*causa sui*). With the being of beings and the highest being understood in terms of cause, we see a second figure of onto-theo-logy in Descartes. Marion is therefore able to describe a "redoubled onto-theo-logy", either branch of which can be followed though the subsequent history of philosophy.[14]

First Cartesian Resistance to Onto-theo-logy: the Freedom of the *Ego*

Having identified ways in which Descartes clearly falls within the scope of metaphysics as onto-theo-logy, Marion then goes on to consider two ways in which Descartes' thought is nevertheless resistant to it. His overarching claim is that neither the *ego* nor God can be entirely contained within Descartes' metaphysical

---

[9] Marion, *Sur le prisme métaphysique* 111; *On Descartes' Metaphysical Prism* 103.

[10] Marion, *Sur le prisme métaphysique* 111ff.; *On Descartes' Metaphysical Prism* 103ff.

[11] Gottfried Leibniz, "Principles of Nature and Grace," *Leibniz: Philosophical Writings*, ed. G. H. R. Parkinson (London: J. M. Dent and Sons, 1973) 199. This definition is quoted in Marion, *Sur le prisme métaphysique* 115n52; *On Descartes' Metaphysical Prism* 108n52.

[12] Marion, *Sur le prisme métaphysique* 116ff.; *On Descartes' Metaphysical Prism* 109ff.

[13] Marion, *Sur le prisme métaphysique* 123; *On Descartes' Metaphysical Prism* 115.

[14] Marion, *Sur le prisme métaphysique* 126–36; *On Descartes' Metaphysical Prism* 117–27.

structure. Chapter 3 of *On Descartes' Metaphysical Prism* is a consideration of the *ego*. Marion determines that Descartes thinks the *ego* as substance; not only does Descartes "deduce" substance from the *ego* but he uses being and substance "synonymously".[15] "Descartes ... establishes the equivalence of Being and thought by constructing a substantiality that owes everything to the *ego* since it is deduced from it ...."[16] Now, Heidegger had argued that part of the weakness of Descartes is his leaving the being of the *res cogitans* undetermined. Marion maintains in response to this argument not only that the being of the *res cogitans* is in fact clearly determined, as substance, but that the real problem is that the two other substances identified by Descartes—extension and God—are themselves left to be thought on the basis of the substance of the thinking thing.[17] None the less, Marion agrees with Heidegger that Descartes thinks substance as permanent presence: "Whatever its origin might be, Cartesian substance manifests its substantiality as the permanence of a subsisting being—this is the sole decisive point according to Heidegger's project in *Sein und Zeit*." Further, and more dramatically, "... Heidegger asks if the *ego*, insofar as it accomplishes the equivalence of Being and thought ... does not mark the apex of the interpretation of the Being of beings as pure and simple persistence in subsistence—and thus does not inaugurate the royal road of erring which, through Kant, ends up at Husserl."[18] Marion argues that the Cartesian *ego* is temporalised in the present because it only exists (or has substance) as long as it thinks, and thought keeps ideas and objects present. This does not mean that its existence has only a successively momentary character, since it is given unity by the duration of thought, a duration that is again understood in terms of the present.[19] For Descartes, time "unfolds in thought"; it "becomes the *ego*'s presence to itself."[20] Anything that exists (or has substance) must persist in this present: "... the insistent persistence, which the temporality of the *ego* puts into operation, is deployed in 'all that is, or exists "according to an egological deduction of presence in the present, which duplicates the egological deduction of the substantiality of all beings."[21]

The description of the substantial presence of the *ego* seems only to confirm the onto-theo-logical character of Descartes' thought. Nevertheless, Marion notes that this presence functions to contradict both the event-character of the past and the possibility of the future. In order for the *ego* to be free, the past and the future must be possible rather than necessary. Two mechanisms allow for this freedom within Descartes' thought. With regard to the past, the mind suspends evidence (in the present) through inattentiveness. With regard to the future, the possible is the necessary that we do not yet know about; freedom becomes possible because we are

---

[15] Marion, *Sur le prisme métaphysique* 175–77; *On Descartes' Metaphysical Prism* 165–66.

[16] Marion, *Sur le prisme métaphysique* 180; *On Descartes' Metaphysical Prism* 169.

[17] Marion, *Sur le prisme métaphysique* 177ff.; *On Descartes' Metaphysical Prism* 167ff.

[18] Marion, *Sur le prisme métaphysique* 181; *On Descartes' Metaphysical Prism* 170.

[19] Marion, *Sur le prisme métaphysique* 184ff.; *On Descartes' Metaphysical Prism* 173ff.

[20] Marion, *Sur le prisme métaphysique* 196, 197; *On Descartes' Metaphysical Prism* 186, 187.

[21] Marion, *Sur le prisme métaphysique* 202; *On Descartes' Metaphysical Prism* 192.

unaware of necessity.[22] In this way, the hold of the *cogitatio* on present evidence is unsettled: "... the *ego* accedes to other modalities of Being besides presence, or to other temporalizations besides the present, by accomplishing a single and unique feat: transgressing the *cogitatio* of present evidence, such as it presents to itself the persisting presence of subsistent beings."[23] The possible exceeds presence. While the *ego* determines Cartesian metaphysics, that metaphysics is flawed because possibility and freedom can only come about if the *cogitatio* is overcome. There is thus a first gap in Descartes' onto-theo-logical constitution.

Second Cartesian Resistance to Onto-theo-logy: The Infinitude of God

In Chapter 4 of *On Descartes' Metaphysical Prism* Marion determines a second gap in Descartes' onto-theo-logy, this time with respect to God's infinitude. Since we are interested not only in the way Descartes exceeds metaphysics, but also and especially in the way he thinks God, we will follow this chapter in some detail.[24] Marion initially associates Descartes' philosophical approach to thinking God with a theology of the divine names.[25] In this regard he identifies three basic formulae used by Descartes to describe God's essence and attributes. All three are found in *Meditation III*, although Marion privileges the first two for much of the discussion: [1] "... the idea that gives me my understanding of a supreme God, eternal, infinite, omniscient, omnipotent and the creator of all things that exist apart from him"; and [2] "By the word 'God' I understand a substance that is infinite, independent, supremely intelligent, supremely powerful, and which created both myself and everything else (if anything else there be) that exists."[26] The third formula concerns God as the most perfect being: [3] "The unity, the simplicity, or the inseparability of all the attributes of God is one of the most important of all the perfections which I understand him to have."[27] In the first half of the chapter, Marion explores ways in which these formulae are meaningful.

The first element that comes under scrutiny is *quaedam* [*substantia*], or *aliquis* [*Deus*]; both these terms are indefinite, translating as "a certain [substance]" or "someone [god, divine]" respectively.[28] Their use "announces, as the first

---

[22] Marion, *Sur le prisme métaphysique* 203ff.; *On Descartes' Metaphysical Prism* 193ff.

[23] Marion, *Sur le prisme métaphysique* 213; *On Descartes' Metaphysical Prism* 203.

[24] Much of this material is also presented in Jean-Luc Marion, "The Essential Incoherence of Descartes' Definition of Divinity," trans. F. Van de Pitte, *Essays on Descartes' Meditations*, ed. Amélie Oksenberg Rorty (Berkeley: University of California Press, 1986) 297–338.

[25] Marion, *Sur le prisme métaphysique* 221; *On Descartes' Metaphysical Prism* 210.

[26] Marion, *Sur le prisme métaphysique* 222; *On Descartes' Metaphysical Prism* 211.

[27] Marion, *Sur le prisme métaphysique* 253; *On Descartes' Metaphysical Prism* 240. Marion also incorporates a fourth formula, from the *Responsiones*, which I do not introduce here, for the sake of clarity. See *Sur le prisme métaphysique* 270ff.; *On Descartes' Metaphysical Prism* 257ff.

[28] The square brackets in "*quaedam* [*substantia*], or *aliquis* [*Deus*]" indicate Marion's interpolations.

determination of God, indetermination itself."[29] This negative idea (indetermination) is used quite distinctively. Marion argues that unlike a theological negation, which would follow and modify a theological affirmation, indetermination comes first in Descartes' philosophical approach to God, and remains an overarching principle: "Imprecision belongs to the concept of God, intrinsically …."[30] He also maintains that this thought of God as indetermination opens for Descartes onto an understanding of God as substance, and especially as infinite substance.[31] While there is considerable theological disagreement historically about the appropriateness of using substance to refer to God, Descartes opens a new possibility because he often uses substance in a very specialised sense, as that which can exist by itself.[32] But since this definition does not necessarily help us to delineate between created and uncreated substance, a further distinction is applied: God is not just substance, but infinite substance, where "infinite" is understood not as an accidental modification of substance but as what it is. "The definition of substance—in a word, the substance of substance—is therefore stated: the infinite. The infinite is not added—regarding God—to substance; it is substance that results from the infinite originally in God, and is suitable to him only in this way."[33] We are no longer to understand substance on the basis of finite substance, but finite substance on the basis of its *a priori*, infinite substance.[34] This means that God as infinite is not ultimately thought by way of negation.

Having considered Descartes' thought of God as infinite, Marion is able to proceed in light of infinitude to consider three further divine [in]-determinations: immensity, incomprehensibility, and independence. Marion again sees these terms as super-eminent, rather than negative.[35] Immensity is understood as that which cannot be measured. Now, since measure relates to order for Descartes, and order to his philosophical method of considering things in the sequence in which they can be known, it is clear that by being immeasurable, God is thereby not subject to the

---

[29] Marion, *Sur le prisme métaphysique* 223; *On Descartes' Metaphysical Prism* 212. It must be noted that while Marion is basically working from the formulae he identifies, he also draws in examples from other texts or other places in the same texts. He is also working in Latin and French, noting certain discrepancies in translations. These factors mean that it is sometimes not as clear to the English-speaking reader how he has arrived at a particular interpretation of the formulae. A more complex problem in this regard is identified in K. Winkler, "Descartes and the Three Names of God," *American Catholic Philosophical Quarterly* 67.4 (1993): 451–65.

[30] Marion, *Sur le prisme métaphysique* 230; *On Descartes' Metaphysical Prism* 218.

[31] Marion, *Sur le prisme métaphysique* 230ff.; *On Descartes' Metaphysical Prism* 218ff.

[32] "Descartes appears to be one of the supporters of a weak sense of substantiality, one that makes it acceptable when speaking of God; namely, no longer the supposed subject of attributes, but subsistence *per se*; not categorical subsistence, but self-subsistence referred to itself …" Marion, *Sur le prisme métaphysique* 235; *On Descartes' Metaphysical Prism* 223.

[33] Marion, *Sur le prisme métaphysique* 239; *On Descartes' Metaphysical Prism* 227.

[34] Marion, *Sur le prisme métaphysique* 241–42; *On Descartes' Metaphysical Prism* 229.

[35] Marion, *Sur le prisme métaphysique* 242; *On Descartes' Metaphysical Prism* 230. In other words, in the same way that infinity is not to be understood as the negation of the finite but as what precedes it and makes it possible, these three terms are to be understood as primary and exemplary, while their finite counterparts are derivative.

method. Similarly, incomprehensibility means that by way of perfection, rather than imperfection, God cannot be understood in terms of the method:

> With divine incomprehensibility, it is not a matter of renouncing the rational knowledge of God, but of allowing rationality to know the infinite, thus to know, beyond the objectivity that it methodically masters, the infinite as such, as incomprehensible to the finite. Incomprehensibility will even become the surest sign that it is indeed God that the *cogitatio* knows, in accordance with the rule that nothing divine can be thought except as incomprehensible, and that nothing truly incomprehensible can be offered to the *cogitatio* without it in the end concerning God.[36]

With regard to the third term, independence, or aseity (*a se*, "from itself"), this has no particular relationship to the method, but once again can be understood only on the basis of the infinite as *a priori*. Infinity expresses the meaning of independence and relegates all else to the status of being dependent.[37]

To this point, Marion has considered those terms from Descartes that would traditionally be interpreted theologically as part of the *via negativa*, although he reads them in an alternative manner by way of eminence or excess. He now turns to examine three terms that would be associated with affirmation in theology, although in the Cartesian setting they are again associated with a certain type of eminence: *summe intelligens*, *summe potens*, and *ens summe perfectum*.[38] "Supreme intelligence" needs no explanation, although Marion does note that while it is mentioned several times in Descartes' work, it is never really discussed. Perhaps God, he wonders, "... is not essentially determined by intelligence ..." for Descartes.[39] "Omnipotence" is a term that appears early in Descartes' writings, and raises a number of questions related to its use on the basis of "opinion" (Descartes speaks of "the long-standing opinion that there is an omnipotent God"), prior to the order of reason (omnipotence precedes hyperbolic doubt), and as the primary name for God (which is elsewhere determined as the infinite).[40] These questions are not immediately resolved. However, omnipotence functions as a hermeneutic key for the title of Creator: "... creation is understood in terms of efficient causality ... which is itself deduced ... from divine omnipotence ...."[41] Marion at a later stage makes stronger this link between omnipotence and causality, with God as *causa sui* who is thus able to meet the principle of sufficient reason.[42] "Most perfect being" is drawn from the third Cartesian formula, but it is set by Marion in the context of a

---

[36] Marion, *Sur le prisme métaphysique* 244; *On Descartes' Metaphysical Prism* 232.

[37] Marion, *Sur le prisme métaphysique* 246; *On Descartes' Metaphysical Prism* 234.

[38] This leads Marion to speculate that there is no "third" way available to Descartes, since both negative and affirmative ways lead to excess. Marion, *Sur le prisme métaphysique* 247; *On Descartes' Metaphysical Prism* 235.

[39] Marion, *Sur le prisme métaphysique* 248; *On Descartes' Metaphysical Prism* 236.

[40] Marion, *Sur le prisme métaphysique* 248ff.; *On Descartes' Metaphysical Prism* 236ff.

[41] Marion, *Sur le prisme métaphysique* 252; *On Descartes' Metaphysical Prism* 239.

[42] Marion, *Sur le prisme métaphysique* 270ff.; *On Descartes' Metaphysical Prism* 256ff. Here I have mixed—for the sake of clarity and brevity—what are essentially two independent sets of deliberations in Marion's texts. In Descartes' works cause and power are linked in *Responsiones I* and *IV*.

series of perfections drawn from many texts. Using formula [3] as a basis, "God thus becomes accessible to thought in a new way: his idea, thus also his existence, is not imposed right away, as previously the idea of infinity was, but can be constructed by the human understanding that counts up the perfections, reconciles them with each other, then attributes them to God."[43] Nevertheless, even the perfections must be thought in relation to infinity, that is, they must be rendered incomprehensible as perfections in order for their use with regard to God to be appropriate.[44]

At the end of his consideration of the various attributes in each of the three passages, Marion determines that there are essentially three Cartesian names for God, although they do not correspond with the individual formulae. These names are [A] the infinite (encompassing substance, infinity, independence, immensity, and incomprehensibility), which Marion associates with the theological *via negativa*; [B] most perfect being (encompassing supreme intelligence, but also all possible perfections), which he associates with the theological *via affirmativa*, and [C] power (encompassing creation and supreme power, or omnipotence, but which Marion later also determines as *causa sui*), which he associates with the theological *via eminentiae*.[45]

In the second part of the chapter, Marion's next aim is to test the compatibility of the three names and to determine the extent to which they are bound up in Descartes' metaphysics. He proposes to do this by way of two procedures. The first of these procedures (the "internal" one) involves determining the compatibility of the three names with reference to the concepts that emerge from the various Cartesian proofs for God. Now, at this point it must be noted that approaching Descartes' thought of God by way of his proofs for God's existence is an alternative strategy that Marion employs here and elsewhere, although often with more of an interest in their coherence than their validity. In "The Idea of God," he explains how and where the proofs are laid out:

> … Descartes proposes three ways for demonstrating the existence of God: (I) the so-called *a posteriori* argument, wherein God is considered the cause of His idea in me (Meditatio III, in two formulations); (2) the so-called *a priori* argument, which deduces God's existence from the very idea of the divine essence (the so-called ontological argument, Meditatio V); and (3) the argument from the principle of (sufficient) reason, which finds the cause of God in God Himself, henceforth named *causa sui* (cause of itself) (Resp. I, IV).[46]

Being cognisant of this alternative strategy enables us to situate *On Descartes' Metaphysical Prism* in a larger context, that is, to relate its conclusions more clearly

---

[43] Marion, *Sur le prisme métaphysique* 253; *On Descartes' Metaphysical Prism* 241.

[44] Marion, *Sur le prisme métaphysique* 254; *On Descartes' Metaphysical Prism* 242.

[45] Marion, *Sur le prisme métaphysique* 244; *On Descartes' Metaphysical Prism* 244. The designations [A], [B], and [C] appear only subsequently in the text.

[46] Marion, "The Idea of God," 275. This text is essentially what appears in French as "Esquisse d'une histoire des définitions de Dieu à l'époque cartésienne," in Marion, *Questions cartésiennes II* 221–79.

to other theo-philosophical analyses.[47] Returning, however, to the examination at hand, the second procedure (the "external" one) involves determining historical (and theological) precedents for the use of the names. What Marion hopes to achieve in the application of the internal and external procedures is a better understanding of the factors influencing the choice of the names and their relative importance, in order to reach his stated aim.

Are the divine names—approached by way of the proofs—ultimately compatible? Marion argues that they are not. After a complex series of comparisons and contrasts, which includes an evaluation of each name according to three criteria (criteria which support the basic principle that " ... the idea of God [is] opposed to every other knowable object"), Marion finds that [A] is the only name to meet all three of the criteria positively.[48] For him, this highlights the contradictions between the three names, and is the basis of an argument that the primary name for God in Descartes' thought is the infinite.[49] But another important insight immediately follows. If we return to Marion's understanding of Descartes' metaphysics as a redoubled onto-theo-logy, we find that [A] is also the only name that resists a metaphysical schema, since [B] is ultimately subject to the *cogitatio*, and [C] to the

---

[47] Such as Marion, "Is the Argument Ontological? The Anselmian Proof and the Two Demonstrations of the Existence of God in the *Meditations*," *Cartesian Questions* 139–60. "The Idea of God" sets out, in quite accessible language, a more global approach to Descartes' thinking of God than *On Descartes' Metaphysical Prism*, although the latter work is useful since it provides a strong articulation of Marion's core arguments, and makes helpful links in the present context with metaphysics and onto-theo-logy.

[48] Marion, *Sur le prisme métaphysique* 286; *On Descartes' Metaphysical Prism* 271.

[49] Other scholars do not entirely agree with Marion on this point. Winkler observes: "I realize that I have done no more than sketch an interpretation according to which God's infinity is, as the *Meditations* proceeds, gradually understood in terms of his perfection. But I hope I have shown that it is premature to say that the two names [that Winkler identifies as "infinite" and "supreme"] are divergent or incompatible. The evidence points instead to the conclusion that the two names are compatible and that Descartes' leading notion of God, in the Third Meditation as well as in the Fifth, is that of supremely perfect being." Winkler, "Descartes and the Three Names," 463–64. Winkler refers to the work of Jean-Marie Beyssade for support on this point, although Beyssade is more guarded: "... Jean-Luc Marion has pointed out the clash between various theological traditions which are partially assimilated in Descartes in a haphazard and unregulated way, and which generate in his system 'irremediable tensions' and 'irreducible inconsistencies,' amounting to nothing less than a 'system of contradictions.'

"I am not entirely confident that the Cartesian system can satisfactorily be defended against objections of this kind. What I am sure of is that any plausible reply must be sought via an explication of Descartes' notion of the 'positive incomprehensibility' of God. For it is this that is the key to the union between the two essential divine attributes *infinite* and *perfect*..." Beyssade later comments in conclusion: "... whether or not there is in fact a contradiction between these two traditions, it would, in my view, be fallacious to infer that this contradiction infects the Cartesian idea of God." Jean-Marie Beyssade, "The Idea of God and the Proofs of his Existence," trans. J. Cottingham, *The Cambridge Companion to Descartes*, ed. J. Cottingham (Cambridge: Cambridge University Press, 1992) 174–99, 186, 192. See also Jean-Marie Beyssade, "On the Idea of God: Incomprehensibility or Incompatibilities?" trans. Charles Paul, *Essays on the Philosophy and Science of René Descartes*, ed. Stephen Voss (New York/Oxford: Oxford University Press, 1993).

causa. Since [A] is not taken up in onto-theo-logy, the idea of infinity "does not arise from the Cartesian constitution of metaphysics."[50] Marion claims:

> ... the divine name drawn from the idea of infinity does not assume a place in any figure of post-Cartesian onto-theo-logy. Therefore it ought to be understood as a nonmetaphysical utterance of Descartes' thought about God, belonging more to the previous theology of the divine names than to the subsequent onto-theo-logies, where the conceptual idol excludes God from the horizon of metaphysics by pretending to sequester him within onto-theo-logical functions.[51]

In Marion's view, the complexities of Descartes' texts reveal not confusion about God but a recognition that to approach the infinite from the perspective of the finite demands "a certain conceptual madness" and the humility of submission.[52] There is, in other words, a way in which Descartes' thought of God exceeds metaphysics, by way of excess.[53] We are reminded here both of the "madness" in relation to God that echoes through the works of Søren Kierkegaard, Jacques Derrida, and John D. Caputo, and of the excess of intuition that is the focus of much of Marion's phenomenological discussion. In spite of its highly specialised context, the analysis of Descartes' metaphysics can be seen to be closely aligned with Marion's work as a whole, and with contemporary debate about the possibility of thinking God.

Pascal and the Destitution of Metaphysics

While Marion has brought us to the point of recognising a Cartesian thought of God that exceeds metaphysics, his stated purpose in the fifth chapter of *On Descartes' Metaphysical Prism* is to establish a non-metaphysical reference point that "... knows Cartesian thought, recognizes it as metaphysics, and criticizes it in terms that, perhaps, permit us to conceive of an overcoming of metaphysics in the

---

50 Marion, *Sur le prisme métaphysique* 288; *On Descartes' Metaphysical Prism* 273.

51 Marion, *Sur le prisme métaphysique* 291; *On Descartes' Metaphysical Prism* 275.

52 Marion, *Sur le prisme métaphysique* 292; *On Descartes' Metaphysical Prism* 276. In "The Idea of God," Marion shows how the other ideas for God are taken up in seventeenth-century philosophy, and why the idea of the infinite suffers a decline: "... after Descartes (and Duns Scotus), infinity is not found among the central notions that make up the idea of the divine essence. This demotion can be compared to the parallel and contemporary abandonment of the doctrine of the creation of the divine truths. One historical factor explains both: the imposition of the principle of sufficient reason as the first metaphysical principle governing essence and existence, and hence all of divine creation. This excludes incomprehensibility from God and His creation. But as 'incomprehensibility is contained in the formal definition of infinity', the requirement of comprehensibility opposes the priority of infinity in the divine nature. The ultimate fulfilment of rationalist metaphysics thus ought to make the infinite God a *persona non grata.*" Marion, "The Idea of God," 265–304, 291–92.

53 See the descriptions of the infinite as incomprehensible at Marion, *On Descartes' Metaphysical Prism* 246–51. While Marion does not use "excess" in this context, it seems to me that the idea of the infinite implies the experience of a positive yet overwhelming intuition. See also the helpful discussions in Beyssade, "The Idea of God," 174–99.

Cartesian epoch of its historical destiny."[54] He finds such a reference point in the work of Blaise Pascal.[55] Having established that Pascal is not only well aware of many of Descartes' concepts, but often utilises them himself, Marion proceeds to show how Pascal renders Cartesian metaphysics destitute. Now, Pascal dismisses the infinite as a name for God on the basis that it can also be used in a much wider sense.[56] But there is something much deeper at stake here. For Pascal, the idea of the infinite is implicated in a metaphysical proof for God's existence, and metaphysics is ultimately an exercise in vanity. Pascal thus judges the idea of the infinite differently to Marion.[57] The central issue for Pascal is that the type of knowledge at which metaphysics arrives is useless because it cannot deliver salvation.[58] Pascal thinks within a framework of three orders, each of which is separated by an incommensurable distance: the order of the body, that of the mind, and that of the heart or will. The order of the body is transgressed by metaphysics, that is, by thought, the order of the mind. Yet metaphysics must also be transgressed. Metaphysics can bring about knowledge, but never the perspective of love. Only that perspective, which puts in question the power of the *ego* and replaces it with a self that "is identified in and with Jesus Christ," has any value or meaning for Pascal.[59] Accordingly, " ... metaphysics must from now on recognize the irreducibility of an order that it does not see, but which sees it, grasps it, and judges it, 'the order of charity.'"[60] This order can only be recognised by loving, through acting according to holiness. "The third order will thus be revealed indirectly, by the distorting effects that its radiance—the luminosity of charity—will have on the elements of the second order."[61] Marion is thus able to propose Pascal as one who thinks in terms of a reduction to charity.[62]

While it is evident to Marion that there is no proof of the Pascalian destitution of metaphysics, he offers three indications of its success. These are articulated in terms of its destitutions of truth, being, and philosophy, all of which provide a critical link with issues addressed in contemporary thought as they were outlined earlier in the present volume.[63] Further, as we will see shortly, these themes also provide a link with passages concerning the overcoming of metaphysics in other works by Marion, particularly *The Idol and Distance* and *God Without Being*. Nevertheless,

---

[54] Marion, *On Descartes' Metaphysical Prism* 279.

[55] The approach is usefully summarised in Marion, "The Idea of God," 265–304, 292.

[56] Marion, *Sur le prisme métaphysique* 305ff.; *On Descartes' Metaphysical Prism* 288ff. "... the concept of infinity does not uniquely pick out God, since numbers, motion, speed, space, and even nature can be infinite as well." Marion, "The Idea of God," 265–304, 292.

[57] It seems to me that in what is otherwise an extraordinary and incisive text, Marion comments insufficiently on this disparity. The only explanation I can find for it is Marion's comment that what is metaphysical has to be determined in every case, which can lead to different determinations.

[58] Marion, *Sur le prisme métaphysique* 310ff.; *On Descartes' Metaphysical Prism* 293ff.

[59] Marion, *Sur le prisme métaphysique* 352; *On Descartes' Metaphysical Prism* 330.

[60] Marion, *Sur le prisme métaphysique* 358; *On Descartes' Metaphysical Prism* 335.

[61] Marion, *Sur le prisme métaphysique* 340; *On Descartes' Metaphysical Prism* 319.

[62] Marion, *Sur le prisme métaphysique* 359; *On Descartes' Metaphysical Prism* 337.

[63] Marion, *Sur le prisme métaphysique* 360ff.; *On Descartes' Metaphysical Prism* 338ff.

we are left with two pressing questions. If Marion argues that Descartes' idea of the infinite exceeds metaphysics, what does it mean for him that this non-metaphysical thought, too, is to be re-included in metaphysics and overcome by Pascal? And with the reduction to charity thought solely on the basis of a religious commitment, we have to wonder how it can be recognised as such, without itself being implicated in the onto-theo-logy it hopes to overcome.

Chapter 8

God Without Being

Introduction

In the previous chapter we observed how Marion locates Descartes within metaphysics understood as onto-theo-logy, while at the same time claiming that Descartes exceeds that metaphysics with a thought of God as the infinite. Nevertheless, even though Marion argues that thinking God as the infinite is a significant moment in the unfolding of philosophy (and one that is not pursued by the philosophers who follow Descartes), he completes *On Descartes' Metaphysical Prism* with a chapter outlining the way in which even the thought of God as infinite is rendered destitute by a belief in God as charity. This argument left a number of questions unanswered, but most important of these is the following: how is the two-staged shift—from metaphysics to non-metaphysical thought, and from non-metaphysical thought (reconceived by Pascal as metaphysics) to charity—to be made without imposing what Graham Ward in another context calls an "uncritical dogmatism"?[1] In other words, how is the order of charity able to fulfil a critical function with regard to metaphysics as Pascal conceives it, without becoming any more than the assertion of a new onto-theo-logical foundation? Marion's theme of Christian love overcoming both metaphysics and "non-metaphysical thought" needs to be examined more closely. While it is evident in a number of texts, here we will examine it in his most well-known and probably most controversial book, *God Without Being*. While this text was essentially completed prior to *On Descartes' Metaphysical Prism*, it has the advantage of bringing together discussions of both medieval and twentieth-century material, and thus serves to frame the Cartesian analysis historically. Sections of *God Without Being* concerned with the icon versus the idol, as well as the theme of distance, have already been considered. What remains to be examined is Marion's reading of two figures that loom large in theological and philosophical history: Heidegger, and Thomas Aquinas. We will then be in a better position to assess, at least in a preliminary way, the possibilities of the theological destitution of metaphysics and "non-metaphysical thought" by love.

When Marion claims, in the preface to the English edition of *God Without Being* from 1991, that his work "remains 'postmodern'" but "does not remain 'postmodern' all the way through," it is on the basis of the destitution by charity both of metaphysics and of "Being, thought as such, without its metaphysical figure."[2] This comment enables us to clarify what was expressed in the previous

---

[1] Graham Ward, "The Theological Project of Jean-Luc Marion," 229. In fact, Ward makes the charge in relation to the text we are about to consider, *God Without Being*.

[2] Marion, *God Without Being* xxi.

paragraph of the present text in terms of a two-stage shift. Left unresolved in *On Descartes' Metaphysical Prism* is the status of what Marion judges to be a non-metaphysical thought of God, despite Pascal's assessment. Another reason why *On Descartes' Metaphysical Prism* remains problematic, then, is because it is unclear whether theology renders only metaphysics destitute (because Pascal includes the infinite within metaphysics), leaving open the possibility of non-metaphysical thought, or whether theology renders all thought destitute (because Pascal perceives all thought to be inherently metaphysical, in spite of Marion's careful delineations). *God Without Being* sets up this issue more clearly. Here Marion first seeks to identify a non-metaphysical thought of being (an overcoming of metaphysics exemplified in Heidegger's work) and then to subject it, in a second stage, to theological destitution. He observes that his work "claims in the end to be able to refer to charity, the *agape* properly revealed in and as the Christ, according to an essential anachronism: charity belongs neither to pre-, nor to post-, nor to modernity; but rather, at once abandoned to and removed from historical destiny, *it dominates any situation of thought*."[3] All thought, then, is subject to a theological overcoming, even if, as we shall see, charity itself is to be thought—as gift.

Heidegger and a Non-Metaphysical Thought of Being (or God?)

The equivocation in the title above reflects something of a tension in Marion's treatment of Heidegger in *God Without Being*: while his stated focus is on a non-metaphysical thought of being (which will be overcome), his overwhelming interest is in the way God has been thought in metaphysics. This leads to something of a reversal of Heidegger's emphasis (Heidegger is primarily concerned with being; the question of God arises only as part of the critique of metaphysics), a reversal of which we must be conscious here. Marion follows Heidegger in relation to the thinking of God in metaphysics, rather than the thinking of being as such. When Marion "overcomes" Heidegger's non-metaphysical thought of being, he does so on the basis of the inadequacy of such a thinking to deal with the question of God.

As observed earlier, Marion argues that the concept of God has been thought idolatrously in modernity both as *causa sui* and as source of morality. He adopts Heidegger's account of the forgetting or obscuring of ontological difference in metaphysics and his critique of onto-theology, where being tends to be thought in terms of beings, and as the ground of beings, the highest being, God: "The advent of something like 'God' in philosophy therefore arises less from God himself than from metaphysics, as destinal figure of the thought of Being." Heidegger sees the need to separate the questions of being and God, while recognising that, in Marion's words, "this liberation is also contrary to the conditions of thought."[4] For Heidegger, being is not God—a thesis with which Marion readily agrees. Nevertheless, while the Heideggerian critique helps to expose the idolatry of

---

[3] Marion, *God Without Being* xxi–xxii. Emphasis added.
[4] Marion, *Dieu sans l'être* 53; *God Without Being* 34.

metaphysics, in Marion's view that idolatry emerges yet again in Heidegger's work. For Heidegger insists that only in the light of the thinking of being can the holy be thought: " 'But the holy, which alone is the essential sphere of divinity, which in turn alone affords a dimension for the gods and God, comes to radiate only when Being itself beforehand and after extensive preparation has been illuminated and is experienced in its truth.'"[5] When considering the question of being, the question of the existence of God becomes secondary. Marion posits that by virtue of this secondariness (where the ontological question has priority over "the so-called ontic question of 'God'"), the thought of being exhibits its own idolatry.[6] There are two ways in particular in which this is confirmed.

In a first idolatry, and even though it seems that Heidegger's "God" of faith or revelation does not depend on the aim of a human gaze, Marion locates in the analytic of *Dasein* this very tendency to reduce the divine to the scope of the human: "… phenomenologically, the anteriority of Being can be developed and justified only by the anteriority of the analytic of *Dasein*."[7] Therefore, it is only on the basis of *Dasein* that any thinking of being, and any investigation of God, could be undertaken. Heidegger's suspension of the God question "implies theologically an instance anterior to 'God,' hence that point from which idolatry could dawn."[8] Marion charges that Heidegger cannot but think of God as a being, and therefore that he has settled for an idol. For Marion, the question is whether or not God can only be thought within the confines of being: "Undoubtedly, if 'God' is, he is a being; but does God have to be?"[9] The second idolatry concerns Heidegger's search for a "more divine God," to which Marion objects on the grounds that the judgement about the measure of divinity again inevitably proceeds on the basis of a human gaze. To look for a more divine God would require, according to Marion, not only going beyond onto-theo-logy, but also beyond ontological difference (and ultimately, to think God under erasure, or "crossed out"—G̶o̶d).[10] But is it possible to think at all outside ontological difference?

Thinking Outside Ontological Difference

For Heidegger, metaphysics has failed to think ontological difference, the difference between being and beings. In seeking to think this difference, and unlike onto-theo-logy, Heidegger does not posit being in a realm beyond beings as if it were the infinite counterpart of the finite. Instead, he thinks being as what brings beings into view, but which itself withdraws in the process. Being is finite, even if it is abyssal, having no ground. Thinking therefore takes place in a matrix that

---

[5] Heidegger, "Letter on Humanism," cited in Marion, *Dieu sans l'être* 62; *God Without Being* 40.

[6] Marion, *Dieu sans l'être* 65; *God Without Being* 41.

[7] Marion, *Dieu sans l'être* 66; *God Without Being* 42.

[8] Marion, *Dieu sans l'être* 67; *God Without Being* 43.

[9] Marion, *Dieu sans l'être* 70; *God Without Being* 44.

[10] Marion, *Dieu sans l'être* 106; *God Without Being* 70.

exceeds the principle of sufficient reason, but not because it has any reference to an infinite transcendence. In asking whether or not it is possible to think outside ontological difference, Marion is trying to think outside this matrix entirely, but also without trying to reinstate the "outside" in metaphysical terms as the infinite realm of a transcendent being. Responding to *God Without Being,* Laurence Hemming nevertheless underlines the fact that Marion does not deny being to God, quoting Marion's steady reassurance of the reader from the preface to the English edition: "The whole book suffered from the inevitable and assumed equivocation of its title: was it insinuating that the God 'without being' is not, or does not exist? Let me repeat now the answer I gave then; no, definitely not. God is, exists, and that is the least of things."[11] Hemming goes on to make a significant criticism in light of this assurance. Marion, he claims, asserts that Heidegger only thinks God within the horizon of being as what ensues from being, a thinking of God that is reductive. Yet Hemming argues that in conceding that God exists, Marion thinks God *as a being* while at the same time attempting that thought beyond the ontological difference. Hemming is occupied with a potential misreading of Heidegger, with pointing out Heidegger's emphasis on *when* rather than *that* God is a being.[12] He ultimately maintains that Heidegger is more radical than Marion because only the former consistently resists the attempt to think God within the *Seinsfrage* (question of being).[13] *Prima facie,* it is difficult to argue with Hemming on the question of whether or not Marion thinks God as a being, not only because of the passage quoted immediately above but also because of the one noted earlier: "Undoubtedly, if 'God' is, he is a being ...." Yet these references are rare in Marion's corpus, and explicitly work against his overall line of reasoning. When they occur, it is as if they serve only as a grudging concession to the uninitiated, as a bracketed acceptance of the ontological assumptions of theology made solely in order to bring the reader past that point and to the threshold of what really matters. While there is an ambiguity in Marion's expression, in other words, I am not sure that it is sufficient to sustain Hemming's case.

Does Marion succeed in thinking outside ontological difference? Can God be thought outside ontological difference without necessarily being thought as being or as a being, and hence brought back within its scope? In an important passage, Marion explains:

> The danger that this critical demand may in fact render thought on the whole immediately impossible cannot be minimized. Indeed, *to think outside of ontological difference eventually condemns one to be no longer able to think at all.* But precisely, *to be no longer able to think, when it is a question of God, indicates neither absurdity nor impropriety,* as soon as God himself, *in order to be thought,* must be thought as ... that which surpasses, detours, and distracts all thought, even non-representational. By definition and decision, God, *if he must be thought,* can

---

[11] Lawrence Hemming, "Reading Heidegger: Is God Without Being? Jean-Luc Marion's Reading of Martin Heidegger in *God Without Being,*" *New Blackfriars* 76.895 (1995): 343–50, 346, quote corrected.

[12] Hemming, "Reading Heidegger," 345–46.

[13] Hemming, "Reading Heidegger," 349–50.

meet no theoretical space to his measure, because his measure exerts itself in our eyes as an excessiveness. Ontological difference itself, and hence also Being, become too limited (even if they are universal, or better: because they make us a universe, because in them the world "worlds") to pretend to offer the dimension, still less the "divine abode" where God would become thinkable.[14]

In the one passage Marion both affirms that thought becomes impossible beyond ontological difference ("to think outside of ontological difference eventually condemns one to be no longer able to think at all"), and that this impossibility of thought is entirely appropriate for a thinking of God. But is there then to be a *thought* of God or not? Is love going to involve a destitution of all thought or simply a new way of thinking?

The passage just quoted has many levels of resonance. In some ways it echoes, albeit in another register, Heidegger's passing from phenomenology to "thought."[15] More strongly, it is reminiscent of Lévinas, for whom being refers to a suffocating totality, and whose project involves the attempt to think otherwise than being: "Language permits us to utter, be it by betrayal, this *outside of being*, this *ex-ception* to being, as though being's other were an event of being."[16] There is also a link to be made with Marion's discussion of Descartes that we have already considered, where the idea of the infinite is still thinkable even while it is without determinable content. Nevertheless, the work of Pascal remains troubling in that context, since Pascal claims to render thought destitute by way of charity. However, it must be noted that in Marion's phenomenology, which will be addressed in subsequent chapters, his aim is, precisely, to think "excessiveness" non-metaphysically, as what he will call the saturated phenomenon. Further, we need to take into account the strategy that Marion has already developed theologically of thinking according to distance, particularly as it is propounded in *The Idol and Distance*, where it is explicitly argued that distance goes beyond ontological difference and even Derridean *différance*—but by way of interruption. There Marion claims: "... one remains all the more inscribed within the ontological difference insofar as one travels through it and pulls it in every direction. Next, and for this very reason, neither *différance* nor the Other avoids the onto-theo-logical idolatry ...." Nevertheless, he goes on to ask rhetorically: "would distance overcome the ontological difference and the Being that is figured metaphysically in it, hence also their idol, not by leaving it, critiquing or inverting it, *but by remaining in it—as not remaining in it?*"[17] This can be compared to a passage in *God Without Being*, where we read:

> ... liberation from Being does not at all mean abstracting from it, precisely because abstraction strictly renders possible one of the metaphysical modes of the Being of beings ... Nor does liberation from Being signify undoing oneself and stealing away from it, since this very evasion opens onto nonbeing, hence remains within

---

[14] Marion, *Dieu sans l'être* 70–71; *God Without Being* 45. Emphasis added.

[15] For an account of this progress, see the classic William J. Richardson, *Heidegger: Through Phenomenology to Thought*, 3rd ed. (New York: Fordham University Press, 2003).

[16] Lévinas, *Otherwise than Being or Beyond Essence* 6.

[17] Marion, *L'idole et la distance* 282, 282–83; *The Idol and Distance:* 233. Emphasis added.

the dominion of the Being of beings. Finally, liberation from Being does not mean that one claims to criticize it or revoke it—for that discourse still supposes a logos and a site from which to set it into operation, hence prerogatives of Being.[18]

In these passages we find affirmed that Marion's attempt to think outside the matrix of ontological difference will not be an attempt simply to reinstate an "outside" as an infinite realm of a transcendent being. Instead, we find again an echo of the Lévinas who writes: "The task is to conceive of the possibility of a break out of essence. To go where? Toward what region? To stay on what ontological plane? But the extraction from essence contests the unconditional privilege of the question 'where?'; it signifies a null-site [non-lieu]."[19] Finally, we might bear in mind Derrida's insight that the impossible is not necessarily the unthinkable, and his noting of the possibility of a "non-dogmatic doublet of dogma ... in any case *thinking*, which 'repeats' without religion the possibility of religion."[20] Here the discussion that takes place between Derrida and Marion in relation to mystical theology is also relevant.[21] In that debate Marion sums up the difficulties very well:

> We agree that there are three ways of speaking about God [affirmative, negative, and mystical], but the difficulty is to understand how it is possible to say that there is a third way. According to metaphysical theory of discourse, there are only two possible ways. So what exactly is the meaning, the status, the legitimacy of the third way? The point is not whether there is a third one, but how to understand that the third one *remains rational, although it does not remain confined within the possibilities opened by metaphysics.* My answer would be that the only way to understand the third way, beyond affirmation and negation, without coming back implicitly or explicitly to affirmation is to take seriously the pragmatic use of language.[22]

It seems to me that Marion is committed to the possibility of a thought that opens onto excessiveness throughout the course of his work, but that he constantly approaches this thought from two points of view. On the one hand, following a philosophical trajectory, an immanent thought of excess (such as the idea of the infinite, or later, the saturated phenomenon) has an intelligible framework but inconceivable content. In this sense it is both possible and impossible: the aporia can be named but not solved. If it exceeds ontological difference, it is because it functions to interrupt that matrix from within, that is, immanently. A thought of excess at once marks the possibility of thought's interruption and the limits of all thought. On the other hand, following a theological trajectory (such as that of *God Without Being*), all thought is rendered

---

[18] Marion, *Dieu sans l'être* 124; *God Without Being* 83.

[19] Lévinas, *Otherwise than Being* 8.

[20] Derrida, *Given Time* 7, 10.

[21] Derrida notes this in relation to Marion and others, a point that is underscored in a very relevant text, Jean-Luc Marion, "Metaphysics and Phenomenology: A Relief for Theology," *Critical Inquiry* 21.4 (1994): 572–91, 590n35. See Jacques Derrida, "Donner la mort," *L'éthique du don. Jacques Derrida et la pensée du don.* Colloque de Royaumont, décembre 1990, eds. Jean-Michel Rabaté and Michael Wetzel (Paris: Métailié-Transition, 1992) 11–108, 52–53.

[22] Marion, "In the Name," 46. Emphasis added.

vain for Marion in the light of Revelation. In this sense thought is exposed as foolishness or meaninglessness, or certainly as no longer important in view of the commandment to love. If ontological difference is exceeded from this perspective, it is because it is no longer a relevant question. Yet we are still left to wonder how a Revelation that exceeds thought and renders it vain is to be given to thought at all. Both perspectives potentially place theology—or theology as it is often understood—in an invidious position. According to the first, the content of (theological) thought cannot be absolutely determined, and so apparently leads only to a type of agnosticism (a "non-dogmatic doublet"?). According to the second, love must affirm what can nevertheless be witnessed to only within the framework of thought (in the broadest sense as language), even if it fundamentally concerns the will. This is why the theological appeal to vanity potentially smacks—for Ward, but also for Derrida, Caputo, Janicaud, and others—of "uncritical dogmatism." In Marion's defence, it could be argued that in more recent works, in particular, he is much more careful when treading this line between undecidability and faith. Better, it becomes clearer that faith is less an exercise in theological certainty than in hermeneutical risk-taking, and that there is a world of difference in between.

In Marion's attempt to overcome the deficiencies in Heidegger's thought of God, he both affirms the inadequacy of metaphysical attempts to think God as being, and then affirms the (as yet unspecified) possibility of overcoming even a non-metaphysical thought of being in order to think God. Within *God Without Being*, that overcoming is largely undertaken from a theological point of view, where all thought is considered ultimately to be in vain. Nevertheless, as we will see, Marion still invokes a thought of God. In the remaining part of the chapter, we have to consider the full unfolding of that theological destitution, which occurs both in relation to Heidegger and in relation to one of theology's favourite sons, Thomas Aquinas. In claiming that God need not be thought as being, Marion stands in conflict with a long tradition of naming God in this way. There are two questions to be considered. First, is Thomas' thinking of God as being part of metaphysics (and therefore, is it overcome by an overcoming of metaphysics)? Second, if Thomas' thinking of God as being is not metaphysical, is it still subject to further philosophical or theological destitution? It is to these questions that we now turn.

Thomas and God as Being

In the transition leading up to the section of text we are about to consider, Marion observes that Heidegger's characterisation of the Christian God is made in the following (highly onto-theo-logical) terms: " 'in Christian theology, we define God, the *summum ens qua summum bonum*, as the highest value'."[23] Marion goes on to comment: "… everything happens as if the primacy of the question of Being (Heidegger) met, without confusion and with the full disparity that separates a thought that recedes from metaphysics from a thought that remains in it, the primacy

---

[23] Heidegger, *The Question Concerning Technology*, quoted in Marion, *Dieu sans l'être* 108; *God Without Being* 72.

of the *ens* over every other divine name (Saint Thomas)." In this way, the Heideggerian critique is linked directly with Thomas' thinking of God, and not simply with the metaphysics of Suarez. Marion questions the priority given to being as a name for God, preferring to speak of God as love, or loving, rather than being. He thus identifies himself with those like Bonaventure and Denys whose first name for God is "the good" (*bonum*), in opposition to those such as Thomas, whose first name for God is being (*esse*, to be, sheer being, but more problematically also *ens*, being in the sense of the being of beings, and any discrete being as well).[24] In Denys' theology, goodness is anterior to being, as well as beings and "non-beings."[25] It is this capacity for indifference to the difference between beings and non-beings which will prove useful for Marion in his theological destitution of metaphysics. For Thomas, on the other hand, being (*esse*) is God's most proper name, since "the being of God is His essence itself."[26] When considering the transcendentals as divine names, Thomas also argues that *ens* has priority over the others (the good, the one, and the true), for "... the *ens* finds itself comprehended in their comprehension, and not reciprocally."[27] Further, the *ens* is logically the first object of the human intellect and therefore has priority.[28] Marion's claim is that the naming of God as *esse/ens* means that with Thomas the Christian God first fully enters into metaphysics, for the belief that God is love can now only be thought by way of being.[29] Theologians and philosophers sympathetic to Thomas typically make two responses to this section of Marion's text. They argue that while he certainly names God *esse*, he never considers God an *ens*, or even *ens* in the sense of the (created) being that beings have in common, *ens commune*.[30] Further, they argue that Thomas does not think *esse* in such a way that it is metaphysical.[31] Before turning to explore these arguments, however, it is first necessary to set out Marion's line of reasoning in the preface to the English edition of *God Without Being*, where Thomas is somewhat rehabilitated.

Conscious of the reaction his work has provoked, in the new preface Marion revises and clarifies his earlier observations, presenting three arguments allowing for a more positive evaluation of Thomas.[32] The first concerns the very distinction

---

[24] Marion, *Dieu sans l'être* 109ff.; *God Without Being* 73ff.

[25] Marion, *Dieu sans l'être* 113–14; *God Without Being* 75.

[26] Marion, *Dieu sans l'être* 114; *God Without Being* 76. Marion refers to a range of texts by Thomas, but here he refers to the *Summa Theologica*, Ia, 13, 11 and Ia, 5, 2.

[27] *Commentary on the Sentences*, I,d.8,q.1,a.3, *solutio*, quoted in Marion, *Dieu sans l'être* 119; *God Without Being* 79.

[28] Marion, *Dieu sans l'être* 119–20; *God Without Being* 80–81. This raises the question for Marion about whether *ens* is therefore to be understood analogically or univocally of God, since we are thinking of God starting from a human construct.

[29] Marion, *Dieu sans l'être* 122–23; *God Without Being* 82–83.

[30] See, for example, Kelly, "The 'Horrible Wrappers' of Aquinas' God" 199–201.

[31] See, for example, Martis, "Thomistic *Esse*—Idol or Icon?"

[32] He also sets out a more comprehensive response and revision in Jean-Luc Marion, "Saint Thomas d'Aquin et l'onto-théo-logie," *Revue Thomiste* XCV (1995): 31–66, which has been included in the 2002 edition of *Dieu sans l'être*. See also Marion, *De surcroît* 175; *In Excess* 145. Parts of the text which follows originally appeared in Robyn Horner, "Rethinking God as Gift: Jean-Luc Marion and a Theology of Donation," Doctoral dissertation, Monash University, 1998, 25ff.

that he had apparently overlooked in the earlier section of text, the distinction between *ens commune* and *esse*: "this 'Being' [*ens commune*] no longer has anything to do with the *esse* that Saint Thomas assigns to the Christian God."[33] It is, however, Heidegger's characterisation of being that is of concern to Marion, a characterisation that has been linked positively in Christian theology with Thomistic *esse*.[34] The second argument is that the Thomistic preference for *esse* can be situated in the context of the debate over divine names, and shown to be but one possible path. And yet, Marion adds (and this can be construed as a third argument), "even when he thinks God as *esse*, Saint Thomas nevertheless does not chain God either to Being or to metaphysics." Marion argues that Thomas "does not chain God to Being because the divine *esse* immeasurably surpasses (and hardly maintains an *analogia* with) the *ens commune* of creatures ...."[35]

Responding not to Marion but to Heidegger, Caputo's interpretation of the *ens/esse* distinction in Aquinas is instructive. While Heidegger accuses Thomas of thinking God as being (where being is reduced to the being of creatures), and of thinking God as the highest being amongst beings, Caputo makes the observation that neither of these accusations is correct.[36] With regard to the first point, Caputo maintains that creatures participate in the *esse* of God only in a causal sense:

> The creature participates in God because the creature is a likeness (*similitude*) of God. But it is a genuine being in its own right, because the similitude which it has of the divine being inheres intrinsically in it (*sibi inhaerens*). The created *esse* formally belongs to the creature. But it originates in God, who is at once the source of all *esse* (*principium*) and the exemplar of all *esse*, the being which is *esse*, purely, subsistently, perfectly ....[37]

With regard to the second point, Caputo observes Thomas' distinction between the finite participation of the creature in *esse*, which is the meaning of *ens*, and *esse* itself, which is unlimited and infinite: "God is not a being, for this implies finitude, the contraction of *esse* to a determinate mode, limitation. God is, not an *ens*, but *esse subsistens*."[38] There is no recuperation of God by the creature who participates in God's *esse*, and we can therefore assert that God is not reduced to the level of the human by virtue of our naming God *esse*.

---

[33] Marion, *God Without Being* xxii.

[34] While Marion is not explicit in warning of "the enthusiastic naïveté of the beginnings" which "has largely given way, among the theologians, to great caution," (xxii) we could think of the ways in which Heidegger's being has been incorporated into the theologies of Karl Rahner and John Macquarrie, for example.

[35] Marion, *God Without Being* xxiii.

[36] John D. Caputo, *Heidegger and Aquinas*. Contrasting Thomas with Heidegger, Caputo states: "In the first place, I want to show that even though creatures participate in Being, and God is Being, the Being of God and the Being of creatures are not to be confused. And secondly, I want to show that for St. Thomas, even though God is distinct from creatures, God is not a being, not even a 'highest being'." (140)

[37] Caputo, *Heidegger and Aquinas* 142.

[38] Caputo, *Heidegger and Aquinas* 144.

In an explicit response to *God Without Being*, Tony Kelly argues that Thomas simply does not create a metaphysical edifice based on a univocal understanding of being. Kelly, like Caputo, insists that Thomas uses *esse* in a non-reductive way: "He is certainly using concepts of causality, perfection, intelligence and so forth; but the way he uses such categories turns on the manner in which his affirmation of God as sheer Be-ing will emerge and function as a kind of clearing space in which the mystery of God can be explored, as affirmed to be, but never known."[39] John Martis' analysis of Marion's three arguments is very helpful in this regard. Martis focuses on Marion's third argument, that is, "that God's *esse* might so surpass the *ens commune* (common being) of creatures that God—even God expressed as *esse*—remains genuinely free from Being."[40] He suggests that this argument offers the possibility of separating God from being while not distinguishing God from *esse*. The difficulty that Martis identifies is that, since Heidegger, the affirmation that God is the giver of being is likely to be inverted—God becomes a gift that is given by being, and is in this way subordinate to being.[41] In Marion's third argument, Martis finds the beginnings of a way of resisting this inversion.

Martis examines the Thomistic understanding of analogical predication, where words that refer to God are used neither univocally nor equivocally but analogically. This leads him to affirm that "*esse* (Being), when predicated of God, is in some sense the same as, but in some sense different from, *ens* (being) when predicated of creatures."[42] The maintenance of these two positions, Martis indicates, involves the holding in tension of the very obvious contradiction that *esse* is "both Being and 'other than Being'." Martis suggests that the only way that both positions can be maintained is through a dynamic that affirms both poles, which he expresses as follows: "*Esse* is the giver of Being: this Being in turn gives *esse* meaning *as* Being, but in a way that also gives *esse* meaning as other than Being. This last giving has in one sense, of course, only the 'shape' of a giving of *esse* as Being; nevertheless, within this shape, the meaning of *esse* as God is successfully indicated as non-identical with its meaning as Being."[43] What Martis propounds is a use of *esse* to refer to God that is both continuous and discontinuous with being: "the meaning of Being *generates the indication, as pre-apprehended, of a meaning which cannot in principle be expressed*—namely the meaning of uncreated *esse*."[44] This continuity, which is at once discontinuous, forbids the return to God of thought, or otherwise expressed, the recuperation of God in meaning.

With his three arguments in the English preface, which by and large affirm and are affirmed by the insights of the authors referred to above, Marion indicates that Thomas' thought of God need not be compromised by metaphysics. At the same time, however, one of Marion's central assertions does not change, which is that even if it is freed from its metaphysical overlay, being is not the most appropriate

---

[39] Kelly, "The 'Horrible Wrappers'" 198.
[40] Martis, "Thomistic *Esse*—Idol or Icon?" 55.
[41] Martis, "Thomistic *Esse*—Idol or Icon?" 60.
[42] Martis, "Thomistic *Esse*—Idol or Icon?" 62.
[43] Martis, "Thomistic *Esse*—Idol or Icon?" 63.
[44] Martis, "Thomistic *Esse*—Idol or Icon?" 64.

name for God.[45] He thus opens the possibility that even a Thomistic thought of God could still be subject to a higher destitution. That destitution is expressed in a rethinking of God as the gift of love.

Indifference and the Gift

It was noted earlier that in attempting to think outside ontological difference, Marion does not envisage that it is a simple case of "stealing away" from being. Instead, he maintains that it is possible to "outwit" being by thinking beings without reference to being:

> Thus it is necessary that being play according to a rule such that its difference does not refer at all to Being; or even that being be disposed and interpreted according to such a difference that it no longer permits Being to recover *itself* in being or permits being to lead itself back to *Being*, so that the play of being can escape *Being*, which no longer would appear therein—not even under the figure of retreat or of the unthought.[46]

Arguing that biblical revelation "does not say a word about Being" and that it "is unaware of ontological difference," Marion nevertheless observes that it has much to say about "being, nonbeing, and beingness."[47] Three texts serve as examples where the Bible plays outside ontological difference. The first is Rom. 4:17, which in the context of faith speaks of God giving life to the dead and calling "the non-beings as beings." Marion observes that the movement from nonbeing to being cannot occur because of any intrinsic potentiality on the part of the nonbeing, but can only happen to it from beyond.[48] For Paul, nonbeings are those subject to death, or the already dead, that is, those who are no longer called by the world. Only God can call the nonbeings from death to being: God calls the nonbeings *as if* they were already beings, not taking into account the difference. God is thus indifferent to ontic difference: "the ontic difference between being and nonbeing indeed intervenes ... however, it no longer functions according to the norms of being [*l'étant*] but to those of operators (faith, call, as if) that ... make it appear indifferent ...."[49] The second text to be examined is 1 Cor. 1:28. Here God is seen to choose the lowly, the nonbeings, in order to confound the beings. Contrary to what we might expect, here nonbeings are those we would ordinarily name beings: the Christians, in the eyes of the world, are less than nothing, nonbeings: "Through the call of God, the 'less than nothing' appear, not in their own eyes or in the eyes of the 'world,' as beings, but inversely, wisdom against wisdom, folly against folly, as

---

45 Marion, *God Without Being* xx.
46 Marion, *Dieu sans l'être* 126; *God Without Being* 85.
47 Marion, *Dieu sans l'être* 128; *God Without Being* 86.
48 "The transition befalls them from the outside; the transition from nonbeing to being goes right through them, issuing from this side and proceeding beyond." Marion, *Dieu sans l'être* 129; *God Without Being* 87.
49 Marion, *Dieu sans l'être* 131; *God Without Being* 88.

nonbeings." Marion further notes here not only an indifference to ontic difference, but an indifference to ontological difference: "the decision on beingness depends neither on the categories of a philosophical discourse nor on Being deploying itself in ontological difference, but on instances separated by the limit between 'the world' and the 'call' of the GXd who gives life."[50] There are thus two different sources of affirmation (or "glory")—the world, or Christ. So there is a new measure, the measure of faith, which defines beings and nonbeings without reference to ontic or ontological difference:[51] "We now see, then, how being and nonbeing can be divided according to something other than Being."[52] For his third and final example, Marion turns to the parable of the loving father (or "prodigal son") in Luke 15:12–32. In this passage both sons get to enjoy the property (*ousia*) of the father, yet both effectively seek to claim it as their own possession. We see this occurring in different ways in the story: the younger son claims his share of the property while he is young, while the older son works diligently in the expectation that what is rightfully his will come to him in the future. The sons effectively see the *ousia* quite differently to the father, who is not looking at the *ousia* in terms of economics but only in terms of gift: "The *ousia* is valuable to him only as the currency in an exchange of which it can mark, at the very best, but a moment …."[53] Marion argues that in this passage the *ousia* in fact operates in defiance of being: "The *ousia* is inscribed in the play of the gift, abandon, and pardon that make of it the currency of an entirely *other* exchange than that of beings." In the most familiar of parables we are finally brought to the point of identification of the game wherein being escapes Being: "And from now on we can delimit even more closely the game that, indifferent to ontological difference, thus causes being to elude Being: it is called the gift. The gift that gave rise to the operations of preceding readings—call, give life, as if, father, and so on—*gives* Being/beings.[54] Taking the final step in the argument, Marion then makes the claim that as the gift has its source in charity, it is ultimately charity that "delivers Being/being"; divine charity renders ontological difference destitute.[55]

Marion thinks the gift of love as a theological destitution not only of metaphysics but also of ontological difference. While it has taken us some time to reach the *dénouement* of the argument that God's self-gift as love outwits ontological

---

[50] Marion, *Dieu sans l'être* 13; *God Without Being* 93.

[51] "A line, along which the 'world' divides into beings and nonbeings that on which it wants to found itself, crosses another line, along which the call reestablishes beings and nonbeings in the measure of their faith. The crossing of these two lines decidedly distorts the play of being by withdrawing it from Being, by undoing being from the rule of Being. This crossing traces a cross over ontological difference, a cross that abolishes it without deconstructing it, exceeds it without overcoming it, annuls it without annihilating it, distorts it without contesting its right." Marion, *Dieu sans l'être* 139; *God Without Being* 95.

[52] Marion, *Dieu sans l'être* 140; *God Without Being* 95.

[53] Marion, *Dieu sans l'être* 145; *God Without Being* 99. "Under the idolatrously charged gaze of the sons, currency obfuscates exchange: to the profoundly iconic gaze of the father, *ousia* never stops the aim of the exchange or circulation of the gift." 145/100.

[54] Marion, *Dieu sans l'être* 146; *God Without Being* 100. First trans. modified.

[55] Marion, *Dieu sans l'être* 148; *God Without Being* 102.

difference, Marion has in fact already stated his conclusions much earlier in the text:

> God can give himself to be thought without idolatry only starting from himself alone: to give himself to be thought as love, hence as gift; to give himself to be thought as a thought of the gift. Or better, as a gift for thought, as a gift that gives itself to be thought. But a gift, which gives itself forever, can be thought only by a thought that gives itself to the gift to be thought. Only a thought that gives itself can devote itself to a gift for thought. But, for thought, what is it to give itself, if not to love?[56]

This tortuous passage is significant not only because it foreshadows the conclusions of *God Without Being*, but also because it places those conclusions within a framework of thought, and thus precisely within the parameters of our questioning. It seems that the theological destitution of thought (metaphysics, but also the thought of ontological difference) still requires, for Marion, a thought that is not in vain—the thought of the gift. How does this thought function? Once again, Marion employs the strategy of thinking according to distance, but it is actually in this context that he identifies (as was noted at the end of Chapter 6) from whence *agape* flows: "everything indicates the direction and meaning of distance."

For the Marion of *God Without Being*, God gives Godself in a gift of love that can be recognised but not appropriated. Yet how are we to be brought to the point of recognition of the gift of love? Marion tells us that we glimpse the crossing of being by love only rarely. *Agape* goes beyond our knowledge, "with a hyperbole that defines it and, indissolubly, prohibits access to it."[57] Given that we are bound to being (and, Marion adds, as sinners), *agape* escapes us in two ways. It escapes us philosophically, because we have a fixed horizon, and it escapes us theologically, because we are finite and sinful.[58] To accede to it, he suggests, we need to develop a totally new way of seeing. Following an analogous path to Heidegger in *Being and Time*, Marion observes that particular moods offer us different perspectives on the meaning of the world. The world can strike us as completely meaningless or vain, for example, from the perspective of boredom or from that of melancholy. Now, the contrary of moods such as these is love, for love is a complete investment in meaning, whereas boredom or melancholy open upon a complete absence of meaning. Nevertheless, love itself can strike the world with vanity, in that all meaning comes to be bound up in the loved one and the lover becomes completely indifferent to the delights or otherwise of the world:

> Vanity covers as much what love includes in its exclusionary logic as what is excluded by this same love. The difference does not at all pass between beings and nonbeings ... it passes between love itself and the world—being—by itself.

---

[56] Marion, *Dieu sans l'être* 75; *God Without Being* 49.

[57] Marion, *Dieu sans l'être* 157; *God Without Being* 108.

[58] "we must recognize that the condition that is as much finite as it is 'sinful' situates us at an infinite distance from *agape* ... ." Marion, *Dieu sans l'être* 158; *God Without Being* 109.

Vanity, which follows and redoubles love as its shadow, has no other function, as long as *agape* has not recapitulated everything under a single authority, than to mark this indifferent difference.[59]

It is possible, in other words, to go beyond metaphysics and ontological difference by learning to see the world from the perspective of infinite meaning, infinite love. But once again, how is this not just to overcome metaphysics by a (Nietzschean) movement of the will? We have been brought by a different route to the same point that we reached at the end of our consideration of *On Descartes' Metaphysical Prism*: Marion claims that theology can render metaphysics destitute, but this can only be so as a result of a decision to see the world in a particular way, a decision that is not ultimately recognised as such. It thus appears as an assertion of a new foundation that risks reincorporation into metaphysics.

---

[59] Marion, *Dieu sans l'être* 195; *God Without Being* 138.

PART III
EXCEEDING EXCESS

Introduction to Part III

In Part II the focus was on Marion's engagement with metaphysics and its overcoming by way of theology. We observed how, for Marion, theology constantly opens onto what exceeds thought, but that its "object" can only be recognised rather than cognised, received rather than appropriated. It is evident that such an overcoming of metaphysics only has a conditional legitimacy. Without a commitment of faith, it remains inaccessible. Further, because it relies on a commitment of faith for its essential moves, it is always subject to the philosophical suspicion that it involves some kind of theological sleight of hand, remaining susceptible to the pressure of a dogma uncomplicated by hermeneutics. And to some extent, the motifs of which it makes use remain un-thought in a broader context, not yet entirely subject to critical examination. This is the case, for example, with Marion's initial use of the gift theme. And with the examination of each theological motif, it became clear that the specificity of the theological reference actually has to be put in question if the motif is going to work without being recuperated by metaphysics. In fine, while Marion's attempt to overcome metaphysics theologically may appear to be unproblematic from the perspective of a faith commitment, by making that perspective absolute, all the difficulties of metaphysics are simply repeated. It seems that Marion recognises this himself where he later observes:

> The critical portion of [*God Without Being*] was accomplished within the field of philosophy, but I could not, at that time, glimpse its constructive side (access to charity) except through recourse to theology ... What was lacking was a nonmetaphysical method of philosophy—phenomenology .... It took twenty years for me to hope to succeed, at least in part. And in fact, *Étant donné*, with the inventory of saturated phenomena, completes, in the particular case of the phenomenon of Revelation, a sketch of what *Dieu sans l'être* bluntly intended through direct recourse to theology.[1]

In Chapters 3 and 4 of the present text I sketched the basic contours of Husserlian phenomenology and sought to show one of the main lines of development from it, extending through Heidegger, Lévinas, and Derrida. In Part III, I will outline Marion's reading of Husserl, as well as the ways in which he adopts or modifies positions of the other three, and draws from thinkers such as Ricoeur and Henry. While Marion's phenomenological interests are foreshadowed in many of his earlier texts, they are represented most systematically in the phenomenological trilogy that comprises *Reduction and Givenness*, *Being Given*, and *In Excess*. Each

---

[1] Marion, "Preface to the American Edition," *Being Given* ix–xi, ix.

part of the trilogy contains its own very detailed phenomenological analyses, but speaking in general terms, Marion has five fundamental arguments with regard to phenomenology. These arguments sometimes undergo development and adjustment over the course of the trilogy, but they are essentially as follows: (i) Although Husserl tends to focus on a reduction to objective, "present" phenomena—which is where he is subject to the heaviest critique by Heidegger and Derrida—his phenomenology at various points opens onto the possibility of exceeding metaphysics. (ii) The proper horizon of the phenomenological reduction is neither presence (Husserl's reduction), nor being (Heidegger's existential reduction), but givenness (*Gegebenheit, donation*) (Marion's reduction). (iii) Givenness implies an emphasis on the self-givenness (*Selbstgegebenheit*) of phenomena, and a consequent recognition that the subject is not first a constituting I but a screen upon which phenomena become visible. In this way, along with being given the phenomena, the subject is simultaneously given to itself, as *l'interloqué* [the interlocuted one], who by the end of the trilogy is referred to as *l'adonné* [the gifted one]. (iv) Some phenomena offer so much to intuition that they cannot be definitively constituted; these phenomena are saturated by intuition (hence, "saturated phenomena"). They include events, idols, flesh, and icons, but potentially also phenomena of r/Revelation.[2] (v) In this way, phenomenology is a kind of philosophical prolegomenon that opens onto theology (my phrase, not Marion's), not because phenomenology has any authority to speak about theology as such, and not because it has any inherent tendency towards the theological, but because it can provide a non-theological context for the consideration of phenomena that are given in excess of our ability to constitute them, which might include revelatory phenomena. It should be apparent from previous chapters that as a theologian, Marion accords Revelation authoritative priority. This is in the sense that he accepts Christian Revelation as given (and in a sense, as given absolutely through [the interpretation of] the Church, which can be hermeneutically problematic), and as determinative for theology. What he attempts to do as a phenomenologist, however, is to show that there is also a way of thinking philosophically about the revelatory phenomena that form the foundations of belief, even though as phenomena of Revelation they are inaccessible to philosophy because of the necessary interpretative gap of faith.

From this vantage point, we can consider the ever-deepening movements of Marion's overcoming of metaphysics as follows:

1 Metaphysics is overcome by the thought of the infinite (Descartes), but even the thought of the infinite is rendered destitute by charity (Pascal) (*On Descartes' Metaphysical Prism*)—yet we are left with the problem of how to think charity in other than dogmatic terms.
2 Metaphysics is overcome to some extent by the thought of Nietzsche, Heidegger, and Derrida, but their thought is similarly rendered destitute by

---

[2] Because Marion sometimes uses the upper case and at other times the lower, and for reasons that will become clear in Chapter 10, most uses of this word will be written as "r/Revelation."

love/the gift (*The Idol and Distance, God Without Being*)—yet the problem of thinking love remains.

3   Metaphysics is overcome by phenomenology, which in turn provides a setting for the thought of love/the gift (as the other person, call, icon, r/Revelation), even if with respect to r/Revelation it confirms only its possibility rather than its actuality ([*La croisée du visible*], *Reduction and Givenness, Being Given, In Excess*).

In Chapter 9 I will sketch Marion's general reworking of phenomenology. This will be followed in Chapter 10 by a closer examination of those phenomena he calls "saturated," which are particularly pertinent with regard to theology. Chapter 11 will then form a study of Marion's consolidation of his thinking on love, *Le phénomène érotique*, which provides the final link between the attempt to overcome metaphysics, theology, and phenomenology.

Chapter 9

Renewals of Phenomenology

Phenomenology and Metaphysics: Rehabilitating Husserl

I often assume that phenomenology makes an exception to metaphysics. I do not, however, defend this assertion in its entirety, since I emphasize that Husserl upholds Kantian decisions (the conditions for the possibility of phenomenality, the horizon, the constituting function of the I) ... It should, therefore, be admitted that phenomenology does not actually overcome metaphysics so much as it opens the official possibility of leaving it to itself. The border between metaphysics and phenomenology runs within phenomenology—as its highest possibility, and I stick with the phenomenological discipline only in search of the way that it opens and, sometimes, closes.[1]

At various points in his phenomenological trilogy, Marion identifies both ways in which Husserlian phenomenology remains part of an unquestionably metaphysical enterprise and ways in which, perhaps in spite of itself, it exceeds metaphysics. Among the ways in which Hussserlian phenomenology remains metaphysical, Marion includes "the unquestioned primacy of the presencing of beings." On Husserl's account this presencing is accomplished by intuition, which he understands in a broadened way, such that Marion can describe it as what "deposits the world into presence, without withdrawal, without remainder, without restraint."[2] Marion further includes as part of a metaphysical enterprise Husserl's reduction to object-ness of what is given to consciousness, or his application of solely an object intentionality to what is given.[3] And Marion includes, as is evident in the quote above, "the conditions for the possibility of phenomenality, the horizon, [and] the constituting function of the I." In Marion's view, phenomenality is ultimately determined for Husserl—as for Kant—by two basic conditions of possibility for experience: a delimiting horizon against which the phenomenon can be contextualised, and a subject without whom no phenomenon can appear.[4] In these ways, Husserlian phenomenology is undoubtedly metaphysical. However, Marion also recognises an ambiguity or an opening beyond metaphysics within Husserl's work: the I who performs the reduction (and is intended to be subject to it) is nevertheless ultimately excluded from it; the I therefore "does not itself have first

---

[1] Marion, *Being Given* 4; *Étant donné* 9.
[2] Marion, *Réduction et donation* 28, 30; *Reduction and Givenness* 15, 17. Marion argues that Husserl allows for signification without intuition. Signification is, however, also included within the realm of presence in its expanded form as givenness (56–57/34–35).
[3] Marion, *Reduction and Givenness* 204; *Réduction et donation* 304.
[4] Marion, *Being Given* 179–89; *Étant donné* 251–64.

to be" and is in this way delivered both from an ontic status and, indeed, from a Heideggerian ontology.[5] Further, the I that is the origin of all constitution in the Cartesian tradition, eventually shows itself incapable of self-constitution. According to Husserl's analysis of internal time-consciousness: "the original impression originally determines consciousness, which henceforth loses its status as origin and discovers itself originally determined, impressed, constituted—transcendentally taken witness."[6] The exception of the I from being and its incapacity to constitute itself suggest to Marion that objective presence for a constituting intention need not be the ultimate horizon of phenomenology. That horizon instead, he claims, is properly givenness.[7]

Givenness as the Ultimate Phenomenological Principle

In accord with Michel Henry, Marion maintains that over the course of Husserl's phenomenological corpus there emerge—explicitly or implicitly—not just one, but four principles, each of which could qualify as the "principle of principles."[8] The first, "so much appearing, so much Being," is dismissed by Marion as inadequate, since it seems to make appearing equivalent to being and thus leaves being indeterminate.[9] Similarly the second principle—"to the things themselves!"—is lacking because appearing seems to have been made redundant, in favour of " 'things' that are supposedly already there, available and accessible if not constituted."[10] The third principle is more complex: "*every originarily giving intuition* is *a source of right for cognition*—that *everything* that offers itself *originarily* to us *in intuition* (in its fleshly actuality, so to speak) *must simply be received for what it gives itself*, but without *passing beyond the limits in which it gives itself.*"[11] This is the only principle for which Husserl actually claims the status "principle of principles." Nevertheless, despite its several advantages over the others, it contains a number of deficiencies: intuition becomes the "measure of phenomenality"; the "source of authority" may be lacking, meaning that intuition

---

[5] Marion, *Reduction and Givenness* 162–166; *Réduction et donation* 240–247.

[6] Marion, *Being Given* 221; *Étant donné* 309.

[7] Marion, *Reduction and Givenness* 32ff.; *Réduction et donation* 52ff.

[8] Michel Henry, "Quatres principes de la phénoménologie," *Revue de Métaphysique et de Morale* 96.1 (1991): 3–26. In this article Henry affirms Marion's enunciation of the fourth principle.

[9] Marion, *Being Given* 11; *Étant donné* 19–20.

[10] Marion, *Being Given* 12; *Étant donné* 20.

[11] In Chapter 3 of the present text the translation used was from Husserl, *Ideas: General Introduction* §24, p.92. Here I have used Kosky's translation from Marion, *Being Given* 12. Marion's footnote is instructive: "In his note to the French translation, Paul Ricoeur observes that the rapprochement of 'giving intuition' and 'what gives itself' not only is 'striking,' but above all 'contains in miniature all the difficulties of a philosophy of constitution that must remain at the same time and from another point of view an intuitionism.' In fact, the two formulations converge easily enough in givenness alone. But another difficulty then arises: is givenness measured solely by intuition (and constitution)?" Marion, *Being Given* 330n7; *Étant donné* 21n1.

may be impoverished; such impoverishment or its varying degrees are not examined; intuition is limited to the fulfilment of an objectifying intentionality, and the principle makes no reference to the phenomenological characteristic *par excellence*, the reduction.[12] Marion is thus led to posit a fourth formulation, "so much reduction, so much givenness" (or, "the more reduction, the more givenness"; as much reduction, as much givenness).[13] He argues for the primacy of this principle on the basis of a number of passages from *The Idea of Phenomenology*, "the very work which, in 1907, practiced for the first time all the figures of the reduction, [and] ... is most insistent in its privilege of givenness."[14] Only this formulation, Marion maintains, can solve the difficulties inherent in the other three, and only this formulation emphasises and effectively protects the self-giving of the phenomenon: "Intuition, in particular, thus also the transcendence of intentionality that it fulfils, can sometimes intervene, but it does not define the given; for, certain apparitions are given without object intentionality, therefore without fulfilling intuition."[15] This idea of phenomena that are given without an adequate concept is of particular importance for Marion. In agreement with Derrida, he also shows the possibility of signification without or prior to intuition in Husserl's work. Yet he further argues that Husserl thinks both signification-intention and intuition on the basis of givenness, albeit a givenness that is ultimately conceived in terms of presence.[16] Possibilities that Marion emphasises are the potential of other-than-object intentionalities (where he can be linked with Lévinas), a givenness that is not simply equal to presence (where he draws from Heidegger), and, of course, situations where the giving intuition is saturated by a phenomenon that gives itself excessively.

The Given

Marion divides his examination of the given into two studies: "Determinations," that is, how the given is given, and "Degrees," which concerns variations in the modes and degrees of the phenomenality which results from givenness. In the first of these studies, Marion proposes five determinations of how a phenomenon is given. It is given anamorphically, which means that it will only appear *as such* from a particular perspective. A phenomenon is also given contingently, as what happens to me or is imposed on me, having an "unpredictable landing," "according to discontinuous rhythms, in fits and starts, unexpectedly, by surprise, detached from the other, in bursts, aleatory."[17] Nevertheless, it is given as a *fait accompli*, a fact, in a very

---

[12] Marion, *Being Given* 12–14; *Étant donné* 20–23.

[13] Marion, *Being Given* 14; *Étant donné* 23; *Reduction and Givenness* 203; *Réduction et donation* 303. "The more reduction, the more givenness" is a translation of "*d'autant plus de réduction, d'autant plus de donation*" given in the text of *Being Given*; my own preference for *autant de réduction, autant de donation*, which is Marion's standard formulation, is "as much reduction, as much givenness."

[14] Marion, *Being Given* 14; *Étant donné* 24.

[15] Marion, *Being Given* 17, see also 191; *Étant donné* 27, 268. Trans. modified.

[16] Marion, *Reduction and Givenness* 34–35; *Réduction et donation* 55–57.

[17] Marion, *Being Given* 132; *Étant donné* 186.

particular sense: "Facticity does not consist in my being reducible to the factuality of a fact, but in exposing me to the fact, which can thus be accomplished only by weighing on me, no longer as a detached observer but as an engaged actor—or better, a critical patient into whom the fact has crashed in being visibly accomplished."[18] The image of the given "crashing" into the patient is one that Marion constantly reinforces and extends: he speaks of the phenomenon that "explodes on the screen" in an incident.[19] The phenomenon is given as an incident, or accident, defined as "a—small—event [or happening] that comes up."[20] And it is finally given as an event, rather than as an object or a thing. The self-giving phenomenon exerts a weight or a pressure on the one to whom it gives itself: "This pressure bears down in such a manner that it makes us feel not only its weight, but also the fact that we cannot in any way master it, that it imposes itself without our having it available to us—we do not trigger it any more than we suspend it."[21] In being given in each of these ways, the phenomenon meets three requirements that Marion imposes: he argues it is given intrinsically (that is, entirely from itself), irrevocably (meaning that it is characterised essentially as given), and radically (appearing in so far as determined by givenness).[22]

Having noted Marion's description of how the phenomenon is given, it remains to consider the question of degrees of phenomenality. Marion frames this second study with a consideration of the possibility of phenomena. Traditionally, possibility has been defined in terms of the conditions of possibility for knowledge of objects (real or ideal) on the part of the subject. Both Kant and Husserl make use of this fundamentally Leibnizian approach.[23] Further, truth has traditionally been defined as adequation, and in Husserlian phenomenology this is expressed in terms of the correspondence between signifying intention and intuitive fulfilment. Yet this correspondence is almost never actually realised for Husserl, for "intuition is (almost) always (partially) lacking to intention, as fulfillment is lacking to signification."[24] Because it is oriented by the possibility of objects, phenomenology has typically focused with greatest certainty on objects (such as mathematical objects) that require the least degree of intuition in order to be fulfilled. Nevertheless, while intuition is subsequently often regarded as limiting and weak, because it is normally inadequate to fulfil concepts, Marion emphasises that concepts are inadequate without intuition:

> To be sure, intuition without concept is as blind as the concept without intuition is empty; but blindness counts more here than vacuity: even blind, intuition still gives, while the concept, even if it alone can make the given see, remains as such perfectly empty, therefore quite incapable of seeing anything whatsoever. Intuition without concept, though still blind, nevertheless gives material to an object, while the concept without intuition, though not blind, sees nothing, since nothing has yet been given it to see.[25]

---

[18] Marion, *Being Given* 146; *Étant donné* 207.
[19] Marion, *De surcroît* 59; *In Excess* 50.
[20] Marion, *Being Given* 151; *Étant donné* 213.
[21] Marion, *Being Given* 159; *Étant donné* 225–26.
[22] Marion, *Being Given* 119–120; *Étant donné* 169–71.
[23] Marion, *Being Given* 179–85; *Étant donné* 251–59.
[24] Marion, *Being Given* 191; *Étant donné* 268.
[25] Marion, *Being Given* 193; *Étant donné* 270–71.

Marion argues that a phenomenology where the reduction is to givenness rather than object-ness can be open to phenomena that saturate intuition even though they are lacking in conceptual clarity or definition. In other words, thinking from givenness allows primacy to be shifted from intention (concept) to intuition (content), which in turn allows for a variation in the degree of intuition in phenomena from a minimal to an immeasurable maximal level.[26] He calls this maximal degree saturation, and describes it as an excess with regard to what he characterises as the two Kantian determinations of possibility: the horizon and the I.

Saturated Phenomena (Paradoxes)

While Marion's examples of saturated phenomena will not be examined in any detail until Chapter 10, the way that he characterises their excessiveness is instructive. In terms of the horizon, he utilises the Kantian categories of quantity, quality, and relation to argue for a phenomenon that exceeds the horizon, at least in the usual sense. First, because the saturated phenomenon cannot be foreseen with regard to its quantity, it cannot be aimed at: "since the intuition that gives it is not limited by its possible concept, its excess can neither be divided nor adequately put together again by virtue of a finite magnitude homogeneous with finite parts. It could not be measured in terms of its parts, since the saturating intuition surpasses limitlessly the sum of the parts by continually adding to them."[27] Second, because intuition cannot anticipate the intensity of the saturated phenomenon (its quality), it cannot be borne: "For the intuition saturating a phenomenon attains an intensive magnitude without measure, or common measure, such that starting with a certain degree, the intensity of the real intuition passes beyond all the conceptual anticipations of perception. Before this excess, not only can perception no longer anticipate what it will receive from intuition; it also can no longer bear its most elevated degrees."[28] Third, because the saturated phenomenon does not allow for any analogy with experience, it "appears *absolute* according to relation."[29] How, nevertheless, could a phenomenon that can neither be foreseen, nor borne, and is absolute, appear as such? Here the relationship with the horizon becomes paramount. Marion argues for three possible scenarios: either the phenomenon is no longer seen against its horizon but as its own horizon and is therefore dazzling; or it is seen against not only one horizon but several, which "paves the way for an infinite hermeneutic"; or it fulfils more than one horizon (the first two alternatives together), where "the hermeneutic adds the bedazzlements in each horizon, instead of combining them."[30] While in this text Marion still at times maintains the necessity of the horizon ("dispensing with a horizon altogether ...

---

[26] Marion, *Being Given* 196–99; *Étant donné* 275–80. Note, nevertheless, Marion's claim that "... it is not a question of privileging intuition as such, but of following in it (indeed eventually without or against it) givenness in its widest possible scope ...." (279/199).

[27] Marion, *Being Given* 200; *Étant donné* 281.

[28] Marion, *Being Given* 203; *Étant donné* 285.

[29] Marion, *Being Given* 206; *Étant donné* 289.

[30] Marion, *Being Given* 211; *Étant donné* 295.

would no doubt forbid any and all manifestation"), he nevertheless also claims that the phenomenon "does not depend on this condition of possibility par excellence—a horizon, whatever it might be," and later says of the paradox or saturated phenomenon that "it makes an exception to every possible horizon."[31] At Villanova Marion notes: "I said to Lévinas some years ago that in fact the last step for a real phenomenology would be to give up the concept of horizon. Lévinas answered me immediately: 'Without horizon there is no phenomenology.' And I boldly assume he was wrong."[32] In short, Marion actually relinquishes the absoluteness of the phenomenological horizon in favour of a hermeneutics of multiple horizons of possibility.[33] This comment is of great pertinence with respect to the question of whether or not givenness is simply a new metaphysical foundation of presence for Marion.

In terms of the I, Marion utilises the Kantian category of modality to argue for a phenomenon that exceeds the I's constitutive functions. While this phenomenon appears ("it must appear in the measure of the excess of giving intuition in it") it cannot be looked at. The saturated phenomenon thus appears as a counter-experience:

> … confronted with the saturated phenomenon, the I cannot not see it, but it cannot any longer gaze at it as its mere object. It has the eye to see but not keep it. What, then, does this eye without gaze see? It sees the superabundance of intuitive givenness; or rather, it does not see it clearly and precisely as such since its excess renders it irregardable and difficult to master. The intuition of the phenomenon is nevertheless seen, but as blurred by the too narrow aperture, the too short lens ….[34]

Perhaps better expressed: "the eye does not see an exterior spectacle so much as it sees the reified traces of its own powerlessness to constitute whatever it might be into an object."[35]

L'adonné

In earlier chapters of the present work we saw that one of the ways in which metaphysics grounds knowledge is on the basis of the transcendental I; this characteristically Cartesian move is repeated—in a slightly different register—by Husserl. We also observed ways in which that grounding has been called into question. Heidegger complains that Descartes leaves unclarified the meaning of the

---

[31] Marion, *Being Given* 209, 212, 287; *Étant donné* 292, 296, 396.

[32] Jean-Luc Marion in "On the Gift: A Discussion between Jacques Derrida and Jean-Luc Marion, Moderated by Richard Kearney," *God, the Gift and Postmodernism*, ed. John D. Caputo and Michael J. Scanlon (Bloomington: Indiana University Press, 1999) 66.

[33] While the language of horizon is still strong in *Being Given*, it plays far less significant a role with *In Excess*, where the language of hermeneutics plays an even more important part. Nevertheless, see the incisive critique in Shane Mackinlay, "Phenomenality in the Middle. Marion, Romano, and the Hermeneutics of the Event," *Givenness and God: Questions of Jean-Luc Marion*, eds. Eoin Cassidy and Ian Leask (New York: Fordham University Press, 2004) forthcoming.

[34] Marion, *Being Given* 215; *Étant donné* 300, 301.

[35] Marion, *Being Given* 216; *Étant donné* 301.

being of the *ego* as *res cogitans*, and thinks it as substantial presence, a complaint with which Marion largely agrees, although he also argues that the subsequently onto-theo-logical constitution of Descartes' thought is nevertheless ruptured by the freedom he attributes to the *ego*. (Ironically, Marion further argues in *Reduction and Givenness* that Heidegger's *Dasein* is ultimately an only slightly remodelled Cartesian *ego*).[36] Commenting on Husserl, Derrida isolates an aporia in subjectivity whereby it cannot ultimately be self-constituting, a reading that Marion confirms even as he also maintains that Husserl does not always think the I according to being. Dissatisfaction with metaphysical characterisations of subjectivity abound in the work of Marion's immediate predecessors and contemporaries. Lévinas resists both the Cartesian subject and Heidegger's attempts to overcome it, preferring instead the always asymmetrical "me" who responds to and is responsible for the other before being able to say "I."[37] Ricoeur argues that the self is not self-identical (in the sense of self-same) but only becomes itself through the other.[38] Henry maintains the primacy of "life," or auto-affection, over self-representation.[39] Marion's response to the question "Who comes after the subject?" develops along these lines, that is, along the lines of thinking who comes *before* the supposedly transcendental, self-identical, self-constituting subject.[40] And while his response often emerges in the context of discussion of the saturated phenomenon, it is clear that his thinking of the one who precedes subjectivity is consistent with his thought of the givenness of all phenomena.

Returning, then, to the context of *Being Given*, who or what experiences the paradox? Where in earlier texts Marion speaks of the interlocuted [*l'interloqué*], here he also speaks of the witness [*le témoin*], the receiver [*l'attributaire*], and *l'adonné* [the gifted, the one given over, the devoted one].[41] In place of the subject

---

[36] See Chapter 3 of Marion, *Réduction et donation*; *Reduction and Givenness*.

[37] See, for example, Lévinas, *Otherwise than Being* 10.

[38] "… identity in the sense of *ipse* [self] implies no assertion concerning some unchanging core of the personality"; "… the selfhood of oneself implies otherness to such an intimate degree that one cannot be thought of without the other, that instead one passes into the other …." Paul Ricoeur, *Oneself as Another*, trans. Kathleen Blamey (Chicago, IL: University of Chicago Press, 1992) 2, 3.

[39] Michel Henry, *Essence of Manifestation*, trans. Girard Etzkorn (The Hague: Martinus Nijhoff, 1973); *The Genealogy of Psychoanalysis*, trans. Douglas Brick (Stanford, CA: Stanford University Press, 1993). In the latter text, Henry writes, for example: "It is impossible, therefore, to apply the laws of *videre*, of the world's finitude, to power. Its 'act' or 'phenomenological actualization' is not its momentary illumination by the light of self-evidence. In fact, *in that light, power, force, and every actual form of energy never arrive. But it is precisely this impossibility of ever arriving in ek-static light that makes them possible as such, as power and force, as actual, efficacious forms of energy.* For if they expose themselves before me, even for a moment, how could I ever rejoin them? On the basis of what power could I move toward grasping them if I didn't already have that power, if I didn't coincide with it in its incoercible self-coherence as the Self that I am?" (321)

[40] Jean-Luc Marion, "The Final Appeal of the Subject," trans. Simon Critchley, *The Religious*, ed. John D. Caputo (Oxford: Blackwell, 2002) 131–44.

[41] While Marion's preference is for a translation of *l'adonné* with "the gifted," I prefer to leave it untranslated and so to maintain its other awkward and ambiguous resonances.

who constitutes a phenomenon we have a witness to it who is constituted by it: "Constituted witness, the subject is still the worker of truth, but he cannot claim to be its producer. With the name *witness* we must understand a subjectivity stripped of the characteristics that gave it transcendental rank."[42] Marion notes four characteristics of the engagement of a witness with a paradox: constitution and synthesis become passive rather than active; intuition exceeds any concept (that is, any "hermeneutic of the concept"); the witness is utterly subject to the paradox ("in space, the saturated phenomenon swallows him with its intuitive deluge; in time, it precedes him with a challenge, always [and] already there"), and the witness lacks every positive function of the I.[43] The image that Marion uses at this point in *Being Given* is that of the witness as a light on a control panel that is switched on in response to a given stimulus.[44] But a vivid passage from *In Excess* gives a better sense of the relationship of the witness (as *l'adonné*) to the given phenomenon:

> ... the given, unseen but received, is projected on *l'adonné* ... as on a screen; all the power of this given comes from crashing down on this screen, provoking all at once a double visibility. *a)* First, that of the given, of course, the impact of which (until then invisible) bursts, explodes and is broken up in its outlines, the first visibles. One could also imagine the model of a prism that stops white light, until then invisible, and breaks it up into a spectrum of elementary colors, colors that are finally visible. *L'adonné* phenomenalizes in receiving the given, precisely because it is an obstacle to it, stops it in blocking it and fixes it in centering it ... *l'adonné* therefore receives the given, receiving it with all the vigor, even the violence of a goal-keeper blocking a shot, of a defender marking, of a receiver sending back a winning return. Screen, prism, frame—*l'adonné* takes the impact of the pure, unseen given, holding back the *momentum* of it in order in this way to transform its longitudinal force into a slack, even, open surface. With this operation—precisely, reception—the given can begin to show *itself* starting from the outlines of visibility that it concedes to *l'adonné*, or rather that it receives from it. *b)* But the visibility risen from the given provokes at the same time the visibility of *l'adonné*. In effect, *l'adonné* does not see itself before receiving the impact of the given. Relieved of its royal transcendental status, it no longer precedes the phenomenon, or even accompanies it any more as a thought already in place. Since it is received from what it receives, it does not precede it and especially not by a visibility prior to the unseen of the given. In fact, *l'adonné* does not show itself more than the given—its screen or its prism remain perfectly unseen as long as the impact, crushed against them, of a given does not illuminate them all at once. Or instead, since, properly speaking, *l'adonné* is not without this reception, the impact gives rise for the first time to the screen against which it is crushed, as it sets up the prism across which it breaks up. In short, *l'adonné* is phenomenalized by the very operation by which it phenomenalizes the given.
>
> The given is therefore revealed to *l'adonné* in revealing *l'adonné* to itself.[45]

---

[42] Marion, *Being Given* 216–17; *Étant donné* 302.

[43] Marion, *Being Given* 217; *Étant donné* 302–303. Trans. modified from "it precedes him with an always already there interpretation."

[44] Marion, *Being Given* 217–18; *Étant donné* 303.

[45] Marion, *De surcroît* 59–60; *In Excess* 50.

This decisive description can be correlated with earlier attempts by Marion to characterise the one who precedes the subject. In *Being Given*, it is the receiver who is the locus of manifestation for the given. But on the same continuum, it is *l'adonné* who receives the saturated phenomenon. The transition from the receiver to *l'adonné* is explained in terms of the call, which is a device employed in relation to *l'interloqué* in *Reduction and Givenness* (and explored more controversially in earlier texts such as *God Without Being*):

> If the receiver is determined as a thought that transforms the given into the manifest and is received from what it receives—in short, if it is born from the very arising of the phenomenon inasmuch as given, that is to say, from a given exerting the mere impact of its event—what will happen when a phenomenon given as saturated arises? The impact will be radicalised into a *call*, and the receiver into *the gifted*.[46]

In something of an understatement, Marion immediately goes on to note: "reference to the call has sometimes been troubling."[47] However, he is at pains to point out that the call is a philosophical (that is, rather than theological) device.[48] Drawing on Lévinas as well as the work of his contemporary, Jean-Louis Chrétien, he maintains that what we might describe as the saturated phenomenon of the call is manifested only in the response.[49] At the same time, the response does not exhaust the call and cannot do justice to it.[50]

This brings us back to a problem in Marion's thought that has persistently been identified throughout the current work, which is the problem of recognising the excessive *as such*. Clearly, what is without horizon cannot be recognised unless we invoke the interruption of experience by excessiveness and an infinite hermeneutics of risk to contextualise it. Yet given the utterly passive characterisation of the witness or *l'adonné*, Shane Mackinlay perceptively asks—in a new register—about the role of hermeneutics in Marion's phenomenology.[51] Drawing from the work of Heidegger and thinking in line with Claude Romano, he suggests that "in place of Heidegger's ontological (or existential) sense of hermeneutics, where hermeneutics is intrinsic to the actual appearing of phenomena, Marion confines hermeneutics to a marginal and derivative sense of 'subsequent interpretation'—after phenomena have already appeared."[52] In other words, we find a conflict between the apparently

---

[46] Marion, *Being Given* 266; *Étant donné* 366.

[47] Marion, *Being Given* 266; *Étant donné* 366. For a discussion of the problems associated with the call, see *Rethinking God as Gift* 98ff.

[48] This is in spite of the fact that in addition to tracing the philosophical pedigree of the call he also uses the biblical example of the call of Samuel.

[49] Marion, *Being Given* 287; *Étant donné* 396. Marion cites Jean-Louis Chrétien, *L'appel et la réponse* (Paris, 1992), now available as *The Call and the Response*, trans. Anne A. Davenport (New York: Fordham University Press, 2004).

[50] Marion, *Being Given* 289; *Étant donné* 398.

[51] Mackinlay, "Phenomenality in the Middle. Marion, Romano, and the Hermeneutics of the Event," forthcoming.

[52] Mackinlay, "Phenomenality in the Middle. Marion, Romano, and the Hermeneutics of the Event," forthcoming.

present and immediate givenness of the phenomenon (as we saw above, "the given, unseen but received, is projected on *l'adonné* ... as on a screen") and the necessary possibility of its multiple interpretations ("[*l'adonné*] responds ... *for* the event as its witness, charged with its reconstitution and its hermeneutic").[53] In my view Marion attempts to resolve this problem by way of the delay he describes between call and response (or responsal), which indicates both the incapacity of *l'adonné* to respond in such a way that the fullness of the call is made manifest, and the fact that *l'adonné* is inscribed in language and hence in a "gap" from the call or in a distance that "arises in the I itself, with it and even before it, since it is hollowed out as soon as the call gives itself, even before the responsal shows it."[54] This latter point is very like Lévinas' distinction between "the Saying" and "the Said," a distinction that is recalled by Marion and compared with Derridean *différance*.[55] If we keep this in mind, together with his insistence that the call only signifies in the response (that is, that what is shown ultimately is the response, not the call as such), and his recognition that the saturated phenomenon—as we noted earlier—"makes an exception to every possible horizon" (which means that the experience is one of interruption), an argument can be mounted that Marion's phenomenology requires a hermeneutics that "is intrinsic to the actual appearing of phenomena" rather than being "marginal and derivative." The point is well made, however, that Marion gives an inconsistent sense of the role of hermeneutics in phenomenology, particularly in the light of some of his theological claims.[56] A further strength of Mackinlay's reading is his questioning of *l'adonné* and its cognate recipients as utterly passive, which is a criticism that has been directed in a slightly different way towards Lévinas. But while passivity might characterise the genesis of what is yet to become the subject, it, too, only signifies in actively responding. This makes sense of a comment from *In Excess*, where Marion suggests that while *l'adonné* loses its transcendental status in the self-giving of the phenomenon, this "does not amount ... to passivity or to the empirical me. In fact, *l'adonné* goes as much beyond passivity as activity, because in being liberated from its royal transcendental status, it annuls the very distinction between the transcendental *I* and the empirical me." He continues shortly after: "*l'adonné* is ... characterized by reception. Reception implies, indeed, passive receptivity, but it also demands active capacity, because capacity ... in order to increase to the measure of the given and to make sure it happens, must be put to work ...."[57]

The Gift

In 1994, Marion weighed into the debate on the gift that had been renewed in France with the publication of Derrida's *Given Time. 1: Counterfeit Money*.[58] With *Being*

---

53 Marion, *Being Given* 293; *Étant donné* 405.

54 Marion, *Being Given* 289, 90; *Étant donné* 399, 400.

55 Marion, *Being Given* 294–96; *Étant donné* 405–408.

56 Especially if we consider a text like Marion, "Christian Philosophy and Charity."

57 Marion, *De surcroît* 57; *In Excess* 48.

58 Derrida, *Given Time*; Marion, "Esquisse d'un concept phénoménologique du don"; "Sketch of a Phenomenological Concept of the Gift."

Given he revised in 1997 what he had only "sketched" earlier, but as I observed in Chapter 6, by the time of the first debate at Villanova later that year he declared himself "at this stage of my work … not interested in the gift and … not interested in the religious meaning of the gift."[59] His interest has apparently since been renewed, with the publication of "The Reason of the Gift" in 2003.[60] In *Being Given*, the question of the gift forms the basis of Book 2, which means that it is placed after the discussion of givenness yet prior to the discussion of the determinations and degrees of the given. I have, in the present context, chosen to consider the gift after these aspects of Marion's renewal of phenomenology. This is because some of the criticisms of *Being Given* relate to the questionability of the semantic linking of givenness, gift, and given, but also and especially to the impression that Marion seeks to think all givens as gifts (of a giver), rather than all gifts as givens.[61] This is, of course, complicated by the way in which the receiver becomes the gifted. Nevertheless, Marion claims that "I am not trying to reduce every phenomenon to a gift and then to say that … there is perhaps a giver behind it all," and we can do no more than both take him at his word and attempt to read the many theological dimensions opened in his phenomenological work in that light.[62] I do not intend to repeat here the detailed analysis of the gift that I have undertaken elsewhere.[63] However, it is necessary to summarise the basic position of Marion in relation to Derrida, and to situate that position in relation to phenomenology and theology.[64] We will also need to note how that position is affected, if at all, by "The Reason of the Gift."

As it is set out by Derrida, the problem of the gift is that its conditions of possibility—that it is completely free and that it is present, or identifiable *as such*—are simultaneously its conditions of impossibility—no gift that is ever present is completely free, and if it is not present then we cannot know it as a gift. The gift structurally exemplifies what he calls "the impossible," where conditions of possibility meet with conditions of impossibility in an aporia. For Derrida, there cannot be a phenomenology of the gift because for him phenomenology attempts to reduce to presence, and a present gift, losing its essential characteristic of freedom, would no longer be a gift.[65] Nevertheless, he does not give up on the gift.[66] If the gift leads to an aporia, then while it may not be known, it might still be thought as the impossible, and risked according to desire and decision. While I could never know for sure whether or not I had given, or whether or not I had received, and would

---

[59] Marion in Richard Kearney, Jacques Derrida, and Jean-Luc Marion, "On the Gift:" 56.

[60] Jean-Luc Marion, "La raison du don," *Philosophie* 78 (2003); "The Reason of the Gift," trans. Shane Mackinlay and Nicholas de Warren, *Givenness and God: Questions of Jean-Luc Marion*, eds. Eoin Cassidy and Ian Leask (New York: Fordham University Press, 2004) forthcoming.

[61] Marion in Kearney, Derrida, and Marion, "On the Gift," 66.

[62] Marion in Kearney, Derrida, and Marion, "On the Gift," 70.

[63] See Horner, *Rethinking God as Gift*.

[64] In what follows, I will draw from and develop Horner, "Aporia or Excess."

[65] Derrida in Kearney, Derrida, and Marion, "On the Gift," 59.

[66] Derrida in Kearney, Derrida, and Marion, "On the Gift," 60.

never be able definitively to identify a gift *as such*, I could risk giving or receiving on the basis of an undecidable trace, and with the same desire that risks the perfection of love, or justice, or forgiveness. For Marion, on the other hand, phenomenology can deliver the gift, since the phenomenological reduction to givenness operates to remove the gift from the schema of causality that implicates it in metaphysics. The problem of the gift as Derrida has articulated it is overcome through the suspension of any one or two of the gift's three constituent elements: the giver, the gift object, or the recipient. It is removed from the cycle of metaphysical causality either because it loses its giver through the reduction of its transcendence, or because it loses its object-ness and is no-thing as such, or because it ultimately has no recipient determinable by the giver. While Derrida requires these three conditions to operate simultaneously, Marion demands that only one or two of the three is operative at any given moment. The difficulty with Derrida's position is that the risk of the gift is also the risk of deception: if I do not know for sure but instead only have a kind of faith in the gift, I may be seriously mistaken about it. Yet for the gift to be possible from Marion's perspective, any one or two of the elements of giving, the gift, or receiving, can always be identified, and always and already undone according to Derrida's conditions.

"The Reason of the Gift" largely repeats, although with renewed clarity and concision, the arguments of Marion's earlier material. Where it goes slightly further is in its claim not only that the gift must be thought from the horizon of givenness (rather than that of the economy), but in its exposition of how the gift contradicts the metaphysical principles of identity, contradiction, and sufficient reason.[67] In line with the last of these, Marion in fact maintains that reason can only be thought on the basis of the gift.[68] "[The gift] delivers its reason at the same time as itself—reason that it gives in giving itself and without asking any other authority than its own advent. The gift coincides with its reason, because its simple givenness suffices as reason for it. Reason sufficing for itself, the gift gives itself reason in giving itself."[69] This helps to clarify what Marion has essentially already propounded in *Being Given* about the relationship between given and gift. While we can say that he is still consistent with the statement that he does not mean to think every given as the gift of a giver, he does indeed think every given as a gift, in the sense that the gift is " … the privileged phenomenon," "the figure of all phenomenality."[70] The gift figures all phenomenality because like any other phenomenon it "shows itself in and on the basis of itself, … gives itself of itself in an accomplished givenness (according to the anamorphosis, the unpredictable landing, the fait accompli, the incident and eventness."[71] And this is especially so, Marion declares, with the saturated phenomenon. There is essentially no advance in the debate between Derrida and Marion in the later text.

---

[67] Marion, "The Reason of the Gift," forthcoming.

[68] Marion, "The Reason of the Gift," forthcoming.

[69] Marion, "The Reason of the Gift," forthcoming.

[70] Marion, "The Reason of the Gift," forthcoming. Cf. also *Being Given* 117–18; *Étant donné* 167–68.

[71] Marion, "The Reason of the Gift," forthcoming.

Where the discussion becomes particularly interesting, however, is when we place it in the context of the possibility of a divine gift. That is the point at which a commitment to the gift's phenomenological possibility meets Marion's early theology of the gift, as well as his thinking of the call, the icon, r/Revelation, the saturated phenomenon more generally, and the gifted. If God were to give Godself (which is at the heart of a Christian theology of grace), then what would this mean in terms of a nominally phenomenological approach? According to Derrida's non-phenomenological strategy, such a giving would be aporetic, unable to be known as such in the present, interruptive of experience, without horizon, the impossible, irresolvable in terms of knowledge but thinkable in terms of the risk of decision in faith. Using Marion's phenomenological schema, however, God's self-gift could be known provided that there was either no recognisable giver, or no recognisable gift, or yet no recognisable recipient. This claim becomes more difficult to sustain, nevertheless, in the light of Marion's strict equivalence between given and gift. We have seen above that the given, especially the saturated phenomenon, inevitably invokes a hermeneutics. If the gift is paradigmatic of the given, then it, too, requires interpretation, and the interpretative process happens at all three points of the gift triangle. Put another way, because each of the elements of giver, gift, and gifted ultimately defy presentation, all three are called into question and put at risk.

In his rethinking of phenomenology, Marion argues that it is not limited to the presentation of objects but opens onto phenomena that exceed our capacity to conceive of them. He claims that it is therefore possible to include religious phenomena within the scope of phenomenology, although he constantly underlines the fact that phenomenology has no authority to rule on their significance, but only on their potential appearance.[72] This raises the question, of course, of whether appearance can only occur in the context of significance.[73] Nevertheless, what he attempts to show is that phenomenology has a preliminary relevance for theology, even if it does not inevitably lead there.[74] This claim will be tested in the following chapter.

---

[72] See, for example, Marion, *Étant donné* 337; *Being Given* 242. See also the extensive footnote on 329n1/367n90, p.367, where Marion is explicit about his "scrupulousness" in utilising the upper and upper cases in maintaining the difference between the possibility of revelation and its actuality as Revelation, as well as the comments on 410/297.

[73] See Horner, "Aporia or Excess."

[74] See my discussion of Janicaud's position in *Rethinking God as Gift*.

Chapter 10

Saturated Phenomena[1]

In this chapter, we turn to examine each of the saturated phenomena identified by Marion—the event, the idol, flesh, the icon, and r/Revelation—particularly as they are described and analysed in *In Excess*, although we will also need to consider *Being Given*. Saturated phenomena (paradoxes) are phenomena where "intuition always submerges the expectation of the intention," and where "givenness not only entirely envelops manifestation but, surpassing it, modifies its common characteristics."[2] *In Excess* defines them as those "where the duality between intention (signification) and intuition (fulfillment) certainly remains, as well as the noetic–noematic correlation, but where, in contrast to poor and common phenomena, intuition gives (itself) in exceeding what the concept (signification, intentionality, aim, and so on) can foresee of it and show."[3] In other words, saturated phenomena disrupt the fulfilment of an intentional aim in intuition, not because intuition is lacking but because it is excessive. Marion goes on to comment: "they are saturated phenomena in that constitution encounters there an intuitive givenness that cannot be granted a univocal sense in return. It must be allowed, then, to overflow with many meanings, or an infinity of meanings, each equally legitimate and rigorous, without managing either to unify them or to organize them."[4]

Saturated phenomena are excessive in that their intuitive content cannot be contained in a single concept, or even by a combination of concepts, but demands an endless hermeneutics. As we saw in Chapter 9, Marion uses Kant's categories to explore this idea of excessiveness. With regard to the event, excessiveness is developed in terms of our inability to foresee the phenomenon and measure it; with the idol, in terms of phenomena that cannot be borne by the look; with flesh, in terms of phenomena that are absolute and without external relation, and with the icon, in terms of phenomena that cannot be looked at or constituted.[5] And

---

[1] Earlier version of parts of this text appear in Horner, "Aporia or Excess?"; "The Face as Icon"; and the "Translator's Introduction" from *In Excess:* ix–xx.

[2] Jean-Luc Marion, *Étant donné* 314; *Being Given*. 225. Trans. modified. For the analyses of each type of saturated phenomenon, see *Étant donné* 318–42; *Being Given* 228–47. The earliest, most explicit exposition of the idea of saturation comes from 1992, Marion, "Le phénomène saturé," *Phénoménologie et théologie* 79–128. The translation appears as Jean-Luc Marion, "The Saturated Phenomenon," *Philosophy Today* 40.1–4 (1996): 103–24.

[3] Marion, *De surcroît* 135; *In Excess* 112. Trans. modified.

[4] Marion, *De surcroît* 135; *In Excess* 112.

[5] Marion, *De surcroît* 135; *In Excess* 112. "If we follow the guiding thread of the Kantian categories, we locate: according to quantity, invisible phenomena of the type of the event (collective or individual); according to quality, phenomena the look cannot bear (the idol and

r/Revelation is understood to be a fifth type of saturated phenomenon that combines the features, not only of the event, the idol, and flesh, but also of the icon; it is saturated "to the second degree."[6] A significant general point about saturated phenomena is that they can only be recognised by the effect that they produce in their witness: "I cannot have vision of these phenomena, because I cannot constitute them starting from a univocal meaning, and even less produce them as objects. What I see of them, if I see anything of them that is, does not result from the constitution that I would assign to them in the visible, but from the effect that they produce on me."[7]

The Event

Under the title of saturated phenomenon as event, Marion examines the historical event (an example of collective phenomena, and which might include "political revolution, war, natural disaster, sporting or cultural performances, and so on"), friendship (an example of intersubjective phenomena), and death and birth (each examples of private phenomena, although Marion does register here the important differences between the death of another and the death of oneself).[8] He distinguishes between an event and an object on three grounds, according to the event's relationship with temporality: it has the character of facticity (it has always already occurred); accomplishment (it is uniquely achieved, "this time, once and for all"), and endlessness (its hermeneutic can never be completed).[9] An event is a *fait accompli* and is characterised as unrepeatable, unable to be assigned a unique cause, and unable to be foreseen.[10] While what gives itself generally shows itself, events like one's death or birth actually never show themselves, or only show themselves in the mode of being given. This is described well in a passage that simultaneously illustrates the relationship of excessive intuition to intention, as well as the gap "between the given and phenomenality" which is a feature of our entry into language (Derrida), the symbolic (Jacques Lacan) or the representational (Henry):[11]

> The excess of intuition over intention bursts open irremediably from the point of my birth—and, moreover, I will speak not only by means of having [repeatedly] intuited in silence, but especially after having heard others speak. Language is first listened to, and only then is it

---

the painting); according to relation, absolute phenomena, because defying any analogy, like flesh *(Leib)*; finally, according to modality, phenomena that cannot be looked at, that escape all relation with thought in general, but which are imposed on it, as the icon of the other person *par excellence*." Note that the icon is understood to combine the features of the previous three types. Marion, *Étant donné* 325; *Being Given* 234.

[6] Marion, *Étant donné* 327; *Being Given* 235; *De surcroît* 34n, 63; *In Excess* 29n41, 53. In Marion's first explorations of the saturated phenomenon, he thought revelation *as* the icon. *De surcroît* vi/n1; *In Excess* xxi/n3.

[7] Marion, *De surcroît* 136; *In Excess* 113.

[8] Marion, *De surcroît* 43; *In Excess* 36.

[9] Marion, *De surcroît* 37–40; *In Excess* 32–34.

[10] Marion, *De surcroît* 43; *In Excess* 36.

[11] Marion, *De surcroît* 58; *In Excess* 49.

uttered. The origin remains to me, indeed, originally inaccessible, not by default, nevertheless, but because the first phenomenon already saturates all intention with intuitions. The origin, which refuses itself, does not nevertheless give *itself* in penury (Derrida), but indeed in excess, determining in this way the regime of all givens to come.[12]

Birth is therefore paradigmatic of a point Marion wants to make about phenomena more generally, that they produce *l'adonné*.[13] The phenomenon of the event testifies, Marion claims, to the self of the phenomenon prior to the self of the *I*.[14] Nevertheless, this apparently involves a "performative contradiction," in that the reduction to givenness produces the very one who carries it out.[15] Where elsewhere Marion has claimed that the *I* is excepted from both Husserl's and Heidegger's reductions, in that it is neither reduced to the horizon of object-ness nor that of being, here he argues that it is included in the third reduction, to givenness: "it is accomplished even in the one who makes it possible."[16] This has to do with the relinquishing by *l'adonné* of its transcendental status in the process of performing the reduction, as well as with its passing beyond, in this relinquishing, the dichotomy between the transcendental *I* and the empirical me. The third reduction works (in a logical sense) retrospectively on *l'adonné*, producing a third figure of subjectivity which is characterised by the active task of bringing the given that it passively receives to phenomenalisation.[17]

The Idol and the Icon

In Chapter 6 we considered the idol and the icon together, since up until the time of *La croisée du visible* Marion generally presented them as opposing figures. *La croisée du visible* is a pivotal work in Marion's corpus. In many ways it could be grouped with his theological texts, but it also reflects aspects of his developing phenomenology, as well as his interest in aesthetics. Significantly, it marks the point at which Marion's thinking of both idol and icon begins to be reframed more explicitly by phenomenological, rather than mainly theological questions. Consequently, any moral overtones—in terms of opening onto transcendence versus merely reflecting an image of the idolater—fall away, and Marion becomes interested in their phenomenality more broadly. These shifts are amplified with the publication of *Being Given* and *In Excess*, which no longer cast the idol in negative contrast to the icon, undoubtedly because theological concerns are no longer paramount in their characterisations. While the present chapter picks up on themes introduced in Chapter 6, I will at this point cease to consider idol and icon together, in order to follow the descriptions and analyses given with *In Excess*.

---

12 Marion, *De surcroît* 52; *In Excess* 44.
13 Marion, *De surcroît* 51; *In Excess* 43.
14 Marion, *De surcroît* 53–54; *In Excess* 45.
15 Marion, *De surcroît* 55; *In Excess* 46.
16 Marion, *De surcroît* 57; *In Excess* 48.
17 Marion, *De surcroît* 57–58; *In Excess* 48–49.

The Idol as Excessive Visiblity

The analysis of the idol found in *In Excess* is extremely powerful. This is due in large part to the extraordinary passages dealing, on the one hand, with the unrelenting wash of visibility, and on the other, with particular works of art. Marion's descriptions are never simple, but they are compelling. With them he makes an important contribution to a phenomenology of art—one in which an ethical component has an important place. He is also able to articulate the role of the artist as one who "tries to receive, in his or her frame, a newcomer, a new seen, and to hold it there in reducing it without remainder to its pure visibility."[18] He emphasises and celebrates the excessive quality of the idol. At the same time, he raises the problem of the representation of the other person, which eventually leads to a consideration of the icon—not in an explicitly religious sense, but as the face of the other.

With *In Excess* the idol still functions as the first visible before which the look is transfixed with fascination, and as the invisible mirror that measures the capacity of the gaze. Hence Marion wryly observes: "name your idol, and you will know who you are."[19] Nevertheless, the idol need not be limited to the dimensions of just one look. A work of art functions as an idol in that it brings visibility to a maximum, making visible what has hitherto remained unseen (*invu*), and becoming the measure of many gazes.[20] "The painter produces absolutely new phenomena, and what phenomena—idols! It is the idols that, in each era, reign over the natural visibles, over the appearance of constituted objects, and that oblige us to see everything starting from the paradigms that their fascination imposes."[21] This radical irruption of the once unseen cannot be exhausted by the limited looks of those who gaze upon it. Marion maintains: "it follows that we cannot see a painting once and for all," or again: "the painting cannot be seen in a single instance, it must be reseen in order to appear, because it appears according to the phenomenality of the saturated phenomenon."[22] This means not only that the painting gives too much visibility for successive looks by the one person, but that it also exceeds the combined capacities of all who come before it.[23] With the idol, the saturation of intuition results in a hermeneutics of the newly visible that can never reach an end point.

---

[18] Marion, *De surcroît* 83; *In Excess* 69.

[19] Marion, *De surcroît* 73; *In Excess* 61: "My idol defines what I can bear of phenomenality—the maximum of intuitive intensity that I can endure while keeping my look on a distinctly visible spectacle, all in transforming an intuition into a distinct and constituted visible, without weakening into confusion or blindness. In this way my idol exposes the span of all my aims—what I set my heart on seeing, and thus also want to see and do. In short, it denudes my desire and my hope. What I look at that is visible decides who I am. I am what I can look at. What I admire judges me."

[20] Marion, *De surcroît* 82–85; *In Excess* 68–71.

[21] Marion, *De surcroît* 83–84; *In Excess* 69.

[22] Marion, *De surcroît* 84; *In Excess* 70.

[23] Marion, *De surcroît* 84–86; *In Excess* 70–71.

Flesh

The study from *In Excess* dealing with flesh is Marion's first extended meditation on the theme in print, and prepares us for the complexities of *Le phénomène érotique*, which will be examined in the next chapter. In the former text he draws together analyses of Descartes and Husserl, but his horizons are often implicitly those of Maurice Merleau-Ponty and Henry. Flesh gives the *ego* to itself; there is no experience of *I* that is not given as flesh. It is also the sole means by which the world is phenomenalised.[24] Flesh is Marion's example of a saturated phenomenon that gives itself without relation: in the Kantian sense, it is given absolutely (that is, without relation to anything other than itself).[25] Here we encounter immediately an aspect of Husserl's difficulty in trying to constitute the other person: I am not given to myself as a body (which is physical and can be considered an object in the world), but as flesh: "My flesh is distinguished from every object of the world, therefore from every body, in such a way that before even being able to perceive itself as a possible external object in the world, it perceives; before even making itself be felt, it allows one to feel ...."[26] Yet we do not phenomenologically reach the other as flesh but only as a body. Flesh is characterised in terms of its passivity and receptivity, and we get a strong sense of this in Marion's descriptions of suffering and aging.[27] Marion's portrayal of the *ego* fixed to itself—or better, riveted to itself—in flesh is reminiscent to some degree of Lévinas' analyses of insomnia and nausea.[28] Time is phenomenologically given in flesh: "*time*, especially according to the having-been, *does not pass*, but ... accumulates .... The past is ... accumulated in the flesh of my members, muscles and bones .... Above all, the weight of time is accumulated there where my flesh is most openly visible—on my face."[29] Or again: "accomplished time only manifests itself in taking flesh in mine, which it defeats, affects, marks. It takes flesh in me."[30] Flesh enables individuation. What individualises is neither thought nor bodily extension but the tension between them that is played out in flesh: "I do not give myself my flesh, it is it that gives me to myself. In receiving my flesh, I receive me myself—I am in this way gifted [*adonné*—given over] to it."[31] Flesh is always and already given in the saturation of intuition prior to becoming the object of an intentional aim.[32]

---

24 Marion, *De surcroît* 107; *In Excess* 89.
25 Marion, *De surcroît* 120; *In Excess* 100.
26 Marion, *De surcroît* 105; *In Excess* 87.
27 Marion, *De surcroît* 105–106; *In Excess* 87.
28 Marion, *De surcroît* 110ff.; *In Excess* 91ff. See also, for example, Emmanuel Lévinas, *Existents and Existence*, trans. Alphonso Lingis (The Hague: Martinus Nijhoff, 1978); or *De l'évasion* (Paris: Fata Morgana, 1982).
29 Marion, *De surcroît* 115; *In Excess* 95.
30 Marion, *De surcroît* 115; *In Excess* 95–96.
31 Marion, *De surcroît* 119; *In Excess* 98.
32 Marion, *De surcroît* 119; *In Excess* 99.

The Face as Icon: Interruption of Visibility by Excess

The analysis of the icon presented in *In Excess* no longer has the theological focus of Marion's earlier works, and is undertaken exclusively in relation to the face. Making clear the distinction between the invisible (which, by definition, cannot be seen) and the unseen (*l'invu*, that remains resistant to a particular type of intentionality, but might still come to visibility), Marion returns to the question of how it is possible to accede phenomenologically to the invisible. In other words, he asks how the invisible might be given *as invisible*. He suggests in response that invisibility gives itself not, as might commonly be assumed, by default, or lack, but by excess.[33] The invisible cannot be looked at, not because—as in the case of the idol—in an excess of visibility no single hermeneutic can exhaust it, but because it interrupts visibility by excess, overwhelming every possible intentional aim. In this case, the face saturates intuition because it bears no relation to thought but is, instead, imposed upon it.[34]

Given that the face is such a strong Lévinasian theme, and that Lévinas' use of the face to open onto the invisible has been criticised for its very phenomenality, we will follow in outline the steps Marion takes in his argument that the face indeed opens onto invisibility.[35] To what extent can the face be considered a phenomenon, and more particularly, to what extent can there be a phenomenology of the invisible? Marion first notes that I am unable to constitute the face as an object phenomenon, since it precedes me; like an unforeseeable event, the face affects me or happens to me.[36] Then he recalls the aporia arrived at in Husserl's attempt to constitute the other person phenomenologically: the flesh of the other can only be inferred, starting from the perception of the other's body, a problem that Husserl's imaginary transposition of points of view reinforces rather than solves[37] "Flesh escapes phenomenality as such (as feeling), because only the felt can show itself by intuition."[38] Marion argues that, as flesh, the face cannot be phenomenalised. Yet the face is distinct from flesh in general, for the face not only feels, but also sees. He maintains that not only can the face not be phenomenalised as felt, but it cannot be phenomenalised as seeing:[39] "[T]his unique characteristic, which suffices to define the face as what looks at me, dictates specifically that I cannot see it, nor look at it in its turn."[40] Finally, Marion observes that in looking into the face of the other I am drawn to the eyes, or more specifically the pupils, the place where, as he earlier notes in *La croisée du visible*, there is nothing to be seen, no object for intentionality to constitute: "Thus, in the face of the other

---

[33] Marion, *De surcroît* 135ff.; *In Excess* 112ff.

[34] Marion, *De surcroît* 135; *In Excess* 112.

[35] Jacques Derrida, "Violence and Metaphysics," trans. Alan Bass, *Writing and Difference* (London: Routledge, 1978) 79–153.

[36] Marion, *De surcroît* 136; *In Excess* 113.

[37] Marion, *De surcroît* 136–37; *In Excess* 113–14.

[38] Marion, *De surcroît* 137; *In Excess* 114.

[39] Marion, *De surcroît* 137–38; *In Excess* 114.

[40] Marion, *De surcroît* 138; *In Excess* 114.

person, we see precisely the point at which all visible spectacle happens to be impossible, where there is nothing to see, where intuition can give nothing [of the] visible".[41]

So, what *can* be seen in my encounter with the other person? While the face cannot be constituted as an object, there is an argument—to be drawn from the work of Lévinas—that the face nevertheless gives itself otherwise. Lévinas claims that the face signifies in so far as it "speaks," and here he invokes the ethical injunction, "thou shalt not kill" as the content of that (possibly silent) speech. Marion makes two points in this regard. First, extending Lévinas' thought, and evidently in view of the icon, he maintains that in the emptiness of the pupils a counter-look rises up that "escapes my look and envisages me in return—in fact, it sees me first, because it takes the initiative."[42] Next, he suggests that "the face (that cannot be looked at) of the other person's look, *only appears when I admit—submitting myself to him or her—that I must not kill.*"[43] In spite of the sequence in which Marion details these ideas, it seems to me that the two moments should not be understood as consecutive but instead as simultaneous, since according to Marion's own definition the counter-look could only appear as such in the act of submission to the injunction. They would, then, coincide in what Marion describes as "an anamorphosis par excellence," where the constituting gaze of the subject is replaced by the perspective of the other, the face revealing itself only in my submission to it.[44]

Marion makes modifications to Lévinas' thought of the face, suggesting that the injunction evoked in the face need not be limited to the ethical, but could be thought more generally in terms of a call.[45] With this he shifts the focus from the other person back to the icon:

> The face, saturated phenomenon according to modality, accomplishes the phenomenological operation of the call more, perhaps, than any other phenomenon (saturated or not) …. That is why what imposes its call must be defined not only as the other person of ethics (Lévinas), but more radically as the icon. The icon gives itself to be seen in that it makes me hear its call.[46]

---

[41] Marion, *De surcroît* 138; *In Excess* 115. In this text I have chosen to translate *autrui* with "the other person," instead of "the Other," which is the usual convention in translations of Lévinas "D'Autrui à l'individu." In contrast, I followed that convention in translating ," since the article largely related to Lévinas' work. Note that Kosky has used "the Other" in *Being Given.*

[42] Marion, *De surcroît* 139; *In Excess* 116.

[43] Marion, *De surcroît* 140; *In Excess* 116. Emphasis added. Trans. modified.

[44] Marion, *De surcroît* 141; *In Excess* 117.

[45] Marion, *De surcroît* 141–42; *In Excess* 117–18. See also Jean-Luc Marion, "D'Autrui à L'Individu"; "From the Other to the Individual"; "The Face: An Endless Hermeneutics," *Harvard Divinity Bulletin* 28.2–3 (1999): 9–10.

[46] Marion, *De surcroît* 142–43; *In Excess* 118–19. In the earlier work, *Prolegomena to Charity*, Marion explores both counter-intentionality and the ethical "summons" of the other. He characterises the encounter as the feeling of the weight of the counter-gaze. Marion, *Prolegomena* 85,88; *Prolégomènes* 105,08.

For Marion, the face only signifies in the effect that it has on me in my hearing of the call. This encounter reverses intentionality, so that I am envisaged rather than primarily envisaging. Nevertheless, Marion still argues that there is a given to envisage, even if it is a given that cannot be definitively interpreted: "The other person only appears to me starting from the moment when I expose myself to him or her, thus when I no longer master or constitute the other and admit that he or she expresses self without signification."[47] This idea is then further refined; it is no longer a question of no signification at all but of a signification that resists clear conceptualisation: "The face expresses an infinity of meanings at each moment and during an indefinite lapse of time. This endless flux of significations, which happens to the other according to the present rising up from original temporality, can never itself be reduced to the concept, nor be said adequately."[48] Now, while the face in this way appropriately resists conceptualisation, we may still ask how the other is given as an individual. Marion's answer is to be found in the submission to the other and to the other's call that is elsewhere more clearly specified as love.[49] Individuation is not opposed to an infinite hermeneutics but demands it:

> There is no way to know the other except by the admission of such an infinite hermeneutic. If you say you know someone and have nothing more to learn from him, no need to know him better, what does that mean? You deny to the other the quality of a face. Any love relationship implies eternity. Why? It is not a question of fidelity or moral standards. It is because, if you have no need of more time to know the other, you are not directly committed to him. To love somebody is always to need more time to know him. You don't have enough information about him. You will never have enough information. This is the infinite hermeneutics of the other.[50]

At this point it becomes necessary to examine briefly Marion's use of the idea of counter-intentionality. It is an idea that he has rehearsed elsewhere and which has drawn some criticism.[51] The potential problem chiefly relates to the question of whether a counter-intentionality first implies or requires an intentionality that prompts it (in much the same way that a reduction requires an operator). If this were the case, Marion's (and Lévinas') attempts to think the subject as responding to and being constituted by the other person would collapse back into a metaphysical framework, where the other is effectively constituted by the self. While there is a certain logic to this position, since the recognition of the other as other demands a recognising self, it need not determine the priority of self in relation to other. Both authors maintain that the injunction of the other is anarchic, preceding the wakening

---

[47] Marion, *De surcroît* 146; *In Excess* 122.

[48] Marion, *De surcroît* 147; *In Excess* 122.

[49] Marion, "D'Autrui à L'Individu"; "From the Other to the Individual"; "The Face: An Endless Hermeneutics"; *Le phénomène érotique.*

[50] Marion, "The Face: An Endless Hermeneutics," 10. See also section VII of Marion, "D'Autrui à L'Individu," 287–308; "From the Other to the Individual".

[51] See *La croisée* and my discussion of John Milbank's position in *Rethinking God as Gift* 172ff.

ego and signifying only in the response to it of the *me*, rather than as a constituted object that arises subsequent to the I. In this regard, it is important to highlight the corresponding idea of submission or exposure: the very appearance of the face in fact depends on the *inability* of the I to constitute it.[52] These two features seem to suggest that while the nomination of "counter-intentionality" may not be ideal, it is not necessary to assume that it simply repeats a metaphysical structure. We might also note here, again, the comments Marion makes about the effect of the reduction on the I: while the I has a logical priority as operator of the reduction, in the very process of the reduction it submits itself to the reduction and is included within its scope, finding itself given to itself and only subsequently actively involved in phenomenalisation.

In thinking the icon as saturated phenomenon, Marion outlines a way for phenomenology to accede to invisibility by way of a call that signifies by putting the self in question. The origin and content of this call remain undecidable, a point that is underlined by the shift Marion makes late in Chapter 5 of *In Excess* to considering the face in terms of the icon rather than the icon in terms of the face.[53] The undecidability of the call is a feature that Marion attempts to highlight in arguments extending over many years, but never quite so successfully as with *In Excess*.[54] Perhaps that is because in this text, which expands similar comments made in *Being Given*, he more clearly distinguishes the saturated phenomenon of the icon from that of r/Revelation.[55] r/Revelation might involve the icon, but the icon need not involve r/Revelation, at least in a religious sense. An icon might bear, in other words, significations that are not interpreted to be revelatory. Ironically, and as we will see shortly, this opening up of the icon to other-than-revelatory meanings also in turn frees up the saturated phenomenon of r/Revelation.[56] Because the icon remains hermeneutically infinite, r/Revelation always and only remains one of its possibilities, and so r/Revelation is protected from any determinate reference that would be the source of its undoing.

A final insight from Chapter 5 of *In Excess* should be mentioned, because it casts light on a difficult theological question, and because Marion's use of philosophy in relation to theology takes an interesting turn at this point. Marion argues that hermeneutics might ultimately come to an end, theologically speaking, in the *parousia*. He then uses a modified form of Kant's argument for the immortality of the soul to present a philosophical version of the same position. Concluding the chapter, Marion maintains in extension to this argument: "the face of the other person compels me to believe in my own eternity, like a need of reason or, what

---

[52] See also the discussion in my introduction to Marion, *In Excess*.

[53] This point is brought out well early in Marion's latest text, where he speaks of the "elsewhere" that assures me that I am loved, indicating that it could be life, nature, the world, a group, society, man or woman, the divine, or even God. Marion, *Le phénomène érotique* 44.

[54] Since the time of *Reduction and Givenness*. See *Réduction et donation* 297–302; *Reduction and Givenness* 198–202.

[55] On Marion's use of revelation and Revelation, see Horner, "Aporia or Excess?".

[56] Marion did try to suggest this in his examination of the icon of the cross in *La crosiée*. Nevertheless, the later works give much more coherence to this thought.

comes back to the same thing, as the condition of its infinite hermeneutic."[57] Christians live in the promise of seeing God face to face (1 John 3:2; 1 Cor. 13:12); belief in the beatific vision can be understood in terms of the desire for an end to all hermeneutics in much the same way that the fall of Adam and Eve can be understood as an entry into the hermeneutic condition.[58] Is the *parousia* to be understood as (the restoration of) absolute presence? Would the *parousia* bring about the conditions for a perfect photology?[59] Does the beatific vision imply that all distinctions between infinite and finite would collapse? Or to use Derrida's frame of reference, would the Messiah finally come? Marion's argument perhaps leads us in this direction, although it can only be articulated in terms of Christian hope rather than philosophical certainty. Yet he will use a similar argument to sustain the ultimate meaningfulness of love in *Le phénomène érotique*.

The Saturated Phenomenon of r/Revelation

While *In Excess* presents chapters on each of the saturated phenomena in turn, the chapter dealing with r/Revelation is markedly different to the others. It is a revised version of the paper Marion delivered at Villanova in 1997, and while it certainly deals with r/Revelation, it is set in the context of a long-standing debate with Derrida on negative and mystical theology, the possibility of naming God, and so on. In the present text I consider the saturated phenomenon of r/Revelation primarily in terms of the problems it raises across Marion's corpus. As I have indicated, Marion seeks to arrive phenomenologically at the possibility of revelation, which, he maintains, is quite different to its actuality (Revelation). We have seen already in our examination of saturated phenomena just how Marion uses phenomenology to allow for what exceeds conceptualisation, and how, particularly, this works in terms of the icon of the face. Given his claim that r/Revelation combines all the other features of saturation, it seems that perhaps there is little more to say. Nevertheless, we must deal with a strong objection that has been made to his work, which is that to identify any particular phenomenon of small r revelation *as such* demands a commitment in advance to its actuality as capital R Revelation.[60] This is complicated by the fact that, despite his protestations to the contrary, small r revelation and capital R Revelation are frequently interwoven in Marion's phenomenological texts in ways that suggest that the possibility of r/Revelation is not so easily separated from its actuality.[61]

---

[57] Marion, *De surcroît*; *In Excess* 127.

[58] See Kevin Hart, *The Trespass of the Sign*, 2nd ed. (New York: Fordham University Press, 2000).

[59] On this question—although it is couched in very different terms—see the comments in Anthony Kelly, *Touching the Infinite: Explorations in Christian Hope* (Blackburn, Vic: Collins Dove, 1991) 203–04.

[60] See my discussion of the main protagonists in *Rethinking God as Gift*.

[61] See, for example, Marion, *Étant donné* 337; *Being Given* 242. See also the extensive footnote on 329/n90/ p. 367, where Marion is explicit about his "scrupulousness" in utilising the upper and lower cases in maintaining this difference, and the comments on 410/297.

What does Marion understand by r/Revelation? In *Being Given* he uses the figure of Christ as "paradigm of the phenomenon of revelation," which he goes on to describe according to the four modes of saturation.[62] So, here as elsewhere, his example of revelation is one that (in another context) is considered Revelation, although we should not find this too surprising. In his earlier texts, examples of revelatory phenomena are often tentatively deprived of their authoritatively Revelatory force by mechanisms such as their strictly provisional phenomenological status, or, better and more widely, by their inherent undecidability, which is ultimately due to their saturation.[63] This also happens here. And as Marion himself comes to observe in the debate at Villanova, "pluralism is implied in the very notion of revelation [lower-case r]. If there is a real revelation [strangely here, still a lower-case r], no concept could achieve to say and to make intelligible in its own way the excess of intuition."[64] By the time of *In Excess*, however, lower-case revelation has been redefined. Now it is simply what happens in the resistance—and he is using the metaphor of electrical resistance—of the *adonné* to the self-giving phenomenon: "The revealed does not thus define an extreme stratum or a particular region of phenomenality, but rather the universal mode of phenomenalization of what gives *itself* in what shows *itself*."[65] Lower-case revelation is finally demythologised, as it were, and Marion soon adds: "philosophy has neither the authority nor the competence to say more."[66] In this new context, Marion none the less insists that he will consider phenomena of capital R Revelation, although he maintains that this is still to be done from the point of view of saturation. Now, if there are phenomena given utterly in excess of my capacity to frame them, what they reveal must be ultimately ambiguous. This means that phenomena of capital R Revelation will therefore still rightfully enter into phenomenology as strictly undecidable, it being the task of theology to determine their status as definitive capital R Revelation. Yet with this approach Marion effectively undoes again the very distinction between lower-case and upper-case Revelation on which he relies. The capital R Revelatory aspect of the phenomenon could still only be one of a range of possibilities of the small r revelatory phenomenon. Significantly, Marion's approach with *In Excess* finally makes much more explicit the inevitably hermeneutical supplement to phenomenology, but it also serves to emphasise that theology, too, is a hermeneutics. Marion recognises this where he discusses the divine names: "The infinite proliferation of names does indeed suggest that they are still there, but it also flags as insufficient the concepts they put in play and thereby does justice to what constantly subverts them."[67] Even upper-case Revelation is not protected from the

---

[62] Marion, *Étant donné* 329; *Being Given* 236.

[63] As I argue of the icon in *Rethinking God as Gift* 172.

[64] Marion in Kearney, Derrida, and Marion, "On the Name" 69.

[65] Marion, *De surcroît* 62; *In Excess* 52. This redefinition can, in fact, already be seen in an earlier work. See Marion, "Le phénomène saturé"; "The Saturated Phenomenon." Here Marion defines revelation phenomenologically as « ... *une apparition purement de soi et à partir de soi ....*», 127/121. To my knowledge, however, this locution does not appear in *Being Given*.

[66] Marion, *De surcroît* 63; *In Excess* 53.

[67] Marion, *De surcroît* 193; *In Excess* 160.

play of *différance*, or to express this more positively, the absolute otherness of God is protected from our references to God.

By way of a possible objection, I note here John D. Caputo's reading of the Villanova texts in his "Apostles of the Impossible: On God and the Gift in Derrida and Marion."[68] Caputo argues that Marion's commitment to the givenness of God also implies a commitment to God's ultimate, if not conceptual, presence:

> We have contended that Marion and Derrida are agreed in regarding the "intention" or the "concept" as an "arrow" which is aimed at the heart of God from which God must be "shielded" ... or kept "safe." For Marion ... this is because the arrow of intentionality is too weak and narrow to penetrate or comprehend the infinite givenness of God; it would compromise the infinite incomprehensibility of God who has utterly saturated the intention "God" in a plenitude of givenness. But for Derrida ... the arrow takes aim at God and never reaches God precisely because the name of God is the name of what we love and desire ... something *tout autre* which is not "present," not only in the narrow conceptual sense of conceptual presentation advanced by Marion, but also not *given*.[69]

The point is a valid one. Marion, of course, argues that givenness is not equivalent to presence, but his argument only works if what is given gives itself as something like a trace, which redoubles the saturation and the need for a hermeneutic supplement. In other words, if God gives Godself in such a way that intuition is saturated, then this is not only because the thought of God is excessive but because we cannot know whether or not that excessiveness even refers us to God. It is the possibility—rather than the actuality—that God gives, which provides a "content without object" for givenness.

---

[68] John D. Caputo, "Apostles of the Impossible," *God, the Gift, and Postmodernism*, eds. John D. Caputo and Michael Scanlon (Bloomington: Indiana University Press, 1999) 185–222.
[69] Caputo, "Apostles of the Impossible," 199.

Chapter 11

A Thought of Love

With *Le phénomène érotique: Six Méditations*, Marion aims to complete a project begun with *The Idol and Distance* and explicitly continued with *Prolegomena to Charity*, but which, he maintains, has essentially marked all his work between and since: the working out of the question of love.[1] But where his earlier material frequently invokes love as a kind of theological imperative that simply overrides metaphysics by claiming to render it destitute, here he attempts a phenomenological thinking of love that addresses the deficiencies of metaphysics as onto-theo-logy on their own terms. While he ultimately calls upon God to guarantee (as a witness) the meaningfulness of love, his *adieu/à Dieu* is a supplication rather than a cognition, more resonant with the tones of Lévinas and Derrida than with Pascal. *Le phénomène érotique* is framed by two basic phenomenological questions: ipseity and alterity. Marion argues that we are assured of ipseity only through being loved, and not through being as such. And we reach the other not through constitution, but by willing-to-love, on the basis of finding ourselves always and already loved. He reaches these claims by way of a series of meditations that tend to function in a spiral rather than a linear fashion; read otherwise they can appear quite confusingly like a sequence of false starts. As we proceed through the book the focus of the questioning shifts around a centre, until we reach a point, as it were, of anamorphosis. In this chapter, we will attempt to follow that movement.

In *Le phénomène érotique*, Marion addresses what he claims to be the complete failure of philosophy to think love; it is hard to take love seriously when we have no real concept of it, or when any concept that we do have has been weakened by the division of love into different types.[2] The basic opposition between *eros* and *agape* reinforces a characterisation of love as passionate (and thereby irrational), or, I might add without further warrant from Marion, as bloodless and sanitised (whereupon it is consigned to the religious in caricature).[3] Marion hopes to achieve a unified "erotic rationality," based on the experience of erotic phenomena, thought in relation to their own horizon—the horizon of "love without being."[4] Descartes' biggest mistake, according to Marion, was to exclude "the tonality of an erotic disposition" from his thinking of the *ego*, constructing certainty in being on the

---

[1] Jean-Luc Marion, *Le phénomène érotique* 22–23.

[2] Marion, *Le phénomène érotique* 14–15.

[3] Of course, the ancient divisions of love are more than two; in *The Four Loves* (Glasgow: Collins, 1960), for example, C. S. Lewis examines not only *eros* and *agape* but also *philia* and *storge*.

[4] Marion, *Le phénomène érotique* 15–16.

basis of knowing.[5] Marion tries to rethink radically the *ego* (and eventually the other person) according to what he calls "the erotic reduction." Nevertheless, just what constitutes the erotic reduction is far from clear. Over the course of the text there are three formulations of this reduction, the first two of which are found to be unsatisfactory. At the same time, however, moving through these reductions is like moving inwards through concentric circles: aspects of the earlier reductions still remain significant in the characterisation of the third. The relationship of the erotic reduction to Marion's phenomenological reduction to givenness is not fully explicated, but the former effectively operates within the general framework of the latter.

Erotic Reduction 1: Am I Loved By Another?

While knowing brings us certainty of the *ego*, it is only the type of certainty we can have of objects poor in intuition, and it only guarantees the *ego* as long as the *ego* sustains itself in thought as an object.[6] Here we see the basic problem of metaphysics: it delivers a certitude that is restricted to objects, but that is nevertheless still contingent on the will to be certain.[7] And as we have seen before in Marion's works, certitude is immediately disqualified by vanity; the question of whether or not I am (according to epistemological or ontological reductions) is less important than the question of whether or not I am loved by another [*m'aime-t-on?* or *m'aime-t-on—d'ailleurs?*] and therefore worthwhile.[8] We shift from the task of establishing certitude in being to that of establishing assurance in love.[9] This shift inevitably makes the I vulnerable and dependent, and the world becomes vain except as ordered completely to the other person who can deliver that assurance. The erotic reduction makes destitute not only space (the other becomes the centre, in comparison to me), but time (I have to wait for the assurance of the other, as an event from elsewhere), and identity (I do not know who I am, save that I take flesh).[10] The kind of reassurance that the I can therefore receive in relation to the question "does someone love me?" comes from elsewhere and introduces into the I a gap or an original alterity. It would seem that this gap should be able to be overcome by self-love, yet Marion goes on to argue that in fact self-love only leads to hate. We are left with an aporia: on the one hand, the assurance of being loved that comes to me from another leads to the recognition of a gap within the I; on the other hand, hate is the only product of the attempt to generate assurance by self-love.[11]

---

[5] Marion, *Le phénomène érotique* 18.

[6] Marion, *Le phénomène érotique* 25–32.

[7] Marion, *Le phénomène érotique* 32–37.

[8] Marion, *Le phénomène érotique* 41, 45, 116. I will continue to refer to "the I" even though Marion sometimes refers to the me, and also to "*l'égo donné (et adonné)*" (41).

[9] Marion, *Le phénomène érotique* 37–48.

[10] Marion, *Le phénomène érotique* 48–69.

[11] Marion, *Le phénomène érotique* 71–109.

Erotic Reduction 2: Can I Love First?

While it enables an erotic reduction to be made, the question of whether or not I am loved by another turns out to be poorly focused, since it is based on the idea that love is essentially reciprocal. A better question is "can I love first?" ["*puis-je aimer, moi le premier?*"].[12] This approach allows for a thinking of love as pure loss rather than as reciprocity (a loss that Marion likens somewhat problematically to the gift), and since it relies on one's own act, it delivers the I to itself.[13] Nevertheless, my own advances in love need to be constantly repeated, since the other person will never ultimately be possessed as an object.[14] Further, in this repeated movement of advancing towards the other, no assurance is delivered of my own loveableness, and there is no certainty that I actually do love, save in my decision to love or to behave as if I love. More problematic still is that I may end up loving only love, rather than a specific individual, for my saturated love intuition will as yet have no determinate corresponding intention, that is, no specific concept or meaning of the other.[15] In order to deliver a specific meaning, the other must somehow first show her or himself to me. This happens in the counter-intentionality of the face, which signifies as "pure exteriority" by way of the ethical injunction (Lévinas). Yet as Marion has shown elsewhere, the ethical injunction signifies in a universal rather than a particular sense.[16] Here instead the exteriority of the other signifies as an oath (a commitment to me) and provides a meaning that nevertheless does not fulfil my excessive intuition.[17] What appears will be an erotic phenomenon, which is produced "without egoic pole" in the crossing of my own decision to love (my oath) and the lover's imposed signification (the other's oath).[18] This crossed phenomenon is held in common between the lovers: it has a common meaning, but involves two separate intuitions:[19] "The lover … sees the unique phenomenon, that he or she loves and who loves him or her, by the grace of this oath."[20] Here we evidently see an advance on the position expressed in *Prolegomena to Charity*, where the crossed phenomenon is described as occurring in feeling the weight of the other's unsubstitutable gaze as it crosses my intentional aim, a weight that is still expressed in Lévinasian terms as the experience of an always-prior injunction that exposes and obliges me.[21] In *Le phénomène érotique*, a development occurs in the provision of a more personal signification of the other in the oath.

The common meaning of the erotic phenomenon depends not on the statement of the oath but on its performance. Here we also find Marion's fuller solution to the

12 Marion, *Le phénomène érotique* 116.
13 Marion, *Le phénomène érotique* 116–33.
14 Marion, *Le phénomène érotique* 133–43.
15 Marion, *Le phénomène érotique* 143–55.
16 Marion, *Le phénomène érotique* 155–61. See also part V of Marion, "D'Autrui à L'Individu"; "From the Other to the Individual."
17 Marion, *Le phénomène érotique* 165–66.
18 Marion, *Le phénomène érotique* 164.
19 Marion, *Le phénomène érotique* 166–68.
20 Marion, *Le phénomène érotique* 168.
21 Marion, *Prolégomènes* 103ff.; *Prolegomena* 83ff.

problem of the individualisation of the I, which he describes as occurring through my desire for the other, my desire that the love be eternal, and by passivity (through dependence, exposure to alterity, and risk).[22] This passivity is like the passivity of flesh in delivering me to myself. It is through flesh, in fact, that not only I but the other will be given. I will access the flesh of the other not according to the horizon of perception (which is limited to the body) but through naked exposure. Flesh is phenomenalised not through being seen, but through being felt without resistance. In eroticisation, the other gives me flesh in allowing me to penetrate his or her flesh, and I give the other flesh.[23] The other person therefore appears as a phenomenon only indirectly, according to flesh, that is:

> ... as the one who phenomenalises me as my flesh. The difficulty of the phenomenon of the other person does not lie in its distancing, poverty or supposed transcendence; on the contrary, it lies in its absolute immanence: the other person appears to the very extent where he gives me my own flesh, which deploys like a screen on which his [flesh] is projected ....[24]

My body becomes flesh, and I become myself, when the flesh of the other is phenomenalised in mine.[25] The other shows her or himself as a face, but not according to the universal ethical injunction, since here there can be no substitution.[26] "The eroticised face also recapitulates all his or her flesh .... I thus see there his or her flesh, insofar as it is felt and is experienced, thus in so far as it is definitively individualised, gifted to itself, in short, in so far as definitively *inaccessible* to mine. I see there the accomplished transcendence of the other person ...."[27] For the duration of the eroticisation, we are no longer in worldly space, for all our coordinates bear a relation only to the other. Neither are we in regular time. But once one partner climaxes, the process of eroticisation has to be recommenced.[28] Once eroticisation ceases, we become naked bodies again, not flesh for one another (I remain flesh for myself, but not eroticised flesh, which requires the resistance of the other). Since there is no substance of eroticisation, I am left with nothing to see: instead of a saturated phenomenon I am left with a

---

[22] Marion, *Le phénomène érotique* 169–78.

[23] Marion, *Le phénomène érotique* 178–90.

[24] Marion, *Le phénomène érotique* 192.

[25] Marion, *Le phénomène érotique* 194–95.

[26] Marion, *Le phénomène érotique* 198–99. "We must recognise that the privilege of the face ... no longer depends *here* on a distance, nor on an ethical height. Here the face of the other person, if it wants or can still speak to me, certainly no longer says to me 'Thou shalt not kill!'; not only because the other person is not in any doubt about this point; not only because he or she says to me, in sighs or in words, 'Here I am, come!' (§28); but especially because we [*lui et moi*] have left the universal, even the universal ethic, in order to strive towards particularity—mine and his or hers, since it is a question of me and of you and surely not of a universally obligating neighbour. In the situation of mutual eroticisation, where each gives to the other the flesh that he or she does not have, each only aims at being individualised in individualising the other person, thus exactly piercing and transgressing the universal." (198)

[27] Marion, *Le phénomène érotique* 200.

[28] Marion, *Le phénomène érotique* 200–11.

"phenomenon under erasure" about which I can say nothing.[29] Erotic speech—which is non-predicative and of which there are three types: obscene, infantile, and hyperbolic—no longer applies.[30] Eroticisation thus attests to finitude, because flesh can excite itself virtually automatically and is thus out of my control, and because each period of eroticisation must literally come to an end.[31]

The Problem of Making Love in Person

In the fifth meditation Marion considers the problems that arise with this characterisation of eroticisation. We want eroticisation to be infinite but it is finite; because it is finite we can tend to become suspicious of the reality of the experience.[32] More problematic again, perhaps, is the fact that orgasm is ultimately impersonal. Since eroticisation, while it individualises, does not yet always reach the other person *in person*, but as flesh, I might be tempted to use people as erotic objects, opening the possibility of the erotic lie.[33] This potentially occurs because of the interior gap between eroticised flesh and the person. The person escapes automatic eroticisation, meaning that it is possible to lie, or even to make a false oath.[34] Further, we cannot actually overcome this gap, especially by force.[35] A final difficulty is that individualisation—even by means of the face as flesh—does not guarantee truth.[36] Both jealousy and hate can also individualise (although this occurs as lack rather than as flesh).[37] (To these problems we might add the one that emerged in the previous chapter: if the other appears in eroticisation as a saturated phenomenon, any "projection" onto the screen of my own flesh will only result in an individualisation by way of hermeneutics.) Marion maintains that the only way to overcome these difficulties seems to be by entry into an eroticisation that is not automatic but free, where not only flesh but access to the person is gained. This, he claims, can occur without physical contact, through words: "my word only aims to touch him, to affect him in the most strict sense, so as to make him feel the weight, the insistence, and the non-resistance of my flesh…." It is "making love *in person*."[38] In this way, Marion proposes that all loving relationships can be subject to the erotic reduction, not simply those that are sexual.[39] While it perhaps seems

---

[29] Marion, *Le phénomène érotique* 211–16, 24–34.

[30] Marion, *Le phénomène érotique* 224–34. Interestingly enough, he compares these to the three types of theological discourse: positive, negative, and mystical. The comparison seems forced, except in so far as language is being used non-predicatively, and except with regard to the mystical and the hyperbolic.

[31] Marion, *Le phénomène érotique* 217–24.

[32] Marion, *Le phénomène érotique* 236.

[33] Marion, *Le phénomène érotique* 238–42.

[34] Marion, *Le phénomène érotique* 242–51.

[35] Marion, *Le phénomène érotique* 253–57.

[36] Marion, *Le phénomène érotique* 257–64.

[37] Marion, *Le phénomène érotique* 265–70, 271–76.

[38] Marion, *Le phénomène érotique* 281.

[39] Marion, *Le phénomène érotique* 283. This would include relationships between parents and children, between friends, and between humanity and God.

unusual, given that he has just deliberated at length on the possibility of the erotic lie, that Marion newly invests the word with "a veracity without weakness," he apparently does this on the basis of the absence of the genital arousal which might otherwise compromise the erotic reduction by its automatic or un-chosen character.[40] Expressed in other terms, "eroticisation" has come to mean giving flesh without physical contact by addressing the person directly. Here is the precise point at which Marion boldly attempts to overcome the division between *eros* and *agape*. He does this by arguing for an eroticisation that can be chaste, that is, he appears to be proposing that all love is on a continuum that includes the sexual as well as the non-sexual.[41] But we have to ask about the kind of address that might occur in such an eroticisation. Marion maintains that it is an address that cannot lie because it does not predicate anything.[42] Is it therefore linked with his earlier description of erotic address—the obscene, the infantile, or the hyperbolic? Presumably, an erotic word that is not destined for genital arousal will not be obscene, while it might possibly be infantile. However, it is more likely to be hyperbolic. Marion does not explicitly make the connection in this context, but such a hyperbolic personal address, of course, bears a striking similarity to the address made to God in mystical theology, a connection he has made earlier.

The Need for Fidelity

According to the erotic reduction, the erotic phenomenon lasts for as long as the oath lasts: fidelity is what allows the phenomenon to be seen: "The erotic phenomenon … demands long and profound fidelity. But fidelity requires nothing less than eternity."[43] Fidelity cannot be proved, but only decided upon (in Derrida's terms, fidelity would be aporetic).[44] It therefore involves a kind of Heideggerian anticipatory resolution, which delivers ipseity:[45] "I thus receive myself, in the end, from the other person. I receive from the other my ipseity, as I have already received my signification in his or her oath, my flesh in the eroticisation of his or hers, and even my proper fidelity in the other's declaration 'You love me truly!'"[46] Nevertheless, fidelity here depends on the temporality of eroticisation. Marion's final challenge is to establish a means of witnessing to fidelity that does not depend on the time of the lovers. Initially he tries to do this with another quasi-Lévinasian move by appealing to the child of a loving union.[47] In doing so he makes a valuable comment on the gift, even if his mechanism to provide for a witness fails:

---

[40] Marion, *Le phénomène érotique* 282.
[41] He comments on 283 that chastity "… is the erotic virtue par excellence." See also 336–39.
[42] Marion, *Le phénomène érotique* 282.
[43] Marion, *Le phénomène érotique* 286.
[44] Marion, *Le phénomène érotique* 293–94.
[45] Marion, *Le phénomène érotique* 294–302.
[46] Marion, *Le phénomène érotique* 302.
[47] See Lévinas' comments on fecundity in *Time and the Other*, trans. Richard Cohen (Pittsburgh, PA: Duquesne University Press, 1987).

The child is no longer defined only as *l'adonné* [the gifted] par excellence (the one who is received perfectly from what is received), but as the one who receives the gift of origin without the power ever to return it to its donor; and who must always re-give it to a recipient, who will never return it to him or her in turn. As the child cannot return the gift, the child must thus convey it—and first in him or her. Because defined as the third from the very beginning, the child definitively ruptures reciprocity by diverting the return of the gift away from the giver, shifting it towards an unknown and as yet non-existent [*non-étant*] recipient (another child, another event still to come). The child thus steals from us, we, the lovers, not only the flesh that our flesh has given to him or her, but especially the return of his or her witness in support of our oath. By definition, the child abandons the lovers to themselves.[48]

The movement of the gift described here is an-economic: it can never be returned to the givers. What Marion elsewhere situates in the context of prior gift as obligation and indebtedness, he now consigns to non-return.[49] But in doing so, he admits that the child cannot ultimately witness to fidelity. He therefore has to shift to another strategy. To avoid the constant repetition of the oath now depends on making each moment the final authority; each moment becomes an eschatological *as if*, so that the lovers make eternity rather than wait for it.[50] Only eternity can assure the permanence of the oath, and here God is invoked as the eternal witness:

> The lovers accomplish their oath in the *adieu*—in the passage to God, who they summon as their final witness, their first witness, the one who never leaves and never lies. Then, for the first time, they say to each other "adieu": next year in Jerusalem—the next time to God. To think to/about God can only be done, erotically, in this "adieu".[51]

Erotic Reduction 3: You Have Loved Me First

Having accomplished fidelity to the oath in a moment that is touched by the eternal, we are finally enabled to discover ourselves as loveable because we have been lovers.[52] Marion here arrives at a new and final formulation of the erotic reduction: "You have loved me first [*Toi, tu m'as aimé le premier*]." My capacity to love, to make an advance in love, is actually made possible by finding myself always and already loved: "To enter into the erotic reduction, there has to have been another lover who has preceded me there and, from there, calls me there in silence."[53] There are Lévinasian antecedents to this position: "love ... designates a movement by which the being searches for that to which it was connected even before having taken

---

[48] Marion, *Le phénomène érotique* 316. Particular thanks to Shane Mackinlay for his assistance with the translation of this complex passage.
[49] See my discussion and comments in Horner, *Rethinking God as Gift* 133.
[50] Marion, *Le phénomène érotique* 321.
[51] Marion, *Le phénomène érotique* 326.
[52] Marion, *Le phénomène érotique* 328.
[53] Marion, *Le phénomène érotique* 331.

the initiative to search ...."[54] Nevertheless, Marion's explication of the universality of the love that enables love, in the final section of the text, rings a little hollow. No one, he maintains, can claim "that no one loves them or has ever loved them." He immediately goes on to qualify this by saying that if I have not been loved in the past then someone may at least love me in the future.[55] And with that, he seems to revert to one of his earlier versions of the erotic reduction: it is not a question of whether or not I have been loved or will be loved, but a question of if, who, and how I love. Ultimately, however, Marion invokes a theological guarantee of love-able-ness. God is the one who loves perfectly, and who always loves before I do: "[God] loves the first and the last ... [T]his first lover, forever, has been named God."[56] This has scriptural echoes: we love God because God first loved us (1 John 4:10). The conclusion of the text could therefore be seen to be problematic in that the apparently phenomenological has been completed by the simple reassertion of the theological.

The À-Dieu

This final point heads the list of difficulties arising from the text. God is used to guarantee love in two ways: as a witness to the faithfulness of love, and as the first lover who enables all other loves. These might be appropriate theological claims, but how are they to be made in the context of a phenomenology that resists metaphysics? Does Marion just repeat the most basic onto-theo-logical move of using God to ground the system? Perhaps we can separate the two instances in our examination. In the first case, where the lovers are said to call upon God as their witness, it is a matter, as I foreshadowed in the introduction to this chapter, of supplication rather than cognition. Here Marion makes use of the *adieu* (farewell), the *à-Dieu* ([un]to God) that is also found in the work of Lévinas, and with a Lévinasian genealogy in the work of Derrida. In his *adieu* to Lévinas, Derrida observes:

> The greeting of the *à-Dieu* does not signal the end. "The *à-Dieu* is not a finality," he says, thus challenging the "alternative between being and nothingness," which "is not ultimate." The *à-Dieu* greets the other beyond being, in "what is signified, beyond being, by the word 'glory.'" "The *à-Dieu* is not a process of being: in the call, I am referred back to the other human being through whom this call signifies, to the neighbor for whom I am to fear."[57]

---

[54] Emmanuel Lévinas, *Totality and Infinity* 254. This text is quoted in part VII of Marion, "D'Autrui à L'Individu"; "From the Other to the Individual."

[55] Marion, *Le phénomène érotique* 332. In human terms, the assertion is just a little bit too universal. Marion refers to the love of parents for their children, which might be the norm, but cannot be guaranteed.

[56] Marion, *Le phénomène érotique* 341.

[57] Jacques Derrida, *Adieu to Emmanuel Lévinas*, trans. Pascale-Anne Brault and Michael Naas (Stanford, CA: Stanford University Press, 1999) 13. Derrida refers to the Lévinas' text, known in English as "Bad Conscience and the Inexorable," in Richard A. Cohen, ed., *Face to Face with Levinas* (Albany, NY: State University of New York Press, 1986). See also Derrida's further commentary on the adieu in "A Word of Welcome," *Adieu* 101–05, 120–22.

This reading of the *à-Dieu*, where the prayer refers beyond being to glory, but where such a reference only has meaning in relation to the other person for whom I am responsible, is coherent with Marion's own reading of prayer, exemplified with "In the Name: How to Avoid Speaking of It." While we have already encountered it as Chapter 6 of *In Excess*, in its original setting, this text is titled "In the Name: How to Avoid Speaking of Negative Theology," and is in some ways a response to Derrida's work, "How to Avoid Speaking."[58] In the latter text, Derrida problematises negative theology in terms of its attempts to refer to what is "not-being" by surreptitiously invoking what is greater than being (the hyper-essential).[59] He also suggests that prayer and praise always have a specific reference or destination in mind, a position that he later modifies in *Sauf le nom*, and which forms a significant part of the discussion at Villanova with regard to the [im]possibility of naming.[60] Marion's claim with "In the Name" is that denomination (in prayer and praise, for example) is always pragmatic, a claim with which Derrida ultimately agrees.[61] To return to the question of the *à-Dieu*, then, it seems to me that Marion uses it in a way that could easily be consistent with a pragmatic or undecideable reference: "Then, for the first time, they say to each other 'adieu': next year in Jerusalem—the next time to God. To think to/about God can only be done, erotically, in this 'adieu'."[62] In calling upon God to guarantee the fidelity of their oath, the lovers are bound in responsibility to each other (where the oath signifies); the eschatological moment is essentially not one that has any other signification.

Nevertheless, we still have the second case to deal with, where Marion invokes God as the first lover who enables all other loves. This case is more difficult, as it resonates with metaphysical determinations of God as first cause, or mover, and at another level with Marion's thinking of the gift as that which emerges always in response to a prior gift, out of the promptings of indebtedness. Perhaps strangely, both the question of the prime mover and that of the enabling gift arise in Derrida's writing, where he thinks the gift as the impossible in relation to the circle, that which enables the circle to begin turning:

> If the figure of the circle is essential to economics, the gift must remain *aneconomic*. Not that it remains foreign to the circle, but it must keep a relation of foreignness to the circle, a relation without relation of familiar foreignness. It is perhaps in this sense that the gift is the impossible.[63]

---

[58] Jacques Derrida, "Comment ne pas parler. Dénégations," *Psyché: Inventions de l'autre* (Paris: Galilée, 1987). This essay is translated by Ken Frieden in *Derrida and Negative Theology*, ed. Harold Coward and Toby Foshay (Albany, NY: State University of New York Press, 1992) 73–142.

[59] See Derrida, "How to Avoid Speaking," 77. In response, see Kevin Hart, *The Trespass of the Sign* (Cambridge: Cambridge University Press, 1989) 202.

[60] Jacques Derrida, "Sauf le nom," trans. John P. Leavey, *On the Name* (Stanford, CA: Stanford University Press, 1995) 35–85. For Derrida's comments in the discussion at Villanova, see Marion, "In the Name," 44–47.

[61] Marion, "In the Name," 46.

[62] Marion, *Le phénomène érotique* 326.

[63] Derrida, *Given Time* 7.

The overrunning of the circle by the gift, if there is any, does not lead to simple, ineffable exteriority that would be transcendent and without relation. It is this exteriority that sets the circle going, it is this exteriority that puts the economy in motion. It is this exteriority that *engages* in the circle and makes it turn .... What is the gift as the first mover of the circle? And how does it contract itself into a circular contract? And from what place? Since when? From whom?[64]

For Derrida, such a first mover will never be available in presence. The "divided Prime Mover" of which he speaks in *The Truth in Painting* is precisely an origin that is never original.[65] Further, as I argue elsewhere, this gift as first mover may be no more than the condition of possibility and impossibility for giving: *différance*.[66] The comparison with Derrida is useful in that it exemplifies a non-metaphysical reference to a first mover and to the first mover as gift. At the same time, however, there is little doubt that Marion's first lover has a theological context: by "God" he is not referring to *"différance."*[67] And there is a strong distinction to be drawn between a gift that gets the circle going—and that may be read impersonally, like the Heideggerian *es gibt*—and love, which cannot be read impersonally. It seems to me that we can read Marion's reference to God as first lover in two ways. According to the first way, God as lover provides a theological solution to the phenomenological problem of how one can be enabled to love, when this can only be the result of always and already finding oneself loved. This solution would be consistent with Marion's earlier writings, and especially with *God Without Being*. It would be a final reassertion of the theological destitution of all thought, including phenomenology. Yet how would we then account for Marion's insistence—in *Being Given* for example—that he now resists the move he made in *Dieu sans l'être*, the "direct recourse to theology"?[68] According to a second way of reading God as first lover, Marion's reference could be interpreted within the trajectory of his later works, that is, in light of his recognition that our references to God are basically pragmatic or undecideable. This requires us to read against the letter of the text at this point, although it is consistent with his earlier use of the *à-Dieu*. In other words, in the same way that the *à-Dieu* appeals to God with an address that will always be a mis-address, the appeal to God as first lover could also find itself diverted to the other person who, I find in every instance of loving, has in fact always loved me first. Evidently, there is no easy way of resolving this problem. *Le phénomène érotique* is not simply another book in the phenomenological series, and Marion has made clear its connections with *The Idol and Distance* and *Prolegomena to Charity*, which are largely theological works. Yet in it he pursues a predominantly phenomenological approach. Undoubtedly it can be seen to bring a highly metaphysical theology to bear, but that is unsettled by the movement within Marion's writing towards a theology that cannot simply be identified with metaphysics.

---

[64] Derrida, *Given Time* 30.
[65] Jacques Derrida, *The Truth in Painting*, trans. Geoffrey Bennington and Ian McLeod (Chicago, IL: University of Chicago Press, 1987) 2.
[66] Horner, *Rethinking God as Gift* 192ff.
[67] He makes clear that God is not *différance* in the later stages of *The Idol and Distance*.
[68] "Preface to the American Translation," in Marion, *Being Given:* ix–xi, x.

A second difficulty that arises in *Le phénomène érotique* relates to the question of the individualisation of the other on the basis of the will to love. As we have earlier seen with the icon of the face, the other is individualised as flesh in *Le phénomène érotique* in part through my decision to love; here the crossed phenomenon appears in the performed crossing of my oath and the other's imposed signification as his or her oath. Further, in *Le phénomène érotique* the other is reached in person through my erotic address to her or him, which becomes possible through my decision to accept the fidelity of the other's oath, finally witnessed by God in the *à-Dieu*. Does individualisation thus depend entirely on my decision, that is, entirely on the will? Is this finally and once again a pseudo-Nietzschean move in the overcoming of metaphysics, one that—Heidegger might suggest—is not an overcoming but a repetition?[69] It seems to me that the difference between Nietzsche's assertion of the will (as the will to power) and Marion's emphasis on decision (which he uses in relation to the gift and to love), is the latter's basis in what Heidegger might call the *Abgrund*, or Derrida the aporia. Marion's decision to "recognise" the other as this particular other always carries an element of risk: it makes us vulnerable rather than strong. In *Le phénomène érotique* he correlates the decision to love with some kind of signification by the other (the other is not simply the product of my imagination), but the imposed signification is matched to an excess of intuition that forbids comprehension, even as it enables individualisation. The decision that individualises is based on endless hermeneutical possibilities. There is always the chance that this type of decision will keep us firmly within the grip of metaphysics, but then there is the chance that it will open onto excess. It will be—using Derrida's way of thinking— a question of faith rather than knowledge. To speak of love overcoming metaphysics, then, will ultimately always be to risk overstating the case, and here we are reminded of Marion's observation that "phenomenology does not actually overcome metaphysics so much as it opens the official possibility of leaving it to itself ...."[70]

A final question must be brought to *Le phénomène érotique*, and that is to do with whether or not Marion has been successful in his thinking of love as a unified phenomenon. The most difficult feature to negotiate in this regard seems to be thinking the continuity of love as both *eros* and *agape*. For much of the book, Marion appears to base his thinking of the latter on the former, which is potentially problematic, as I noted above concerning the appropriateness of erotic address. However, in the latter stages of the text the argument about love is essentially recast in terms of fidelity. All love can be thought in relation to faithfulness; to do so is neither to tame passion nor to undervalue the love of parents and children, friends for friends, or Christ for the other *par excellence*. While much of the contemporary narrative about love rests on the significance of emotion, Marion's basic insight is that no matter what initially motivates it, love depends on choice: the choice to be faithful, a choice that has no ground at all. To this extent, it seems to me that he achieves his goal.

---

[69] I am indebted here to my conversations with Lawrence Hemming and Joeri Schrivers in Leuven. On Heidegger's reading of Nietzsche, see Martin Heidegger, "The Word of Nietzsche 'God is Dead.'"

[70] Marion, *Being Given* 4; *Étant donné* 9.

With *Le phénomène érotique*, Marion essentially argues that metaphysics is deficient because it cannot think what matters, and that what matters is loving and being loved. For much of the book he takes a phenomenological approach to determining how love signifies in the I and in the other person. This is in contrast to his theological works, where he asserts the destitution of metaphysics by love but does not provide a context for thinking love apart from the affirmation of Christian faith. While the case could easily be put forward that the two appeals to God (as a witness, and as first lover) at the end of the text constitute a reversion to dogmatic solutions, and hence a reversion to metaphysics, it could also be argued that in the context of Marion's later works these appeals remain undecidable. Oddly enough, the latter argument amounts to the recognition that metaphysics can only be unsettled by a kind of faith—not a determinate faith, but a faith that admits the ungrounded nature of its appeal. This is a faith that is solely characterised in terms of a leap.

POSTSCRIPT

POSTSCRIPT

Postscript

In the introduction to the present work, I raised the question of how it is possible to do theology in the wake of the postmodern, or more specifically, in the wake of various critiques of metaphysics. It was with this question in mind that I referred to Jean-Luc Marion as a theologian whose work might suggest a way forward. Over the course of this volume, it has been observed that some of Marion's initial optimism with regard to the possibilities offered by theology for overcoming metaphysics, has given way to a recognition that a theology that asserts itself as a kind of absolute knowledge—however that is configured—is doomed to repeat metaphysics in another register. While many theologians would contest that theology actually makes such absolute claims, it is apparent, even in the work of one so sensitive to the subtleties of metaphysics as Marion, that it is very hard to avoid them, at least by implication. When Marion shifts to a phenomenological approach to the overcoming of metaphysics, the energy of his work is directed towards the possibility of thinking alterity by way of the saturated phenomenon. To do phenomenology is clearly no longer to do theology, but by pursuing phenomenology's capacity to open onto excess, he creates a space where the task of theology can begin.

The theology to emerge from such a space would be characterised by its lack of a metaphysical ground. In other words, it would not be able to refer to God by any analogy of being or on the basis of a self-present subject for whom language could in any circumstances communicate absolutely (thereby also ruling out any analogy of faith in the sense it has come to assume). It would be able to deliver no guarantees. But that is not to say that it would be empty. According to the schema that Marion suggests, the experience of faith would arise in response to the exposure of the self to "phenomena" that exceed the capacities of conceptuality to determine them. They would signify as a call that would be heard only in the response (in the same way that the oath of the other person only signifies in my decision to accept it as such). Such phenomena would therefore yield no absolute meaning, but would instead give rise to an infinite hermeneutics of faith. The logic of this position, re-expressed using the terms of a theology of revelation, is as follows. The necessary corollary of revelation is experience, and if experience is characterised primarily as exposure, rather than as seeing (according to a horizon), then any phenomenon of "revelation" would be subject to potentially infinite interpretative possibilities.

One of the major questions that was provoked by the exposition of Marion's work concerned the extent to which it relies on a quasi-Nietzschean re-assertion of the will. In the setting of his early theology, this question arose with regard to the overriding of metaphysics by the mere assertion of faith, that is, by a faith that asserted itself as knowledge rather than as faith. It has become evident that such a position is untenable. But in the setting of Marion's phenomenology, the same question was related to the capacity of the self to recognise the other as any particular other (which includes God). Two factors can be seen to ameliorate this difficulty. In the first place, we are not talking about an experience without content, even if we are talking about experience that has no object. This is why, in the context of the other person, Marion's shift to speaking of some kind of imposed signification, even and especially in so far as it does not fulfil intuition, is important. Saturated phenomena are not simply imagined, even if they may give rise to interpretations that are no more than wish-fulfilment. This relates to the second factor. What we have not explored here is the likelihood that the infinite interpretative possibilities prompted by the saturated phenomenon would ultimately be re-limited to some extent, nevertheless, by the fact that interpretation is never purely private but involves a world of shared meaning. Here the role of faith communities and interpretative traditions in identifying phenomena of revelation would again become significant, and the work of Ricoeur in this regard is extremely relevant. But also important would be the way in which the self was shaped by the experience of exposure, which is why, for all the problems that Marion's idea of knowing as loving occasions, it has a place as we search for theological coherence. In this sense, we can agree with Marion that love is the essential criterion.

Appendix 1

Primary Bibliography of Jean-Luc Marion

The bibliographies have been put together on the basis of a number of resources: Marion's own records, which are sometimes incomplete, including a list compiled by Marc Loriaux; an online bibliography compiled by James K. A. Smith; and independent searches completed by myself, Mark Manolopoulos, and Glenn Morrison. Where possible, entries in the primary bibliography have been cross-referenced, although later translations falling into the same category (for either book chapters or articles) have been listed with the originals rather than re-entered. The primary bibliography is chronological and the secondary alphabetical by author and then chronological. While every effort has been made to track down primary and secondary works, these bibliographies are, doubtlessly, not exhaustive. Special thanks to Stijn Van den Bossche, Peter Howard, and Luz Imbriano for their proofreading assistance.

1.1 Books in French and their English Translations

Marion, Jean-Luc. *Sur l'ontologie grise de Descartes. Science cartésienne et savoir aristotélicien dans les 'Regulae'*. Paris: J. Vrin, 1975. Rev. ed. 1981. 3rd ed. Paris: J. Vrin, 1993. 4th ed., 2000. *Sobre a ontologia cinzenta de Descartes*. Lisbonne: Instituto Piaget, 1997. *Descartes' Grey Ontology. Cartesian Science and Aristotelian Thought in the* Regulae. Trans. S. Donohue. South Bend, IN.: St. Augustine's Press, 2004.
——. *L'idole et la distance: cinq études*. Paris: B. Grasset, 1977. 2nd ed. 1989. 3rd ed. Paris: Livre de Poche, 1991. *L'idolo e la distanza*. Trans. A. dell'Asta. Milan: Jaca Book, 1979. *El ídolo y la distancia*. Trans. M. Pascual and N. Latrille. Salamanque: Ediciones Segime, 1999. *The Idol and Distance: Five Studies*. Trans. Thomas A. Carlson. Perspectives in Continental Philosophy. Ed. John D. Caputo. New York: Fordham University Press, 2001.
——. *Sur la théologie blanche de Descartes. Analogie, création des vérités éternelles et fondement*. 1981. Rev. ed. Paris: Presses Universitaires de France, 1991. English translation forthcoming.
——. *Dieu sans l'être. Hors-texte*. Paris: Arthème Fayard, 1982. Rev. ed. Paris: Presses Universitaires de France, 1991. *Dio senza essere*. Trans. A. dell'Asta. Milan: Jaca Book, 1987. *God Without Being*. Trans. Thomas A. Carlson. Chicago: University of Chicago Press, 1991. Japanese translation by S. Nagai

and M. Nakajima. Tokyo: Hosei University Press, 1995. *Bog bez bycia.* Trans. M. Franiewicz and K. Tarnowski. Carcovie: Znak, 1996. *Dieu sans l'être. Horstexte.* 2nd ed. Paris: Presses Universitaires de France, 2002. Chinese translation forthcoming. Japanese translation forthcoming.

——. *'Ce que cela donne.' Jean-François Lacalmontie.* Paris: Éditions de la Différence, 1986. Completely revised in *La croisée du visible.* 1991. Rev. ed. Paris: Éditions de la Différence, 1996.

——. *Prolégomènes à la charité.* 1986. 2nd ed. Paris: Éditions de la Différence, 1991. *Prolegomenos a la Caridad.* Trans. C. Diaz. Madrid: Caparros editores, 1993. *Prolegomena to Charity.* Trans. Stephen Lewis. Perspectives in Continental Philosophy. Ed. John D. Caputo. New York: Fordham University Press, 2002.

——. *Sur le prisme métaphysique de Descartes. Constitution et limites de l'ontothéo-logie dans la pensée cartésienne.* Paris: Presses Universitaires de France, 1986. *Il prismo metafisico di Descartes.* Trans. F. Ciro Papparo and G. Belgioioso. Milan, 1998. *On Descartes' Metaphysical Prism: The Constitution and the Limits of the Onto-theo-logy of Cartesian Thought.* Trans. Jeffrey L. Kosky. Chicago, IL: University of Chicago Press, 1999.

——. *Réduction et donation: recherches sur Husserl, Heidegger et la phénoménologie.* Paris: Presses Universitaires de France, 1989. Japanese translation. Tokyo: Kora Sha, 1995. *Reduction and Givenness: Investigations of Husserl, Heidegger and Phenomenology.* Trans. Thomas A. Carlson. Evanston, IL: Northwestern University Press, 1998.

——. *La croisée du visible.* 1991. Rev. ed. Paris: Éditions de la Différence, 1996. Presses Universitaires de France, 1996. *Crucea vizibilului. Tablou, televiziune, iciana—o privire fenomenologica.* Trans. M. Neauytu. Sibiu: Deisis, 2000. *Atvaizdo dovana.* Trans. N. Keryté. Vilnius: Vertimas, 2002. *The Crossing of the Visible.* Trans. James K. A. Smith. Stanford: Stanford University Press, 2004. Romanian translation forthcoming.

——. *Questions cartésiennes. Méthode et métaphysique.* Paris: Presses Universitaires de France, 1991. *Cartesian Questions: Method and Metaphysics.* Trans. Jeffrey L. Kosky, John Cottingham, and Stephen Voss. Chicago, IL: University of Chicago Press, 1999.

——. *Questions cartésiennes II. Sur l'ego et sur Dieu.* Paris: Presses Universitaires de France, 1996.

——. *Étant donné. Essai d'une phénoménologie de la donation.* Paris: Presses Universitaires de France, 1997. *Being Given: Toward a Phenomenology of Givenness.* Trans. Jeffrey L. Kosky. Stanford, CA: Stanford University Press, 2002. Italian translation by R. Caderone. Turin: S.E.I., 2002.

——. *De surcroît: études sur les phénomènes saturés.* Paris: Presses Universitaires de France, 2001. *In Excess: Studies of Saturated Phenomena.* Trans. Robyn Horner and Vincent Berraud. Perspectives in Continental Philosophy. Ed. John D. Caputo. New York: Fordham University Press, 2002. *In plus. Studii asupra fenomenelor saturata.* Trans. I. Biliuta. Sibiu: Deisis, 2003.

——. *Le phénomène érotique: Six méditations.* Paris: Grasset, 2003. Romanian translation forthcoming. English translation forthcoming.

1.2 Books Translated into English

Marion, Jean-Luc. *God Without Being*. Trans. Thomas A. Carlson. Chicago, IL:
University of Chicago Press, 1991.

——. *Reduction and Givenness: Investigations of Husserl, Heidegger and
Phenomenology*. Trans. Thomas A. Carlson. Evanston, IL: Northwestern
University Press, 1998.

——. *Cartesian Questions: Method and Metaphysics*. Trans. Jeffrey L. Kosky, John
Cottingham, and Stephen Voss. Chicago, IL: University of Chicago Press, 1999.

——. *On Descartes' Metaphysical Prism: The Constitution and the Limits of Onto-
theo-logy in Cartesian Thought*. Trans. Jeffrey L. Kosky. Chicago: University of
Chicago Press, 1999.

——. *The Idol and Distance: Five Studies*. Trans. Thomas A. Carlson. Perspectives
in Continental Philosophy. Ed. John D. Caputo. New York: Fordham University
Press, 2001.

——. *Being Given: Toward a Phenomenology of Givenness*. Trans. Jeffrey L.
Kosky. Stanford, CA: Stanford University Press, 2002.

——. *In Excess: Studies of Saturated Phenomena*. Trans. Robyn Horner and
Vincent Berraud. Perspectives in Continental Philosophy. Ed. John D. Caputo.
New York: Fordham University Press, 2002.

——. *Prolegomena to Charity*. Trans. Stephen Lewis. Perspectives in Continental
Philosophy. Ed. John D. Caputo. New York: Fordham University Press, 2002.

——. *The Crossing of the Visible*. Trans. James K. A. Smith. Stanford, CA: Stanford
University Press, 2004.

——. *Descartes' Grey Ontology. Cartesian Science and Aristotelian Thought in the
Regulae*. Trans. S. Donohue. South Bend, IN.: St. Augustine's Press, 2004.

1.3 Co-authored Books

Marion, Jean-Luc, and Alain de Benoist. *Avec ou sans Dieu?* Carrefour des Jeunes.
Ed. Guy Baret. Paris: Beauchesne, 1970.

Marion, Jean-Luc, and Jacques Lacourt. *La difficulté de croire*. Limoges: Droguet
et Ardant, 1980. *Foi à l'épreuve de l'incroyance*. Limoges: Droguet et Ardant,
1990.

Marion, Jean-Luc, and Alain Bonfand. *Hergé: Tintin le Terrible ou l'alphabet des
richesses*. Paris: Hachette, 1996.

1.4 Edited Books and Translations

Marion, Jean-Luc, ed. *Emmanuel Lévinas: Positivité et transcendence. Suivi de
Lévinas et la phénoménologie*. Paris: Presses Universitaires de France, 1999.

Marion, Jean-Luc, and Jean-Robert Armogathe, eds. *Index des 'Regulae ad
directionem ingenii' de René Descartes*. Rome: Edizioni dell'Ateneo, 1976.

Marion, Jean-Luc, trans. and ed., and Pierre Costabel. *René Descartes. Règles utiles et claires pour la direction de l'esprit en la recherche de la vérité.* The Hague: Martinus Nijhoff, 1977.

Marion, Jean-Luc, and Jean Deprun, eds. *La passion de la raison. Hommage à Ferdinand Alquié.* Paris: Presses Universitaires de France, 1983.

Marion, Jean-Luc, and Guy Planty-Bonjour, eds. *Phénoménologie et métaphysique.* Paris: Presses Universitaires de France, 1984.

Marion, Jean-Luc, Alain Bonfand, and Gérard Labrot, eds. *Trois essais sur la perspective.* 2nd ed. Paris: Éditions de la Différence, 1985.

Marion, Jean-Luc, and Nicolas Grimaldi, eds. *Le discours et sa Méthode.* Paris: Presses Universitaires de France, 1987.

Marion, Jean-Luc, and Jean-Marie Beyssade, eds. *Descartes: objecter et répondre.* Paris: Presses Universitaires de France, 1994.

Marion, Jean-Luc, and Marc B. de Launay, trans. and eds. *Edmund Husserl: Méditations cartésiennes.* Paris: Presses Universitaires de France, 1994.

Marion, Jean-Luc, et al., eds. *René Descartes: Index des Meditationes de prima Philosophia de R. Descartes.* Besançon: Annales littéraires de l'université de Franche-Compté, 1996.

Marion, Jean-Luc, and P. F. Moreau, eds. and trans. *Spinoza. Cogitata Metaphysica.* In *Spinoza. Oeuvres Complètes.* Paris: Presses Universitaires de France, 2000.

Marion, Jean-Luc, and Vincent Carraud. *Montaigne. Scepticisme, métaphysique et théologie.* Paris: Presses Universitaires de France, 2004.

1.5 Book Sections

Marion, Jean-Luc. "La rigueur de la louange." *Confession de la foi chrétienne.* Ed. Claude Bruaire. Paris: Fayard, 1977. 261–76. Trans. L. Wenzler. *Gott nennen. Phänomenologische Zugänge.* Ed. Bernhard Casper. Freiburg/München: Alber Verlag, 1981. Revised in *Dieu sans l'être. Hors-texte.* Paris: Arthème Fayard, 1982.

——. "La double idolâtrie. Remarques sur la différence ontologique et la pensée de Dieu." *Heidegger et la question de Dieu.* Eds. Richard Kearney and Joseph S. O'Leary. Paris: B. Grasset, 1980. Revised in *Dieu sans l'être. Hors-texte.* Paris: Arthème Fayard, 1982. Castilian translation. "La doble idolatria: Observaciones sobre la diferencia ontologica y el pensamiento de Dios" *Nombres* 96.

——. "L'instauration de la rupture: Gilson à la lecture de Descartes." *Étienne Gilson et nous: la philosophie et son histoire.* Ed. M. Couratier. Paris: J. Vrin, 1980. 13–34.

——. "Quelques objections à quelques réponses." *Heidegger et la question de Dieu.* Eds. Richard Kearney and Joseph S. O'Leary. Paris: B. Grasset, 1980. 304–09.

——. "Die Strenge der Liebe." *Gott nennen: Phänomenologische Zugänge.* Ed. Bernhard Casper. Freiburg/München: Alber Verlag, 1981. 165–87.

——. "Idol und Bild." *Phänomenologie des Idols.* Ed. Bernhard Casper. Freiburg/München: Alber Verlag, 1981. 107–32.

———. "Une nouvelle morale provisoire: la liberté d'être libre." *La morale, sagesse et salut.* Ed. Claude Bruaire. Paris: Communio Fayard, 1981.

———. "Avertissement." *E. Gilson. La liberté chez Descartes et la théologie.* Paris: J. Vrin, 1982. i–v.

———. "La vanité d'être et le nom de Dieu." *Analogie et dialectique. Essais de théologie fondamentale.* Eds. P. Gisel and P. Secretan. Geneva: Labor et Fides, 1982. 17–49. Revised in *Dieu sans l'être. Hors-texte.* Paris: Arthème Fayard, 1982. 17–50.

———. "Du pareil au même, ou: comment Heidegger permet de refaire de l'histoire de la philosophie." *Martin Heidegger.* Ed. Michel Haar. Paris: Éditions de l'Herne, 1983. 177–91.

———. "Les trois songes ou l'éveil du philosophe." *La passion de la raison. Hommage à Ferdinand Alquié.* Eds. J. Deprun and Jean-Luc Marion. Paris: Presses Universitaires de France, 1983. *Questions cartésiennes. Méthode et métaphysique.* Paris: Presses Universitaires de France, 1991.

———. "Avant propos." *Phénoménologie et métaphysique.* Eds. Jean-Luc Marion and Guy Planty-Bonjour. Paris: Presses Universitaires de France, 1984. 7–14.

———. "L'étant et le phénomène." *Phénoménologie et Métaphysique.* Eds. Jean-Luc Marion and G. Planty-Bonjour. Paris: Presses Universitaires de France, 1984. 159–209. Revised in *Réduction et donation.* Paris: Presses Universitaires de France, 1989.

———. "L'intentionnalité de l'amour." *Emmanuel Lévinas.* Ed. Jacques Rolland. Lagrasse: Éditions Verdier, 1984. 225–45. "L'intenzionalità dell'amore." *E si sporco le mani ... Prossimità ed estraneità.* Perugia: Collevanlenza, 1984. Hungarian translation in *Pannonhalmi Szemle,* 1994. Revised in *Prolégomènes à la charité.* Paris: Éditions de la différence, 1986.

———. "Splendeur de la contemplation eucharistique." *La politique de la mystique. Hommage à Mgr Maxime Charles.* Limoges: Critérion, 1984. 17–28.

———. "La croisée du visible et l'invisible." *Trois essais sur la perspective.* Eds. Jean-Luc Marion, A. Bonfand, and G. Labrot. 2nd ed. Paris: Éditions de la Différence, 1985. Revised in *La croisée du visible.* 1991. Paris: Presses Universitaires de France, 1996.

———. "Wahrheit in der europäischen Geschichte: Grund oder Gabe?" *Das europäische Erbe und seine christliche Zukunft.* Ed. N. von Lobkowicz. München, 1985.

———. "De la 'mort de Dieu' aux noms divins. L'itinéraire théologique de la métaphysique." *L'être et Dieu.* Ed. D. Bourg. Paris: Cerf, 1986.

———. "The Essential Incoherence of Descartes' Definition of Divinity." Trans. F. Van de Pitte. *Essays on Descartes' Meditations.* Ed. Amélie Oksenberg Rorty. Berkeley: University of California Press, 1986. 297–338.

———. "Aspekte der Religionsphänomenologie: Grund, Horizont und Offenbarung." *Religionsphilosophie heute: Chancen und Bedeutung in Philosophie und Theologie.* Eds. Lois Halder, Klaus Kienzler, and Joseph Möller. Düsseldorf, 1987. 84–102.

———. "La situation métaphysique du *Discours de la Méthode.*" *Le discours et sa*

Méthode. Eds. Jean-Luc Marion and Nicolas Grimaldi. Paris: Presses Universitaires de France, 1987. 365–94. "The Metaphysical Situation of the *Discourse on Method.*" Trans. Rosalind Gill and Roger Gannon. *René Descartes: Critical Assessments.* Ed. G. Moyal. London/New York: Routledge, 1991. Revised in *Questions cartésiennes. Méthode et métaphysique.* Paris: Presses Universitaires de France, 1991.

——. "Le prototype de l'image." *Nicée II, 787–1987. Douze siècles d'images religieuses.* Ed. F. Bloesflug and N. Lossky. Paris: Cerf, 1987. 451–70. Revised in *La croisée du visible.* 1991. Rev. ed. Paris: Éditions de la Différence, 1996.

——. "Descartes à l'encontre d'Aristote." *Aristote aujhourd'hui.* Ed. M. A. Sinaceur. Paris: Érès, 1988. 326–30.

——. *Emmanuel Lévinas: Autrement que Savoir.* Eds. G. Petitdemande and J. Rolland. Paris: Éditions Osiris, 1988. 74–6.

——. "L'interloqué." *Après le sujet qui vient?* Ed. Jean-Luc Nancy. Paris: Aubier, 1989. *Who Comes After the Subject?* Eds. E. Cadava, P. Connor, and J.-L. Nancy. London/New York: Routledge, 1991. "Podmiot w Wezwaniu." *Zawierzyc czlowiekowi. Ksiedzu Jozefowi Tischerowi na szescdziesiate urodziny.* Crocovie: Znaxk, 1992. Revised in "Le sujet en dernier appeal." *Revue de Métaphysique et de Morale.* 96.1 (1991): 77–96. "L'essere e la rivendicazione." *Heidegger e la metafisica.* Ed. M. Ruggenini. Gênes, 1991. "El sujeto en última instancia." Trans. R. Rodriguea. *Revista de Filosofía.* VI.10 (1993). "The Final Appeal of the Subject." Trans. Simon Critchley. *Deconstructive Subjectivities.* Ed. Simon Critchley and Peter Dews. 85–104. Albany, NY: State University of New York Press, 1996. Reprinted in *The Religious.* Ed. John D. Caputo. Oxford: Blackwell, 2002. 131–44.

——. "Phänomenologie und Offenbarung." Trans. R. Funk. *Religionsphilosophie heute: Chancen und Bedeutung in Philosophie und Theologie.* Eds. Lois Halder, Klaus Kienzler, and Joseph Möller. Düsseldorf, 1988. "Filosofia e Rivelazione." Trans. F. Volpi. *Studia Patavina. Revista di Scienze religiose.* XXXI.3 (1989). "Le possible et la Révélation." *Eros et Eris. Contributions to a Hermeneutical Phenomenology. Liber amicorum for Adriaan Peperzak.* Ed. P. J. M. van Tongeren et al. The Hague: Kluwer Academic, 1992. 217–32.

——. "… plus en pratique qu'en théorie." *Problématique et réception du Discours de la Méthode et des Essais.* Ed. H. Méchoulan. Paris: J. Vrin, 1988.

——. "Préface." *René Descartes et Martin Schook. La querelle d'Utrecht.* Ed. T. Verbeek. Paris: Les impressiones nouvelles, 1988. 7–17.

——. "Théo-logique." *Encyclopédie philosophique universelle.* Ed. André Jacob and Jean-François Mattei. Vol. I. Paris: Presses Universitaires de France, 1989. 17–25.

——. "L'interprétation criticiste de Descartes et Leibniz: Critique d'une critique." *Ernst Cassirer. De Marbourg à New York: L'itinéraire philosophique.* Ed. Jean Seidengart. Paris: Les éditions du Cerf, 1990. 29–42.

——. "Spinoza et les trois noms de Dieu." *Herméneutique et ontologie: mélanges en hommage à Pierre Aubenque.* Eds. Remi Brague and Jean-François Courtine. Paris: Presses Universitaires de France, 1990. 225–45. "The Coherence of

Spinoza's Definitions of God in *Ethics I*, Proposition 11." *God and Nature: Spinoza's Metaphysics*. Ed. Yirmayhu Yovel. Leiden: E. J. Brill, 1991. 61–77.

——. "Cartesian Metaphysics and the Role of the Simple Natures." *The Cambridge Companion to Descartes*. Ed. J. Cottingham. New York: Cambridge University Press, 1992. *Questions cartésiennes. Méthode et métaphysique*. Paris: Presses Universitaires de France, 1991. Metodo e metafisica: la nature simplici. *Cartesiana*. Ed. Giulia Belgioioso. Lecce: Università degli Studi di Lecce, 1992.

——. "Constitution et crise de la métaphysique." *Le XVIIè siècle. Diversité et cohérence*. Ed. J. Truchet. Paris: Berger-Levrault, 1992.

——. "Heidegger and Descartes." *Martin Heidegger: Critical Assessments*. Ed. Christopher Macann. London: Routledge, 1992. 178–207.

——. "Le colloque de Lecce et les perspectives des études cartésiennes." *Cartesiana*. Ed. Giulia Belgioioso. Lecce: Università degli Studi di Lecce, 1992.

——. "Le phénomène saturé." *Phénoménologie et théologie*. Ed. Jean-François Courtine. Paris: Critérion, 1992. 79–128. "The Saturated Phenomenon." Trans. Thomas A. Carlson. *Philosophy Today* 40.1–4 (1996): 103–24. "Fenomenaul saturat." Trans. N. Ionel. *Fenomenoolgie si Teologie*. Iasi, 1996.

——. "Vorwort." Michel Henry. *Radikale Lebensphänomenologie*. Freiburg: Alber Verlag, 1992. 9–16.

——. "Generosity and Phenomenology: Remarks on Michel Henry's Interpretation of the Cartesian *Cogito*." Trans. Stephen Voss. *Essays on the Philosophy and Science of René Descartes*. Ed. Stephen Voss. New York: Oxford University Press, 1993. 52–74. *Questions cartésiennes. Méthode et métaphysique*. Paris: Presses Universitaires de France, 1991.

——. "L'image et la liberté." *Saint Bernard et la philosophie*. Ed. Remi Brague. Paris: Presses Universitaires de France, 1993. 49–72.

——. "Note sur l'indifférence ontologique." *Emmanuel Lévinas. L'éthique comme philosophie première*. Eds. Jean Greisch and Jacques Rolland. Paris: Cerf, 1993. 47–62. Trans. Jeffrey L. Kosky. *The Graduate Faculty Philosophy Journal* (New School for Social Research). (1996).

——. "Métaphysique et phénoménologie: une relève pour la théologie." *L'avenir de la métaphysique*. Toulouse: Bulletin de littérature ecclésiastique, 1993–94. 189–206. "Metaphysics and Phenomenology: a Relief for Theology." Trans. Thomas A. Carlson. *Critical Inquiry* 20.4 (1994): 572–91. "Metaphysics and Phenomenology: A Summary for Theologians." Trans. A. McGeoch. *The Postmodern God: A Theological Reader*. Ed. Graham Ward. Oxford: Blackwell, 1997. 279–96.

——. "*Aporias* and the Origins of Spinoza's Theory of Adequate Ideas." *Spinoza on Knowledge and the Human Mind*. Ed. Y. Yovel. Leiden: E. J. Brill, 1994. 129–58. "Aporie ed origini della teoria spinoziana dell'idea adeguata." *L'etica e il suo altro*. Ed. C. Vigna. Milan, 1994. "Apories et origines de la théorie spinoziste de l'idée adéquate." *Philosophiques*. Paris: Kimé, 1998.

——. "Entre analogie et principe de raison suffisante: la *causa sui*." *Descartes. Objecter et répondre*. Eds. Jean-Luc Marion and Jean-Marie Beyssade. Paris:

Presses Universitaires de France, 1994. 305–35. *Questions cartésiennes II. Sur l'ego et sur Dieu.* Paris: Presses Universitaires de France, 1996.

——. "Konstanten der kritischen Vernunft." *Vernunftbegriffe in der Moderne.* Eds. H. F. Fulda and R. P. Hortsmann. Stuttgart: Hegel-Vereinigung, 1994. 104–26. Revised in *Questions cartésiennes II. Sur l'ego et sur Dieu.* Paris: Presses Universitaires de France, 1996.

——. "Le statut originairement responsorial des *Meditationes.*" *Descartes. Objecter et répondre.* Eds. Jean-Luc Marion and Jean-Marie Beyssade. Paris: Presses Universitaires de France, 1994. 3–19. "The Place of the *Objections* in the Development of Cartesian Metaphysics." *Descartes and His Contemporaries: Meditations, Objections and Replies.* Ed. R. Ariew and M. Grene. Chicago: University of Chicago Press, 1995. *Questions cartésiennes II. Sur l'ego et sur Dieu.* Paris: Presses Universitaires de France, 1996.

——. "L'ego cartesiano e le sue interpretazioni fenomenologiche: al di là della representatione." *Descartes metafisico. Interpretationi del Novecento.* Eds. Jean-Robert Armogathe and Giulia Belgioioso. Roma, 1994.

——. "Préface." Philippe Cormier. *Généalogie de personne.* Paris: Critérion, 1994.

——. "Tintin le terrible." Jean-Luc Marion and Alain Bonfand, eds. *Hergé: Tintin le Terrible ou l'alphabet des richesses.* Paris: Hachette, 1996.

——. "Nothing and Nothing Else." *The Ancients and the Moderns.* Ed. Reginald Lilly. Studies in Continental Thought. Bloomington: Indiana University Press, 1996. 183–95.

——. "The Idea of God." Trans. Thomas A. Carlson and Daniel Garber. *The Cambridge History of Seventeenth-Century Philosophy.* Eds. Daniel Garber and Michael Ayers. Vol. I. Cambridge: Cambridge University Press, 1998. 265–304. Revised in *Questions cartésiennes II. Sur l'ego et sur Dieu.* Paris: Presses Universitaires de France, 1996.

——. "La 'règle générale' de vérité. Meditatio III, AT VII, 34–36." *Lire Descartes Aujourd'hui.* Eds. O. Depré and D. Lories. *Actes du Colloque de Louvain-la-Neuve.* June, 1996. Louvain-Paris, 1997. *Questions cartésiennes II. Sur l'ego et sur Dieu.* Paris: Presses Universitaires de France, 1996.

——. "Notes sur les modalités de l'ego." *Chemins de Descartes.* Eds. P. Soual and Miklos Vetö. Paris: L'Harmattan, 1997.

——. "Justice et transcendance." *Difficile Liberté. Dans la trace d'Emmanuel Lévinas.* Paris: Albin Michel, 1998. 53ff.

——. "La voix sans nom." *Rue Descartes: Emmanuel Lévinas.* Paris: Collège International de Philosophie, 1998. 11–26. "The Voice Without Name: Homage to Lévinas." *The Face of the Other and the Trace of God: Essays on the Philosophy of Emmanuel Lévinas.* Ed. Jeffrey Bloechl. New York: Fordham University Press, 2000. 224–242.

——. "La création des vérités éternelles—le réseau d'une 'question'." *La biografia intelletuale di René Descartes Attraverso la correspondance.* Eds. Jean-Robert Armogathe, Guilia Belgioioso, and C. Verti. Naples: Vivarium, 1999.

——. "La prise de chair comme donation de soi." *Encyclopédie philosophique universelle*. Ed. Jean-François Mattei. Vol. IV. Paris: Presses Universitaires de France, 1999. "La prise de chair comme donation de soi." *Incarnation. Archivio di Filosofia*. Ed. Marco M. Olivetti. Roma, 1999. Revised in *De surcroît: études sur les phénomènes saturés*. Paris: Presses Universitaires de France, 2001.

——. "Specificità filosofica della storia delle filosofia." *La filosofia e le sue storie*. Lecce, 1998. "D'une quadruple méthode pour lire les textes de la philosophie: la pertinence d'Henri Gouhier." *Le regard d'Henri Gouhier*. Ed. Denise Leduc-Fayette. Paris: J. Vrin, 1999. 103–20.

——. "'Christian Philosophy': Hermeneutic or Heuristic?" *The Question of Christian Philosophy Today*. Ed. Francis J. Ambrosio. Perspectives in Continental Philosophy. Ed. John D. Caputo. New York: Fordham University Press, 1999. 247–64.

——. "In the Name: How to Avoid Speaking of 'Negative Theology' (including Derrida's Response to Jean-Luc Marion)." *God, the Gift and Postmodernism*. Eds. John D. Caputo and Michael Scanlon. Bloomington, IN: Indiana University Press, 1999. 122–53. Revised in *In Excess: Studies of Saturated Phenomena*. Trans. Robyn Horner and Vincent Berraud. Perspectives in Continental Philosophy. Ed. John D. Caputo. New York: Fordham University Press, 2002.

——. "La science toujours recherché et toujours manquante." *La métaphysique. Son histoire, sa critique, ses enjeux (Acts of the XXVIIth Congress of the Association des sociétés de philosophie de langue française)*. Eds. Jean-Marc Narbonne and Luc Langois. Québec-Paris: Vrin/Presses de L'Université Laval, 1999. 13–36. "La scienza sempre cercata e sempre mancante." *Ri-pensar Diritto*. Ed. P. Ventura. Turin: G. Giappichelli, 2000.

——. "The Original Otherness of the Ego: A Re-reading of Descartes' Meditatio II." *The Ethical*. Eds. Edith Wyschogrod and G. McKenny. Oxford: Blackwell, 1999. *Questions cartésiennes II. Sur l'ego et sur Dieu*. Paris: Presses Universitaires de France, 1996.

——. "D'Autrui à L'Individu." *Emmanuel Lévinas: Positivité et transcendence*. Ed. Jean-Luc Marion. Paris: Presses Universitaires de France, 2000. 287–308. "From the Other to the Individual." Trans. Robyn Horner. *Transcendence*. Ed. Regina Schwartz. London: Routledge, 2004.

——. "Descartes et l'expérience de la finitude." *L'Esprit cartésien*. Ed. Berard Bourgois and J. Havet. Paris: Vrin, 2000.

——. "Préface." *Pétrarque: Le repos religieux*. Ed. and Trans. Christophe Carraud. Grenoble: J. Millon, 2000.

——. "La conscience du don." *Le don. Théologie, philosophie, psychologie, sociologie*. Ed. J.-N.Dumont. Colloque interdisciplinaire sous la direction de J.-L. Marion. Lyon, 2001. "L'incoscienza del dono." *Il codice del dono. Verità e gratuità nelle ontologie del novecento*. Ed. G. Ferretti. Atti del IX Colloquio su Filosopfia e Religione. Macerata, 2003. Revised in *Die Normativität des Wirklichen. Robert Spaemann, zum 75.Geburtstag*. Eds. T. Buchheim, R. Schönberger, and W. Schweidler. Stuttgart, 2002. 458–482.

——. "Ils le reconnurent et lui-même leur devint invisible." *Demain l'église*. Eds. Jean Duchesne and Jacques Ollier. Paris: Flammarion, 2001. 134–43. "They

Recognized Him; and He Became Invisible to Them." *Modern Theology* 18.2 (2002): 145–52.

——. "The Formal Reason For the Infinite." *The Blackwell Companion to Postmodern Theology.* Ed. Graham Ward. Blackwell Companions to Religion. Oxford: Blackwell, 2001. "La raison formelle de l'infini." *Christiannisme. Héritages et destins.* Paris: Le livre de poche, 2002.

——. "La fenomenalita del sacramento: essere e donazione." *Il mondo del sacramento. Teologia e filosofia a confronto.* Ed. Nicola Reali. Milano: Paoline, 2001. 134–54. "La phénoménalité du sacrement: être et donation." *Communio* XXVI.5 (2001).

——. "Phänomen und Transzendenz." *Mythisierung Der Transzendenz als Entwurf ihrer Erfahrung: Arbeitsdokumentation eines Symposiums.* Eds. Gerhard Oberhammer and Marcus Schmeicher. Verlag der Österreichischen Akademie der Wissenschaften, 2003.

——. Préface. Emmanuel Housset. *L'Intelligence de la Pitié. Phénoménologie et Communauté.* Paris: Cerf, 2003.

——. "The End of Metaphysics as a Possibility." *Religion After Metaphysics.* Ed. Mark A. Wrathall. Cambridge: Cambridge University Press, 2003. 166–89.

——. "The Original Otherness of the *Ego*: a Rereading of Descartes' *Meditation II*." *The Ethical.* Eds. E. Wyschogrod and G. McKenny. Oxford: Blackwell, 2003.

——. "From the Other to the Individual." Trans. Robyn Horner. *Transcendence.* Ed. Regina Schwartz. London: Routledge, 2004.

——. "Objectivité et donation." *Le souci du passage. Hommage à Jean Greisch.* Eds. Ph. Capelle, G. Hébert, and M.-D. Popelard. Paris, 2004. 43–59.

——. "Qui suis-je pour ne pas dire *ego sum, ego existo*?" *Montaigne: scepticisme, métaphysique, théologie.* Eds. V. Carraud and J.-L. Marion. Paris: Presses Universitaires de France, 2004.

Marion, Jean-Luc, and Jean-Robert Armogathe. "Contribution à la sémantèse d'*ordre/ordo* chez Descartes." *Ordo Atti del II Colloquio Internationale del Lessico Intellectuale Europeo.* Rome, 1980.

Kearney, Richard, Jacques Derrida, and Jean-Luc Marion. "On the Gift: A Discussion between Jacques Derrida and Jean-Luc Marion, Moderated by Richard Kearney." *God, the Gift and Postmodernism.* Eds. John D. Caputo and Michael J. Scanlon. Bloomington, IN: Indiana University Press, 1999. 54–78.

1.6 Journal Articles

Marion, Jean-Luc. "Distance et béatitude: sur le mot capacitas chez Saint Augustin." *Résurrection* 29 (1968): 58–80.

——. "La saisie trinitaire selon l'Esprit de saint Augustin." *Résurrection* 28 (1968): 66–94.

——. "Remarques sur le concept de Révélation chez R. Bultmann." *Résurrection* 27 (1968): 29–42.

——. "Ce mystère qui juge celui qui le juge." *Résurrection* 32 (1969): 54–78.

——. "La splendeur de la contemplation eucharistique." *Résurrection* 31 (1969): 84–88.

——. "Penser juste ou trahir le mystère: notes sur l'elaboration patristique du dogme de l'incarnation." *Résurrection* 30 (1969): 68–93.

——. "Amour de Dieu, amour des hommes." *Résurrection* 34 (1970): 89–96.

——. "Distance et louange." *Résurrection* 38 (1971): 89–118.

——. "Généalogie de la 'Mort de Dieu'." *Résurrection* 36 (1971): 30–53.

——. "Note sur l'athéisme conceptuel." *Résurrection* 38 (1971): 119–20.

——. "Note sur le choix d'un analogon." *Résurrection* 38 (1971): 121–22.

——. "Le fondement de la *cogitatio* selon le *De Intellectus Emendatione*: Essai d'une lecture des §§104–105." *Les Études Philosophiques* (1972): 357–68.

——. "Les deux volontés du Christ selon saint Maxime le Confesseur." *Résurrection* 41 (1972): 48–66.

——. "A propos d'une sémantique de la Méthode." *Revue Internationale de Philosophie* 27.103 (1973): 37–48.

——. "De la divinisation à la domination: étude sur la sémantique de *capax/capable* chez Descartes." *Revue philosophique de Louvain* (1973). Revised in *Questions cartésiennes. Méthode et métaphysique.* Paris: Presses Universitaires de France, 1991.

——. "Ordre et relation. Sur la situation aristotélicienne de la théorie cartésienne de l'ordre selon les *Regulae V* et *VI*." *Archives de Philosophie* 37 (1974): 243–74.

——. "Présence et distance: remarques sur l'implication réciproque de la contemplation eucharistique et de la présence réelle." *Résurrection* 43–44 (1974): 31–58.

——. "Bulletin cartésien IV." *Archives Philosophie* 38 (1975): 253–309.

——. "Droit à la confession." *Communio* 1 (1975): 17–27.

——. "Heidegger et la situation métaphysique de Descartes." *Archives de Philosophie* 38.2 (1975): 253–63.

——. "Intimität durch Abstand: Grundgesetz christlichen Betens." *Internationale Katholische Zeitschrift 'Communio'* 4 (1975): 218–27.

——. "Le verbe et le texte." *Résurrection* 46 (1975): 63–80.

——. "Après Ecône." *Communio* I.8 (1976): 87–91.

——. "L'ambivalence de la métaphysique cartésienne." *Les Études Philosophiques* 4 (1976): 443–60.

——. "Le présent et le don." *Revue Catholique Internationale Communio* II.6 (1977): 50–70. Reprinted in *L'eucharistie, pain nouveau pour un monde rompu.* Paris: Fayard, 1980. Revised in *Dieu sans l'être. Hors-texte.* Paris: Arthème Fayard, 1982. Rev. ed. Paris: Presses Universitaires de France, 1991.

——. "De connaître à aimer: l'éblouissement." *Revue Catholique Internationale Communio* III (1978): 17–28. "L'évidence et l'éblouissement." *Prolégomènes à la charité.* 2nd ed. Paris: Éditions de la Différence, 1986.

——. "A interdisciplinaridade como questao para a filosofia." *Presença filosofica* 1 (1978): 15–27. French text in *A Filosofía e as ciencias.* IV. Rio de Janiero: Semana Internacional de Filosofía, 1978.

——. "Clavel philosophe?" *Revue Catholique Internationale Communio* IV (1979): 73–75.

——. "De l'éminente dignité des pauvres baptisés." *Revue Catholique Internationale Communio* IV.2 (1979): 27–44.

——. "Fragments sur l'idole et l'icone." *Revue de Métaphysique et de Morale* 84.4 (1979): 433–45. Trans. L. Wenzler. *Phänomenologie des Idols*, ed. Berhard Casper. Freiburg/München: Alber Verlag, 1981. "Ce que montre l'idole." *Rencontres de l'École du Louvre. L'idolatrie*. Paris: Documentation française, 1990. 23–34. Trans. A. Vassiliu. *Viata Româneasca* (1996). Revised in *Dieu sans l'être. Hors-texte*. Paris: Arthème Fayard, 1982. Rev. ed. Paris: Presses Universitaires de France, 1991.

——. "Le mal en personne." *Revue Catholique Internationale Communio* IV.3 (1979): 28–42. "Das Böse in Person." *Internationale Katholique Zeitschrift Communio* 8 (1979) 243–50. *Prolégomènes à la charité*. 1986. 2nd ed. Paris: Éditions de la Différence, 1991.

——. "L'angoisse et l'ennui. Pout interpréter 'Was ist Metaphysik?'" *Archives de Philosophie* 43.1 (1980): 121–46.

——. "Le système ou l'étoile. Étude de l'ouvrage de F. Rosenzweig, *Der Stern der Erlösung*." *Archives de Philosophie* 43.1 (1980).

——. "Les chemins de la recherche sur le jeune Descartes. Notes bibliographiques sur quelques ouvrages récents (1966–1977)." *XVIIe siècle* 1 (1980).

——. "L'être et l'affection. A propos de *La conscience affective* de F. Alquié." *Archives de Philosophie* 43.1 (1980): 433–41.

——. "L'idéologie, ou la violence sans ombre." *Revue Catholique Internationale Communio* V.6 (1980): 82–92.

——. "Paradoxe sur une doctrine." *Revue Catholique Internationale Communio* VI.2 (1981): 2–5. "Paradox van een benaming." *Internationale Katholique Zeitschrift Communio* 6 (1981): 81–6.

——. "Descartes et l'onto-théologie." *Bulletin de la Société française de Philosophie* 76.4 (1982): 117–71. *Giornale di Metafisica* (1984). "Die cartesianische Ontotheologie." *Zeitschrift für philosophische Forschung* (1984). *Auslegungen. Descartes.* Ed. T. Keutner. Frankfurt am Main: Peter Lang, 1993. "Descartes and Onto-theo-logy." Trans. B. Bergo. *Post-Secular Philosophy: Between Philosophy and Theology.* Ed. Phillip Blond. London: Routledge and Paul, 1998. Revised in *Sur le prisme métaphysique de Descartes. Constitution et limites de l'onto-théo-logie dans la pensée cartésienne.* Paris: Presses Universitaires de France, 1986

——. "Le présent de l'homme." *Revue Catholique Internationale Communio* VII.4 (1982): 2–9.

——. "La crise et la Croix." *Revue Catholique Internationale Communio* VIII.3 (1983): 8–22. *Prolégomènes à la charité*. 1986. 2nd ed. Paris: Éditions de la Différence, 1991.

——. "Le don glorieux d'une présence." *Revue Catholique Internationale Communio* VIII (1983): 35–51. *Prolégomènes à la charité*. 1986. 2nd ed. Paris: Éditions de la Différence, 1991.

——. "Le système ou l'étoile. Étude de l'ouvrage de F. Rosenzweig, *Der Stern der Erlösung* dont une traduction française vient de paraître." *Archives de Philosophie* 46.3 (1983): 429–43.

——. "La percée et l'élargissement. Contribution à l'interprétation des *Recherches Loqiques* de Husserl." *Philosophie* 2 (1984): 67–91, 3 (1984): 67–88. *Réduction et donation*. Paris: Presses Universitaires de France, 1989.

——. "L'âme et la paix. A propos du pacifisme." *Commentaire* 7.26 (1984): 237–42. *Identit`culturale dell'Europa. La vie della pace*. Turin: A.I.C., 1984. "Limpegno del cristiano." *Strumento internazionale per un lavoro teologico Communio* 83–84 (1985). "Per costruire la pace." *Strumento internazionale per un lavoro teologico Communio* 104 (1989). "Das Herz des Friedens. Anmerkungen zum Pazifismus. *Internationale katholische Zeitschrift Communio*. (1985). "El alma de la paz. A propósito del pacifismo." *Revista Católica Internacional Communio* V.7 (1985).

——. "L'autre regard." *Presença filosofica* 10.3–4 (1984): 60–65.

——. "De la création des vérités au principe de raison suffisante. Remarques sur l'anti-cartésianisme de Spinoza, Malebranche et Leibniz." *XVIIè siècle* 147.2 (1985): 143–64. Revised in *Questions cartésiennes II. Sur l'ego et sur Dieu*. Paris: Presses Universitaires de France, 1996.

——. "De la 'mort de Dieu' aux noms divins. L'itinéraire théologique de la métaphysique." *Laval Théologique et Philosophique* 41.1 (1985): 25–41. *L'être et Dieu*. Ed. D. Bourg. Paris: Cerf, 1986.

——. "L'avenir du catholicisme." *Revue Catholique Internationale Communio* X.5–6 (1985): 38–47.

——. "La fin de la fin de la métaphysique." *Laval Théologique et Philosophique* 42.1 (1986): 23–33. "The End of the 'End of Metaphysics'." *Epoche: A Journal for the History of Philosophy* 2 (1996): 1–22.

——. "L'unique ego et l'altération de l'autre." *Archivio di Filosofia* 54.1–3 (1986): 607–24. Revised in *Questions cartésiennes. Méthode et métaphysique*. Paris: Presses Universitaires de France, 1991.

——. "On Descartes' Constitution of Metaphysics." *The Graduate Faculty of Philosophy Journal* 11.1 (1986): 21–33.

——. "Sur les figures de la relation entre rationalité et progrès." *Revue tunisienne des Études Philosophiques* 5 (1986).

——. "Différence ontologique ou question de l'être; une indécidé de *Sein und Zeit*." *Tijdschrift voor Filosofie* 49.4 (1987): 602–45. Revised in *Réduction et donation*. Paris: Presses Universitaires de France, 1989.

——. "La conversion de la volonté selon 'L'action'." *Revue Philosophique de la France et de l'Étranger* (1987): 33–46. *Maurice Blondel: une dramatique de la modernité*. Ed. D. Folscheid. Paris: Presses Universitaires de France, 1990. 154–65.

——. "L'aveugle à Siloé ou le report de l'image à son original." *Revue Catholique Internationale Communio* XII.6 (1987): 17–34. Revised in *La croisée du visible*. 1991. Rev. ed. Paris: Éditions de la Différence, 1996.

——. "L'*ego* et le *Dasein*. Heidegger et la 'Destruktion' de Descartes dans *Sein und*

Zeit." *Revue de Métaphysique et de Morale* 92.1 (1987): 25–53. *Réduction et donation.* Paris: Presses Universitaires de France, 1989. *Critical Heidegger.* Ed. C. McCann. London: Routledge and Paul, 1996.

——. "L'exactitude de l'ego." *Les Études Philosophiques* (1987): 3–10. *Destins et enjeux du XVIIIe siècle.* Paris: Presses Universitaires de France, 1985. "The Exactitude of the 'Ego'." Trans. Stephen Voss. *American Catholic Philosophical Quarterly* 67.4 (1993).

——. " 'Ego autem substantia.' Überlegungen über den metaphysischen Status des ersten Prinzips bei Descartes." *Philos. Jahrb.* 95 (1988): 54–71.

——. "Générosité et phénoménologie. Remarques sur l'interprétation du *cogito* cartésien par Michel Henry." *Les Études Philosophiques* 1 (1988). Revised in *Questions cartésiennes. Méthode et métaphysique.* Paris: Presses Universitaires de France, 1991. *Essays on the Philosophy and Science of René Descartes.* Ed. S. Voss. New York/Oxford: Oxford University Press, 1993. Greek translation by D. Rosakis. Athens, 1997. *Cartesian Questions: Method and Metaphysics.* Trans. Jeffrey L. Kosky, John Cottingham and Stephen Voss. Chicago, IL: University of Chicago Press, 1999.

——. "L'interloqué." Trans. E. Cadava and A. Tomiche. *Topoi* 7.2 (1988): 175–80. French version in *Confrontation.* Cahier 20. Paris, 1989. *Après le sujet qui vient?* Ed. Jean-Luc Nancy. Paris: Aubier, 1989. "El Interpelado." Trans. J.-L. Vermal. *Taula. Quaderns de pesament.* Palma de Majorque: Universitat de les Illes Balears, 1990. "L'interloqué." *Who Comes After the Subject?* Eds E. Cadava, P. Connor, and J.-L. Nancy. London/New York: Routledge, 1991. "Podmiot w Wezwaniu." *Zawierzyc czlowiekowi. Ksiedzu Jozefowi Tischerowi na szescdziesiate urodziny.* Crocovie: Znaxk, 1992. Revised in "Le sujet en dernier appeal." *Revue de Métaphysique et de Morale.* 96.1 (1991): 77–96. "L'essere e la rivendicazione." *Heidegger e la metafisica.* Ed. M. Ruggenini. Gênes, 1991. "El sujeto en última instancia." Trans. R. Rodriguea. *Revista de Filosofía.* VI.10 (1993). "The Final Appeal of the Subject." Trans. Simon Critchley. *Deconstructive Subjectivities.* Eds. Simon Critchley and Peter Dews. 85–104. Albany, NY: State University of New York Press, 1996. Reprinted in *The Religious.* Ed. John D. Caputo. Oxford: Blackwell, 2002. 131–44.

——. "À Dieu, rien d'impossible." *Revue Catholique Internationale Communio* XIV.5 (1989): 43–58.

——. "L'analogie." *Les Études Philosophiques* 3.4 (1989).

——. "L'argument relève-t-il de l'ontologie?" *Archivio di Filosofia* 57 (1990). *L'argomento ontologico. The Ontological Argument. L'argument ontologique. Der ontologische Gottesbeweis.* Roma: Biblioteca dell' "Archivio di Filosofia," 1990. *Questions cartésiennes. Méthode et métaphysique.* Paris: Presses Universitaires de France, 1991. "Is the Ontological Argument Ontological?" *The Journal of the History of Philosophy* 28 (1992). *Cartesian Questions: Method and Metaphysics.* Trans. Jeffrey L. Kosky, John Cottingham, and Stephen Voss. Chicago, IL: University of Chicago Press, 1999. "Is the Ontological Argument Ontological? The Argument According to Anselm and Its Metaphysical Interpretation According to Kant." *Flight of the Gods: Philosophical*

Perspectives on Negative Theology. Eds. Ilse N. Bulhof and Laurens ten Kate. New York: Fordham University Press, 2000. 78–99.

——. "Réponses à quelques questions." *Revue de Métaphysique et de Morale* 96 (1991): 65–76.

——. "Apologie de l'argument." *Revue Catholique Internationale Communio* XVII.2–3 (1992): 12–33.

——. "Christian Philosophy and Charity." *Communio* XVII (1992): 465–73.

——. "Esquisse d'une histoire du nom de Dieu dans la philosophie du XVII siècle." *Nouvelles de la République des Lettres* 2 (1993). Revised in "The Idea of God." Trans. Thomas A. Carlson and Daniel Garber. *The Cambridge History of Seventeenth-Century Philosophy.* Eds. Daniel Garber and Michael Ayers. Vol. I. Cambridge: Cambridge University Press, 1998. 265–304. *Questions cartésiennes II. Sur l'ego et sur Dieu.* Paris: Presses Universitaires de France, 1996.

——. "Philosophie chrétienne et herméneutique de la charité." *Revue Catholique Internationale Communio* XVIII.2 (1993): 89–96.

——. "Erkenntnis durch Liebe." *Internationale Katholische Zeitschrift 'Communio'* (1994): 387–99.

——. "Esquisse d'un concept phénoménologique du don." *Archivio di Filosofia* LXII.1–3 (1994): 75–94. *Phénoménologie et herméneutique.* Lausanne: Payot, 1997. "Sketch of a Phenomenological Concept of the Gift." *Postmodern Philosophy and Christian Thought.* Eds. J. Conley and D. Poe. Bloomington, IN: Indiana University Press, 1999.

——. "La connaissance de la charité." *Revue Catholique Internationale Communio* XIX.6 (1994): 27–42. "What Love Knows." *Prolegomena to Charity.* Trans. Stephen Lewis. New York: Fordham University Press, 2002. 153–69.

——. "Le concept de métaphysique selon Mersenne." *Les Études Philosophiques* 106.1–2 (1994): 129–43. Revised in *Questions cartésiennes II. Sur l'ego et sur Dieu.* Paris: Presses Universitaires de France, 1996.

——. *Philosophie. Phénomenologie et théologie.* Vol. 42. Paris: Minuit, 1994.

——. "A propos de Descartes et Suarez. *Revue Internationale de Philosophie.* (1996). "Sostanza e sussistenza. Suarez e il tratatto della substantia nei Principia I, §51–54." *Descartes: Principia Philosophiae.* Ed. Jean-Robert Armogathe and Guilia Belgioioso. Naples: Vivarium, 1996. *Questions cartésiennes II.* Paris: Presses Universitaires de France, 1996.

——. "L'obscure évidence de la volonté. Pascal au-delà de la *regula generalis* de Descartes." *XVIIè siècle* 185.4 (1994). Revised in *Questions cartésiennes II. Sur l'ego et sur Dieu.* Paris: Presses Universitaires de France, 1996.

——. "Réponses à J.-L. Vieillard-Baron à propos d'une hypothèse sur saint Bernard et l'image de Dieu." *Philosophie* 42 (1994): 62–68.

——. "Saint Thomas d'Aquin et l'onto-théo-logie." *Revue Thomiste* XCV (1995): 31–66. *Dieu sans l'être. Hors-texte.* 2nd ed. Paris: Presses Universitaires de France, 2002. "Saint Thomas Aquinas and Onto-theo-logy." Trans. B. Gendreau, R. Rethty, and M. Sweeney. *Mystic: Presence and Aporia.* Ed. M. Kessler and C. Sheppard. Chicago, IL: University of Chicago Press, 2003.

——. "L'altérité de l'ego. Une relecture de Descartes, Meditatio II." *Archivio di Filosofia* VXIV.1–3 (1996): 583–602.

——. "L'autre philosophie première et la question de la donation." *Philosophie* 49 (1996). Revised in *Le statut contemporain de la philosophie première.* Ed. P. Capelle. Paris: Beauchesne, 1996. "La donazione in filosofia." *Annuario filosofica* 12 (1996). German translation in *Festschrift für Bernhard Casper.* Freibourg. "The Other First Philosophy and the Question of Givenness." Trans. Jeffrey L. Kosky *Critical Inquiry* 25.4 (1999): 784–800. *De surcroît: études sur les phénomènes saturés.* Paris: Presses Universitaires de France, 2001.

——. "Présentation de travaux actuels." *Les Études Philosophiques* 1–2 (1996): 1–2.

——. "À propos de Descartes et Suarez." *Revue Internationale de Philosophie* 50.1 (1996): 109–31. Revised in *Questions cartésiennes II. Sur l'ego et sur Dieu.* Paris: Presses Universitaires de France, 1996.

——. "Quelques règles en l'histoire de la philosophie." *Les Études Philosophiques* 4 (1996): 495–510.

——. "The Saturated Phenomenon." *Philosophy Today* 40.1–4 (1996): 103–24.

——. "Le paradigme cartésien de la métaphysique." *Laval Théologique et Philosophique* 53.3 (1997): 785–91.

——. "A Note Concerning the Ontological Difference." *The Graduate Faculty of Philosophy Journal* 20.2 (1998): 25–40.

——. "Au nom. Comment ne pas parler de 'théologie négative'." *Laval théologique et philosophique* 55.3 (1999): 339–63. "In the Name: How to Avoid Speaking of 'Negative Theology' (including Derrida's Response to Jean-Luc Marion)." *God, the Gift and Postmodernism.* Eds. John D. Caputo and Michael Scanlon. Bloomington, IN: Indiana University Press, 1999. 122–53. Revised in *De surcroît: études sur les phénomènes saturés.* Paris: Presses Universitaires de France, 2001.

——. "État des études philosophiques dans la revue XVIIe siècle: Acquis, déficits et prospective." *XVIIe siècle* 51.203 (1999): 227–33.

——. "Le visage, une herméneutique sans fin." *Conférences* 9 (1999). "The Face: An Endless Hermeneutics." *Harvard Divinity Bulletin* 28.2–3 (1999): 9–10. Revised in *De surcroît: études sur les phénomènes saturés.* Paris: Presses Universitaires de France, 2001.

——. "L'évènement, le phénomène, et le révélé." *Transversalités: Revue de L'Institut Catholique de Paris* 70 (1999): 4–26. Revised in *De surcroît: études sur les phénomènes saturés.* Paris: Presses Universitaires de France, 2001. "The Event, the Phenomenon, and the Revealed. *Transcendence in Philosophy and Religion.* Ed. James E. Faulconer. Bloomington: Indiana University Press, 2003.

——. "Quelques règles en l'histoire de la philosophie." *Les Études Philosophiques* 109.4 (1999): 495–510.

——. "Le paradoxe de la personne." *Études* (1999). Spanish translation in *Criterio* 2251 (2000).

——. "Ratiunea formalata a infintului." *Echinox* XXXI.1–3 (2000). "The Formal

Reason For the Infinite." *The Blackwell Companion to Postmodern Theology.* Ed. Graham Ward. Blackwell Companions to Religion. Oxford: Blackwell, 2001.

———. "Remarques sur des questions." *Annales de Philosophie* 21 (2000).

———. "The Blind Man of Siloe." *Image* 29 (2001).

———. "La phénoménalité du sacrement: être et donation." *Communio* XXVI.5 (2001).

———. "Réaliser la présence réelle." *La Maison-Dieu* 225 (2001).

———. "Ce qui ne se dit pas: Remarques sur l'apophase dans le discours amoureux." *Théologie négative.* Ed. M.-M. Ollivetti. *Actes du Colloque «Castelli.»* Rome, 4–7 janvier 2002.

———. "Parlare d'amore." *Il Regno* 901 (2002).

———. "Notes sur le phénomène et son évènement." *Iris. Annales de philosophie. Université Saint-Joseph Beyrouth.* Vol. 23. Beyrouth, 2002. Revised in "Le phénomène et l'évènement." *Quaes* (2003). *L'existenzia/L'existence/Die Existenz/Existence.* Eds. C. Esposito and P. Porro. Bari: Turnhout, 2004.

———. "La raison du don." *Philosophie. Jean-Luc Marion.* Vol. 78. Paris: Minuit, 2003. 3–32. "The Reason of the Gift." Trans. Shane Mackinlay and Nicholas de Warren. Bijdragen 65.1 (2004): 5–37. *Givenness and God: Questions of Jean-Luc Marion.* Eds. Eoin Cassidy and Ian Leask. New York: Fordham University Press, 2004. Forthcoming.

———. "On Love and Phenomenological Reduction." Trans. Anne Davenport. *The New Arcadia Review* (2004).

Marion, Jean-Luc, and Michel Henry et al. "Préalables philosophiques à une lecture de Marx." *Bulletin de la Société française de Philosophie* 77.4 (1983): 117–51.

Marion, Jean-Luc, and Vincent Carraud. "De quelque citations cartésiennes de l'Écriture Sainte." *Archives de Philosophie* 59.1 (1996).

1.7 Interviews

"La modernité sans avenir." *Le Débat. Histoire, Politique, Société* septembre 1980: 54–60.

"Phénoménologiques." *Magazine Littéraire* novembre 1986: 47–48.

"Si tu m'aimes ou si tu me hais." *Art Pressï* juin 1987.

"La fin de la bêtise." *Le Nouvel Observateur* 22–28 décembre 1988.

"Pour une philosophie de la charité." *France Catholique* 15 mai 1992.

"De l'histoire de l'être à la donation du possible." *Le Débat. Histoire, Politique, Société* novembre–décembre 1992.

"Ni passion, ni vertu." *La charité.* Revue *Autrement* avril 1993.

"Si je veux." *Libération* 30 août 1993.

"Descartes." *Le Point* 1995.

"Descartes—à revoir." *Magazine littéraire* mars 1996: 31–32.

"La fin de la métaphysique?" *Page* janvier–février 1996.

"Interview with Jean-Luc Marion." *The Leuven Philosophy Newsletter* 6 (1997).

"Après tout, l'être se donne." *Le Nouvel Observateur* 1998.

"La fin de la métaphysique ouvre une nouvelle carrière à la métaphysique." *Le Monde* 22 septembre 1998.

"Auf der Suche nach einer neuen Phänomenologie" (Paris, 17 juin 1997); "Ruf und Gabe als formale Bestimmung der Süjektivität» in der Phänomenologie" (Bonn, 25 juin 1998). Jean-Luc Marion and Josef Wolmuth. *Ruf und Gabe. Zum Verhältnis von Phänomenologie und Theologie.* Bonn: Borengässer, 2000.

"Le paradoxe de la personne." *Etudes* octobre 1999.

"A quoi pensez-vous?—A penser." *Libération* 1 janvier 2000.

Entretien avec V. Citôt et P. Godo. *Le philosophoire* printemps–été 2000.

"Les vrais sujets sont délaissés." *Le Figaro* 27 septembre 2000.

"Réaliser la présence réelle." *La Maison-Dieu* 1er trimestre 2001.

"Entretien avec D. Janicaud." *Heidegger en France. II. Entretiens.* Paris, 2001. 210–227.

"Un moment français de la phénoménologie." *Phénoménologies françaises. Revue Descartes* 35. Paris, 2002.

"Qu'est-ce que l'amour?" *Le Nouvel Observateur* 17–23 avril 2003.

"L'amour et ses raisons." *Valeurs Actuelles* 20 juin 2003.

"Un clair devoir d'universalité." *Le Figaro* 19 août 2003.

"Le phénomène érotique." *Etudes* novembre 2003.

"The Hermeneutics of Revelation." *Debates in Continental Philosophy. Conversations with Contemporary Thinkers.* Ed. R. Kearney. New York: Fordham University Press, 2004.

Appendix 2

Secondary Bibliography of Jean-Luc Marion

Many of these works are substantial studies of Marion, but in line with Marion's own records, entries include texts where he is briefly mentioned.

Rev. of Jean-Luc Marion. *God Without Being.* Trans. Thomas A. Carlson. Chicago, IL: University of Chicago Press, 1991. *First Things.* (1996): 67–73.

Rev. of Jean-Luc Marion. *Prolegomena to Charity.* Trans. Stephen Lewis. New York: Fordham University Press, 2002. *First Things* 20.3 (2003): 75–79.

Aguti, A. "Jean-Luc Marion. Una fenomenologia dell'inapparente." *Hermeneutica. Annuario di filosofia e teologia.* Urbino, 2000.

Ahn, Taekyun. "The Gift and the Understanding of God: Iconic Theology of J. L. Marion." Doctoral dissertation. Drew University, 2003.

Alessi, A. *Salesianum* 52.1 (1990): 53–111.

Alliez, Eric. *De l'impossibilité de la phénoménologie. Sur la philosophie française contemporaine.* Paris: J. Vrin, 1995.

Ambrosio, Francis J. "Concluding Roundtable Discussion (R. Adams, A. Peperzak, M. Adams, J. Ladriere, J. Richardson, L. Dupré, J.-L. Marion)." *The Question of Christian Philosophy Today.* Ed. Francis J. Ambrosio. New York: Fordham University Press, 1999.

Ansaldi, Jean. "Approche doxologique de la Trinité de Dieu: Dialogue avec Jean-Luc Marion." *Études théologiques et religieuses* 62.1 (1987): 81–95.

Armour, Ellen T. "Beyond Belief? Sexual Difference and Religion After Ontotheology." *The Religious.* Ed. John D. Caputo. Oxford: Blackwell, 2002. 212–26.

Audi, P. "S'adonner à la phénoménologie." *Le Monde* 21 novembre 1997.

Ayres, Lewis, and Gareth Jones, eds. *Christian Origins: Theology, Rhetoric and Community.* London/New York: Routledge, 1998.

Badiou, Alain. *Saint Paul: The Foundation of Universalism.* Trans. Paul Brassier. Stanford, CA: Stanford University Press, 2003.

Barber, Michael D. "Theory and Alterity: Dussel's Marx and Marion on Idolatry." *Thinking from the Underside of History: Enrique Dussel's Philosophy of Liberation.* Ed. Linda Martin Alcoff. Rowman and Littlefield: Lanham MD, 2000.

Batstone, David, et al., eds. *Liberation Theologies, Postmodernity, and the Americas.* London/New York: Routledge, 1997.

Bauerschmidt, Frederick Christian. "Aesthetics. The Theological Sublime."

Radical Orthodoxy. Eds. John Milbank, Catherine Pickstock, and Graham Ward. London/New York: Routledge, 1999. 201–19.

Beaufret, Jean. "Heidegger et la théologie." *Heidegger et la question de Dieu.* Eds. Richard Kearney and Joseph S. O'Leary. Paris: B. Grasset, 1980. 19–35.

Begbie, Jeremy S. *Theology, Music and Time.* Cambridge: Cambridge University Press, 2000.

Belgioioso, Giulia. "L'année Descartes 1996: un bilan historiographique." *Nouvelles de la République des Lettres* (1996).

Bella, S. di. *Le Meditazioni Metafisiche di Cartesio. Introduzione alla lettura.* Roma, 1997.

Ben-Smit, Peter. "The Bishop and His/Her Eucharistic Community: A Critique of Jean-Luc Marion's Eucharistic Hermeneutic." *Modern Theology* 19.1 (2003): 29–40.

Benoist, Jocelyn. "Répondre de soi." *Philosophie* 34 (1992): 37–44.

——. "Vingt ans de phénoménologie française." *Philosophie Contemporaine en France.* Paris: Ministère des Affaires Étrangères, 1994.

——. "Qu'est ce qui est donné? La pensée et l'évènement." *Archives de Philosophie* 59.4 (1996).

——. "Le tournant théologique." *L'Idée de phénoménologie.* Paris: Beauchesne, 2001.

——. "Les voix du soliloque. Sur quelques interprétations récentes du *cogito.*" *Les Études Philosophiques* 4 (1997): 541–55.

——. "L'écart plutôt que l'excédent." *Philosophie. Jean-Luc Marion.* Vol. 78. Paris: Minuit, 2003.

Benson, Bruce Ellis. *Graven Ideologies: Nietzsche, Derrida and Marion on Modern Idolatry.* Downers Grove, IL: InterVarsity Press, 2002.

——. "Jean-Luc Marion Tests the Limits of Logic: Love is a Given." *The Christian Century* 120.3 (2003): 22–25.

Beyssade, Jean-Marie. "The Idea of God and the Proofs of his Existence." Trans. J. Cottingham. *The Cambridge Companion to Descartes.* Ed. J. Cottingham. Cambridge: Cambridge University Press, 1992. 174–99.

——. "On the Idea of God: Incomprehensibility or Incompatibilities?" Trans. Charles Paul. *Essays on the Philosophy and Science of René Descartes.* Ed. Stephen Voss. New York/Oxford: Oxford University Press, 1993.

——. "Méditer, objecter, répondre." *Descartes. Objecter et répondre.* Eds. Jean-Luc Marion and Jean-Marie Beyssade. Paris: Presses Universitaires de France, 1994. 21–38.

Bloechl, Jeffrey. "Dialectical Approaches to Retrieving God After Heidegger: Premises and Consequences (Lacoste and Marion)." *Pacifica: Journal of the Melbourne College of Divinity* 13 (2000): 288–298.

——. "The Postmodern Context and Sacramental Presence: Disputed Questions." *The Presence of Transcendence.* Eds. Lieven Boeve and John C. Ries. Leuven: Uitgeverij Peeters, 2001. 3–17.

——. "Translator's Introduction." *Jean-Louis Chrétien. The Unforgettable and the Unhoped For.* New York: Fordham University Press, 2002. vii–xv.

Bloesch, Donald G. *God the Almighty: Power, Wisdom, Holiness, Love*. Downers Grove, IL: Intervarsity Press, 1995.

Blond, Philip, ed. *Post-Secular Philosophy: Between Philosophy and Theology*. London/New York: Routledge, 1998.

——. "Perception: From Modern Painting to the Vision in Christ." *Radical Orthodoxy: A New Theology*. Eds. John Milbank, Catherine Pickstock, and Graham Ward. London: Routledge, 1999. 220–42.

Boeve, Lieven. "Method in Postmodern Theology: A Case Study." *The Presence of Transcendence*. Eds. Lieven Boeve and John C. Ries. Leuven: Uitgeverij Peeters, 2001. 19–39.

Boldor, Marius. "O incursiune fenomenologică în lumea vizibilului împreună cu Jean-Luc Marion." *Studia Theologica* Anul 1.4 (2003): 178–95.

Bonfand, Alain. *L'ombre de la nuit. Essai sur la mélancolie et l'angoisse dans les oeuvres de Mario Sironi et de Paul Klee entre 1933 et 1940*. Paris, 1993.

——. *L'expérience esthétique à l'épreuve de la phénoménologie. La tristesse du roi*. Paris: Presses Universitaires de France, 1995.

Bottum, J. "Christians and Postmodernists." *First Things* 40 (1994): 28–32.

Bouttes, M. "Analogie et question de l'infini chez Descartes." *Cartesiana*. Eds. M. Bouttes and G. Granel. Mauvezin: TER, 1984. 69–85.

Bracken, Joseph A. "Toward a New Philosophical Theology Based on Intersubjectivity." *Theological Studies* 59.4 (1998): 703–19.

Bradley, Arthur. "God *Sans* Being: Derrida, Marion and 'a Paradoxical Writing of the Word *Without*'." *Literature and Theology* 14.3 (2000): 299–312.

Brennan, Teresa, and Martin Jay, eds. *Vision in Context: Historical and Contemporary Perspectives on Sight*. London/New York: Routledge, 1996.

Bres, Yvon. "L'avenir du judéo-christianisme (suite et fin)." *Revue Philosophique de la France et de l'Étranger*. (2002): 65–83.

Breton, Stanislas. Rev. of Jean-Luc Marion. *L'idole et la distance*. Paris: Grasset, 1977. *Archives de Philosophie* 43 (1980): 152–57.

——. "La querelle des dénominations." *Heidegger et la question de Dieu*. Eds. Richard Kearney and Joseph S. O'Leary. Paris: B. Grasset, 1980. 248–68.

Brito, Emilio. "La réception de la pensée de Heidegger dans la théologie catholique." *Nouvelle Revue Théologique* 119.3 (1997): 352–74.

——. *Heidegger et l'hymne du sacré*. Louvain: Peeters, 1999.

Broughton, Janet. *Descartes's Method of Doubt*. Princeton, NJ: Princeton University Press, 2003.

Bulhof, Ilse N. "Being Open As a Form of Negative Theology: On Nominalism, Negative Theology, and Derrida's Performative Interpretation of 'Khôra'." *Flight of the Gods: Philosophical Perspectives on Negative Theology*. Eds. Ilse N. Bulhof and Laurens ten Kate. New York: Fordham University Press, 2000. 194–221.

Bulhof, Ilse N., and Laurens ten Kate, eds. *Flight of the Gods: Philosophical Perspectives on Negative Theology*. New York: Fordham University Press, 2000.

Bultmann, Rudolf, et al. *Philosophie. Phénomenologie et théologie*. Vol. 42. Paris: Minuit, 1994.

Burrell, David B. "Reflections on 'Negative Theology' in the Light of a Recent

Venture to Speak of 'God Without Being'." *Postmodernism and Christian Philosophy.* Ed. R. T. Ciapalo. Washington, DC: The Catholic University of America Press, 1997. 58–67.

Cacciari, M. "Il problema del sacro in Heidegger." *La recezione italiana di Heidegger.* Ed. Marco Olivetti. Padua: Cedam, 1989. 203–17.

Calderone, R. "Donazione e Indondatezza." *Giornale di Metafisica* XXI (1999).

Canziani, G. "Ermeneutica cartesiana. In margine ad un recente libro di J.-L. Marion [*Sur la théologie blanche de Descartes*, vol. I, no.5]." *Rivista di Storia della Filosofia.* (1984).

Caputo, John D. "How to Avoid Speaking of God: The Violence of Natural Theology." *Prospects for Natural Theology.* Ed. E. T. Long. Washington, DC: The Catholic University of America Press, 1992.

——. "God is Wholly Other-Almost: 'Différance' and the Hyperbolic Alterity of God." *The Otherness of God.* Ed. O. F. Summerell. Charlottesville: University Press of Virginia, 1998. 190–205.

——. "Apostles of the Impossible." *God, the Gift and Postmodernism.* Eds. John D. Caputo and Michael Scanlon. Bloomington: Indiana University Press, 1999. 185–222. "Apôtres de l'impossible: sur Dieu et le don chez Derrida et Marion." *Philosophie. Jean-Luc Marion.* Vol. 78. Paris: Minuit, 2003.

Caputo, John D., Mark Dooley, and Richard Kearney, eds. *Questioning God.* Bloomington: Indiana University Press, 2001.

Caputo, John D., and Michael Scanlon. "Apology for the Impossible: Religion and Postmodernism." *God, the Gift, and Postmodernism.* Eds. John D. Caputo and Michael Scanlon. Bloomington: Indiana University Press, 1999. 1–19.

——, eds. *God, the Gift, and Postmodernism.* Bloomington: Indiana University Press, 1999.

Carabine, Deirdre. *John Scottus Eriugena.* Great Medieval Thinkers. Oxford: Oxford University Press, 2000.

Carlson, Thomas A. "Finitude and the Naming of God: A Study of Ontotheology and the Apophatic Traditions." Doctoral dissertation. The University of Chicago, 1995.

——. *Indiscretion: Finitude and the Naming of God. A Study of Onto-theology and the Apophatic Traditions.* Chicago, IL: University of Chicago Press, 1999.

——. "Translator's Introduction." *The Idol and Distance: Five Studies.* New York: Fordham University Press, 2001. xi–xxxi.

Carraud, Vincent. "Descartes appartienne alla storia della metafisica?" *Descartes metafisico. Interpretationi del Novecento.* Eds. Jean-Robert Armogathe and Guilia Belgioioso. Roma: Instituto della Enciclopedia Italiana, 1995.

Cassidy, Eoin, and Ian Leask, eds. *Givenness and God: Questions of Jean-Luc Marion.* New York: Fordham University Press. Forthcoming.

Cavanaugh, William T. "The City: Beyond Secular Parodies." *Radical Orthodoxy.* Eds. John Milbank, Catherine Pickstock, and Graham Ward. London/New York: Routledge, 1999. 182–200.

Chambers, Iain. *Migrancy, Culture, Identity.* London: Routledge, 1994.

Chararot, M. *L'art du comprendre* 8 (1999).

Chevalley, C. "Remarques sur la topique des phénomènes dans *Etant donné.*" *Hermeneutica. Annuario di filosofia e teologia.* Urbino, 2000.

Chrétien, Jean-Louis. *The Call and the Response.* Trans. Anne A. Davenport. New York: Fordham University Press, 2004.

Cislaghi, A. *Il sapere del desiderio. Libertà metafisica e saggezza etica.* Assise, 2002.

Clark, David A. "Otherwise than God: Schelling, Marion." *Trajectories of Mysticism in Theory and Literature.* New York: St. Martin's Press, 2000. 133–76.

Coda, P. "Dono e abbandono: con Heidegger sulle tracce dell'Essere." *La Trinità e il pensare: figure percorsi prospettive.* Eds. P. Coda and A. Tapken. Roma: Città Nuovo, 1994. 165–70.

Colette, Jacques. "Phénoménologie et métaphysique." *Critique* 548–549 (1993): 56–73.

Corbin, Michel. "Négation et transcendance dans l'oeuvre de Denys." *Revue des sciences philosophiques et théologiques* 69.1 (1985): 41–75.

Corvet, M. *Revue Théologique* 1 (1979): 124–32.

Cottingham, John. ed. *The Cambridge Companion to Descartes.* Cambridge: Cambridge University Press, 1992.

——. Rev. of Cartesian Questions: Method and Metaphysics. Trans. Jeffrey L. Kosky, John Cottingham, and Stephen Voss. Chicago, IL: University of Chicago Press, 1999. *Mind* 111.442 (2002): 447–49.

——. Recension de *Cartesian Questions. Mind,* 2000.

Courtine, Jean-François, et al. *Phénoménologie et théologie.* Paris: Critérion, 1992.

Craig, Edward, ed. *Routledge Encyclopedia of Philosophy.* London/New York: Routledge, 1998.

Critchley, Simon, and Robert Bernasconi, eds. *The Cambridge Companion to Levinas.* Cambridge: Cambridge University Press, 2002.

Crockett, Clayton. *Secular Theology: American Radical Theological Thought.* London/New York: Routledge, 2001.

——. *A Theology of the Sublime.* London/New York: Routledge, 2001.

Crowell, Steven-Galt. "Authentic Thinking and Phenomenological Method." *The New Yearbook for Phenomenology and Phenomenological Philosophy.* Ed. Burt C. Hopkins. Seattle, WA: Noesis-Press, 2002. 23–37.

Crump, Eric H. Rev. of Jean-Luc Marion. *God Without Being.* Trans. Thomas A. Carlson. Chicago, IL: University of Chicago Press, 1991. *Modern Theology* 9.3 (1993): 309.

Cunningham, Conor. *Genealogy of Nihilism: Philosophies of Nothing and the Difference of Theology.* Radical Orthodoxy. London: Routledge, 2002.

Davenport, John, et al., eds. *Kierkegaard After MacIntyre: Essays on Freedom, Narrative, and Virtue.* Chicago, IL: Open Court, 2001.

Davis, Stephen T., Daniel Kendall, and Gerald O'Collins, eds. *The Trinity: An Interdisciplinary Symposium on the Trinity.* Oxford: Oxford University Press, 2002.

Decartes, René. *Discourse on Method and Related Writings.* Trans. Desmond M. Clarke. Penguin Classics. New York: Penguin, 2000.

DeHart, Paul J. *Beyond the Necessary God: Trinitarian Faith and Philosophy in the Thought of Eberhard Jungel.* Reflection and Theory in the Study of Religion, No 15: American Academy of Religion, 2000.

——. "The Ambiguous Infinite: Jungel, Marion, and the God of Descartes." *The Journal of Religion* 82.1 (2002): 75–96.

Delacampagne, Christian. *A History of Philosophy in the Twentieth Century.* Trans. M. B. Debevoise. Reprint ed. Baltimore, MD: Johns Hopkins University Press, 2001.

Depraz, Natalie. "Gibt es eine Gebung des Unendlichen." *Perspektiven der Philosophie.* Ed. R. Berlinger. Amsterdam: Rodopi, 1997.

——. "The Return of Phenomenology in Recent French Moral Philosophy." *Phenomenological Approaches to Moral Philosophy.* Ed. John Drummond. Dordrecht: Kluwer Academic Publishers, 2002.

Derrida, Jacques. *Donner le temps. I. La fausse monnaie.* Paris: Galilée, 1991. *Given Time. I. Counterfeit Money.* Trans. Peggy Kamuf. Chicago, IL: University of Chicago Press, 1992.

Deverell, Gary. "The Bonds of Freedom: Vow, Sacraments, and the Formation of the Christian Self." Doctoral dissertation. Monash University, 1998.

Devillairs, Laurence. "Le phénomène érotique. Entretien avec Jean-Luc Marion. *Études* 10 (2003): 483–494.

Dostal, Robert J., ed. *The Cambridge Companion to Gadamer.* Cambridge: Cambridge University Press, 2002.

Drabinski, J. E. "Sense and Icon: The Problem of *Sinngebung* in Lévinas and Marion." *Philosophy Today* 42 SPEP Supplement (1998): 47–58.

Duquesne, Marcel. "À propos d'un livre récent: Jean-Luc Marion, *Dieu sans l'être* (à suivre)." *Mélanges de Science Religieuse* XLII.2 (1985): 57–76.

——. "À propos d'un livre récent: Jean-Luc Marion, *Dieu sans l'être.*" *Mélanges de Science Religieuse* XLII (1985): 127–40.

English, Adam C. "Structure, mystery, power: The Christian ontology of Maurice Blondel (John Milbank, Henri de Lubac, Karl Rahner, Jean-Luc Marion)." Doctoral dissertation. Baylor University, 2003.

Esposito, C. "Ritorno a Suarez. Le Disputationes Metaphysicae *nella critica contemporanea.*" *La filosofia nel siglo de Oro. Studi sul tardo rinascimento spagnolo.* Bari, 1995.

Ewbank, Michael B. "Of Idols, Icons, and Aquinas's Esse: Reflections on Jean-Luc Marion." *International Philosophical Quarterly* 42.2 (2002): 161–75.

Fabrègues, J. de. "Non à l'idole, oui à l'icône." *France Catholique-Ecclesia* 24 septembre 1982,: 12–13.

Fagenblat, Michael. "Rage Against Order: On Recent Work by Jean-Luc Marion." *Verse* 20.3–4. 188–199.

Falque, Emmanuel. *Saint Bonaventure et l'entrée de Dieu en théologie.* Paris: Vrin, 2000.

——. "Phénoménologie de l'extraordinaire." *Philosophie. Jean-Luc Marion.* Vol. 78. Paris: Minuit, 2003.

Faulconer, James E., ed. *Transcendence in Philosophy and Religion*. Bloomington: Indiana University Press, 2003.

Fédier, F. "Heidegger et Dieu." *Heidegger et la question de Dieu*. Eds. Richard Kearney and Joseph S. O'Leary. Paris: B. Grasset, 1980. 37–45.

Ferretti, G., ed. *Fenomenologia della donazione a proposito di Dato ché di Jean-Luc Marion.*

Fletcher, Paul. "Writing of(f) Victims: hors texte." *New Blackfriars* 78.916 (1997): 267–78.

Floucat, Y. "Chronique de philosophie." *Revue Théologique* (1983).

Ford, David F. *Self and Salvation: Being Transformed*. Cambridge: Cambridge University Press, 1999.

Fountain, J. Stephen. "Postmodernism, A/Theology, and the Possibility of Language as Universal Eucharist." *The Nature of Religious Language*. Ed. Stanley E. Porter. Sheffield: Sheffield Academic Press, 1996. 131–47.

Foutz, S. D. "Postmetaphysic[al?] Theology—A Case Study: Jean-Luc Marion." *Quodlibet: Online Journal of Christian Theology and Philosophy* 1.3 (1999).

Frank, Daniel H., and Oliver Leaman, eds. *History of Jewish Philosophy*. Vol. 2. London/New York: Routledge, 1997.

Gabellieri, E. "De la métaphysique à la phénoménologies: une 'relève'?" *Revue philosophique de Louvain* 94.4 (1996): 625–45.

Gagnon, M. "La phénoménologie à la limite." *Eidos: The Canadian Graduate Journal of Philosophy* 11 (1993): 111–30.

Gamba, F. "Della reduzione alla donazione: Svilluppi della fenomenologia contemporanea." *Filosofia* 49.3: 315–31.

Garber, Daniel. "Foreword." *Cartesian Questions: Method and Metaphysics*. Chicago, IL: University of Chicago Press, 1999. ix–xiii.

——. *Descartes Embodied: Reading Cartesian Philosophy through Cartesian Science*. Cambridge: Cambridge University Press, 2000.

Garcia Murga, Jose R. "Como decir hoy que Dios es amor." *Miscelanea Comillas* 45 (1987): 289–321.

Gaukroger, Stephen, John Schuster, and John Sutton, eds. *Descartes' Natural Philosophy*. London/New York: Routledge, 2000.

Gicquel, Herve-Marie. "L'intervention de l'inconnu dans la vie personnelle." Doctoral dissertation. University of Ottawa, 1996.

——. et S. Petrosino. *Le don. Amitié et paternité*. Paris, 2003.

Gilbert, Paul. "Substance et présence: Derrida et Marion, critiques de Husserl." *Gregorianum* 75.1 (1994): 95–133.

Godo, P. "Rire de la métaphysique/Rire de Dieu. Nietzsche: dernier métaphysicien?" *Le Philosophoire. Le lisible et l'illisible* 9, (1999).

Godzieba, Anthony J. "Ontotheology to Excess: Imagining God Without Being." *Theological Studies* 56 (1995): 3–20.

Goodchild, Philip. *Capitalism and Religion: The Price of Piety*. London/New York: Routledge, 2002.

Goudriaan, A. "Marion en de problematiek vande analogie bij Descartes." *Il Cannocchiale. Rivista di studi filosopfici*. Rome, 2000/3.

Greisch, Jean. "Actualité ou inactualité de la théologie naturelle?" *Revue des sciences philosophiques et théologiques* 67.3 (1983): 443–53.

——. "L'herméneutique dans la 'phénoménologie comme telle'." *Revue de Métaphysique et de Morale* 96.1 (1991): 43–76.

——. "Index sui et non dati: Les paradoxes d'une phénoménologie de la donation." *Transversalités: Revue de L'Institut Catholique de Paris* (1999): 27–54.

——. *Le cogito herméneutique: l'herméneutique philosophique et l'heritage cartésien.* Paris: J. Vrin, 2000.

——. "Bulletin de philosophie de la religion." *Revue des Sciences Théologiques et Philosophiques* 85/3 (2001): 548-552.

——. *Le buisson ardant et les lumières de la raison. L'invention de la philosophie de la religion.* Vol. II. *Les approches phénoménologiques et analytiques,* Paris, 2002.

Grene, Marjorie Glicksman, Lewis Edward Hahn, and Randall E. Auxier, eds. *The Philosophy of Marjorie Grene.* Chicago, IL: Open Court Publishing Company, 2003.

Grimwood, Steven. "Iconography and Postmodernity." *Literature and Theology* 17.1 (2003): 76–97.

Grondin, Jean. Rev. of Jean-Luc Marion, *Sur le prisme métaphysique de Descartes.* Paris: Presses Universitaires de France, 1986. *Laval Théologique et Philosophique* 43.3 (1987): 409–13.

——. "La phénoménologie sans herméneutique." *L'horizon herméneutique de la pensée contemporaine.* Paris: J. Vrin, 1993. 81–90.

——. "La tension de la donation ultime et de la pensée herméneutique de l'application chez Jean-Luc Marion." *Dialogue* 38.3 (1999): 547–59.

Gschwandtner, Christina Margrit. "Sparks of meaning at the points of friction: At the boundary between philosophy and theology in the work of Jean-Luc Marion (René Descartes)." Doctoral dissertation. Depaul University, 2003.

Guarino, Thomas. "Postmodernity and Five Fundamental Theological Issues." *Theological Studies* 57.4 (1996): 654–89.

Guitton, Jean. "Le fini de l'homme et l'infini de Dieu." *France Catholique-Ecclesia* 24 septembre 1982: 12–13.

Gutting, Gary. *French Philosophy in the Twentieth Century.* Cambridge: Cambridge University Press, 2001.

Hankey, Wayne J. "The Postmodern Retrieval of Neoplatonism in Jean-Luc Marion and John Milbank and the Origins of Western Subjectivity in Augustine and Eriugena." *Hermathena* 165 (1998): 9–70.

——. "Theoria Versus Poesis: Neoplatonism and Trinitarian Difference in Aquinas, John Milbank, Jean-Luc Marion and John Zizoulas." *Modern Theology* 15.4 (1999): 387–415.

——. "Between and Beyond Augustine and Descartes: More than a Source of the Self." *Augustinian Studies* 32.1 (2001): 65–88.

——. "Why Philosophy Abides for Aquinas." *Heythrop Journal* 42.3 (2001): 329–48.

Hannay, Alastair, and Gordon Daniel Marino, eds. *The Cambridge Companion to Kierkegaard.* Cambridge: Cambridge University Press, 1997.

Hanson, J. A. "Jean-Luc Marion and the Possibility of a Postmodern Theology." *Mars Hill Review* 12 (1998): 93–104.

Happel, Stephen. *Metaphors for God's Time in Science and Religion.* Houndmills, Hampshire: Palgrave Macmillan, 2003.

Heinich, Nathalie. *The Glory of van Gogh.* Trans. Paul Leduc Browne. Princeton, NJ: Princeton University Press, 1997.

Hemming, Laurence. "Reading Heidegger: Is God Without Being? Jean-Luc Marion's Reading of Martin Heidegger in *God Without Being.*" *New Blackfriars* 76.895 (1995): 343–50.

——. "To say nothing of the existence of God." Doctoral dissertation. Cambridge, 1999.

——. "Nihilism. Heidegger and the Grounds of Redemption." *Radical Orthodoxy.* Eds. John Milbank, Catherine Pickstock, and Graham Ward. London: Routledge, 1999. 91–108.

——. *Heidegger's Atheism. The Refusal of a theological voice.* South Bend, IN: University of Notre-Dame Press, 2002.

Hengel, John van den. "God With/out Being." *Method: Journal of Lonergan Studies* 12.2 (1994): 251–79.

Henry, Michel. "Quatres principes de la phénoménologie." *Revue de Métaphysique et de Morale* 96.1 (1991): 3–26.

Hoff, A. E. van. "Sein als Idol? Erwägungen zu Jean-Luc Marion, *Dieu sans l'être.*" *Archivio di Filosofia* 54 (1986).

Höhn, G. "Suche nach Ursprünglichkeit. Die Wiedergeburt der Metaphysik aus dem Erbe der Phänomenologie." *Frankfurter Rundschau* (1994).

Holzer, Vincent. "Phénoménologie radicale et phénomène de révélation." *Transversalités: Revue de L'Institut Catholique de Paris* (1999): 55–68.

Horner, Robyn. "Rethinking God as Gift: Jean-Luc Marion and a Theology of Donation." Doctoral dissertation. Monash University, 1998.

——. "The Eucharist and the Postmodern." *Eucharist: Experience and Testimony.* Ed. Tom Knowles. Ringwood, VIC: David Lovell, 2001. 3–24.

——. *Rethinking God as Gift: Marion, Derrida, and the Limits of Phenomenology.* Perspectives in Continental Philosophy. Ed. John D. Caputo. New York: Fordham University Press, 2001.

——. "Problème du mal et péché des origines." *Recherches de Science Religieuse* 90.1 (2002): 63–86.

——. "Translator's Introduction." *Jean-Luc Marion. In Excess: Studies of Saturated Phenomena.* New York: Fordham University Press, 2002. ix–xx.

——. "Aporia or Excess: Two strategies for Thinking/Revelation." *Other Testaments: Derrida and Religion.* Eds. Kevin Hart and Yvonne Sherwood. London: Routledge, 2004.

——. "The Betrayal of Transcendence." *Transcendence.* Ed. Regina Schwartz. New York: Routledge, 2004.

——. "The Face as Icon." *Australasian Catholic Record* 82.1. (2005).

Houtepen, A. *God, een open vraag. Theologische perspectieven in een cultuur van agnosme.* Zoetermeer: Meinema, 1997.

Hutter, Reinhard. Rev. of Jean-Luc Marion. *God Without Being. Hors-Texte.* Trans. Thomas. A. Carlson. Chicago, IL: University of Chicago Press, 1991. *Pro-Ecclesia* 3 (1994): 239–44.

Iezzoni, E. *Il Dar-si dell' Essere nell' ecstasi del' altro. Antropologia filosofics e ontologia trinitaria nel peniero di Jean-Luc Marion e Klaus Hemmerle.* University of Chieti, 1997.

Inglis, John, ed. *Medieval Philosophy and the Classical Tradition In Islam, Judaism and Christianity.* London: Curzon Press, 2001.

Janicaud, Dominique. Rev. of Jean-Luc Marion. *L'idole et la distance.* Paris: Grasset, 1977. *Les Études Philosophiques* 2 (1979): 250–52.

——. Rev. of Jean-Luc Marion. *Dieu sans l'être.* Paris: Fayard, 1982. *Les Études Philosophiques* 4 (1983): 496–98.

——. *Le tournant théologique de la phénoménologie française.* Combas: Éditions de l'Éclat, 1991.

——. *La phénoménologie éclatée.* Combas: Éditions de l'éclat, 1998.

——. "'Veerings' from *The Theological Turn of French Phenomenology.*" *The Religious.* Ed. John D. Caputo. Oxford: Blackwell, 2002. 145–58.

Janicaud, Dominique, et al. *Phenomenology and the 'Theological Turn': The French Debate.* Perspectives in Continental Philosophy. Ed. John D. Caputo. New York: Fordham University Press, 2001.

Janz, Denis R. "Syllogism or Paradox: Aquinas and Luther on Theological Method." *Theological Studies* 59.1 (1998): 3–21.

Jaran, F. "Heidegger et la constitution onto-théo-logique de la métaphysique cartésienne." *Heidegger Studies/Heidgger Studien/Etudes Heidegerriennes.* Vol.19. Berlin, 2003. 65-80.

Javaux, J. Rev. of Jean-Luc Marion. *L'idole et la distance.* Paris: Grasset, 1977. *Nouvelle Revue Théologique* 100.2 (1978): 297–99.

——. Rev. of Jean-Luc Marion. *Dieu sans l'être.* Paris: Fayard, 1982. *Nouvelle Revue Théologique* 105.5 (1983): 731–32.

Jenson, Robert W. *Systematic Theology: The Triune God.* Oxford: Oxford University Press, 2001.

Jonkers, Peter, and Ruud Welten, eds. *God in Frankrijk. Zes hedendaagse Franse filosofen over God.* Damon, 2003.

Kal, Victor. "Being Unable to Speak, Seen As a Period: Difference and Distance in Jean-Luc Marion." *Flight of the Gods: Philosophical Perspectives on Negative Theology.* Eds. Ilse N. Bulhof and Laurens ten Kate. New York: Fordham University Press, 2000. 143–64.

Kalinowski, G. "Discours de louange et discours métaphysique: Denys l'aréopagite et Thomas D'Aquin." *Rivista di Filosofia Neo Scolastica* 73 (1981): 399–404.

Kate, Laurens ten. "The Gift of Loss: A Study of the Fugitive God in Bataille's Atheology, with Reference to Jean-Luc Nancy." *Flight of the Gods: Philosophical Perspectives on Negative Theology.* Eds. Ilse N. Bulhof and Laurens ten Kate. New York: Fordham University Press, 2000. 249–91.

Kearney, Richard. *The God Who May Be: A Hermeneutics of Religion.* Bloomington: Indiana University Press, 2001.

——. "Eschatology of the Possible God." *The Religious*. Ed. John D. Caputo. Oxford: Blackwell, 2002. 175–96.

——. *Strangers, Gods, and Monsters*. London/New York: Routledge, 2002.

Kearney, Richard, Jacques Derrida, and Jean-Luc Marion. "On the Gift: A Discussion between Jacques Derrida and Jean-Luc Marion, Moderated by Richard Kearney." *God, the Gift and Postmodernism*. Eds. John D. Caputo and Michael J. Scanlon. Bloomington: Indiana University Press, 1999. 54–78.

Kearney, Richard, and Mark Dooley, eds. *Questioning Ethics: Contemporary Debates in Philosophy*. London/New York: Routledge, 1999.

Kearney, Richard, and Joseph S. O'Leary, eds. *Heidegger et la question de Dieu*. Paris: Grasset, 1980.

Kelly, Anthony (Tony). "A Trinitarian Moral Theology." *Studia Moralia* 39 (2001): 245–89.

Kelly, Tony. "The 'Horrible Wrappers' of Aquinas' God." *Pacifica: Journal of the Melbourne College of Divinity* 9.2 (1996): 185–203.

Kelly, Tony, and Francis J. Moloney. *The Experience of God in the Gospel of John*. New York: Paulist, 2003.

Kerr, Fergus. "Aquinas After Marion." *New Blackfriars* 76.895 (1995): 354–64.

Kinnard, Jacob N. *Imaging Wisdom: Seeing and Knowing in the Art of Indian Buddhism*. London: Curzon Press, 1999.

Klein, Julie Rachel. "Descartes' Occluded Metaphysics." Doctoral dissertation. Vanderbilt University, 1996.

Kosky, Jeffrey L. "The Disqualification of Intentionality: the Gift in Derrida, Lévinas, and Michel Henry." *Philosophy Today* 41 SPEP Supplement (1997): 186–97.

Kraftson-Hogue, Mike. "Predication Turning to Praise: Marion and Augustine on God and Hermeneutics (Giver, Gift, Giving)." *Literature and Theology* 14.4 (2000): 399–411.

Kroesen, J. O. *Kwaad en Zin. Over de betekenis van de filosofie van Emmanuel Lévinas voor de theologische vraag van het kwade*. Kampen, 1991.

Kühn, R. *Philosophischer Literaturanzeiger* 44.4 (1991).

——. *Französische Reflexions-und Geisterphilosophie*. Frankfurt: Anton Hain, 1993.

——. "Langweile und Anruf. Eine Heidegger-und Husserl-Revision mit dem Problemhintergrund 'absoluter Phänomene' bei Jean-Luc Marion." *Philosophisches Jahrbuch* 102.1 (1995): 144–55.

——. " 'Sättinung' als absolutes Phänomen. Zur Kritik der klassische Phänomenalität (Kant, Husserl) bei Jean-Luc Marion." *Mesotes. Zeitschrift für philosophischen Ost-West-Dialog* 3 (1995).

——. *Radikalisierte Phänomenologie*, Frankfurt a.M., 2002.

Labarrière, Pierre-Jean. Rev. of Jean-Luc Marion. *Dieu sans l'être*. Paris: Fayard, 1982. *Études: Revue Mensuelle*. (1983): 285–88.

Lacocque, André, and Paul Ricoeur. *Penser la Bible*. Paris: Éditions du Seuil, 1998.

Lacoste, Jean-Yves. Rev. of Jean-Luc Marion. *L'idole et la distance*. Paris: Grasset, 1977. *Résurrection* 56 (1977): 78–83.

——. "Penser à Dieu en l'aimant: philosophie et théologie de Jean-Luc Marion." *Archives de Philosophie* 50 (1987): 245–70.

Lafont, Ghislain. "Mystique de la croix et question de 'être. À propos d'un livre récent de Jean-Luc Marion." *Revue Théologique de Louvain* (1979): 259–304.

——. "Écouter Heidegger en théologien." *Revue des sciences philosophiques et théologiques* 67.3 (1983): 371–98.

Laird, Martin. "'Whereof We Speak': Gregory of Nyssa, Jean-Luc Marion and the Current Apophatic Rage." *The Heythrop Journal* 42.1 (2001): 1–12.

Lakeland, Paul. "Is the Holy Wholly Other, and is the Wholly Other Really Holy?" *Divine Aporia.* Lewisberg, PA: Bucknell University Press, 2000. 57–69.

Lamore, C. Rev. of Jean-Luc Marion. *Sur la théologie blanche de Descartes.* Paris: Presses Universitaires de France, 1981. *The Journal of Philosophy* 81.3 (1984): 156–62.

Laramée, Martin. Rev. of *De surcroît: études sur les phénomènes saturés.* Paris: Presses Universitaires de France, 2001. *Religiologiques* 26 (2002).

Laruelle, François. "L'Appel et le Phénomène." *Revue de Métaphysique et de Morale* 96.1 (1991): 27–42.

Launay, M. B. de. *Le Figaro* 22 septembre 1997.

Laurens, Camille. "Qu'est-ce que l'amour?" *Le Nouvel Observateur* 17 April 2003.

Lee, Richard A. *Science, the Singular, and the Question of Theology.* Houndmills, Hampshire: Palgrave Macmillan, 2002.

Lévinas, Emmanuel. *Entre Nous.* Trans. Michael B. Smith and Barbara Harshav. New York: Columbia University Press, 2000.

Lilly, R. *The Ancients and the Moderns.* Bloomington: Indiana University Press, 1996.

Lindbeck, George A., Dennis L. Okholm, and Timothy R. Phillips, eds. *The Nature of Confession: Evangelicals & Postliberals in Conversation.* Downers Grove, IL: Intervarsity Press, 1996.

Llewelyn, John. "Meanings Reserved, Re-served, and Reduced." *Southern Journal of Philosophy* XXXII, Supplement (1994): 27–54.

Lock, Charles. "Against Being: An Introduction to the Thought of Jean-Luc Marion." *Saint Vladimir's Theological Quarterly* 37.4 (1993): 370–80.

Lojacono, E. "Le letture delle *Meditationes* di Jean-Luc Marion." *Descartes metafisico. Interpretationi del Novecento.* Eds. Jean-Robert Armogathe and Giulia Belgioioso. Roma: Instituto della Enciclopedia Italiana, 1994. 129–51.

Long, D. Stephen. *Divine Economy: Theology and the Market.* Radical Orthodoxy. London/New York: Routledge, 2000.

Longhitano, T. "I paradossi del dare. Spunti per una ricerca sul dono in Marcel Mauss, Jacques Derrida e Jean-Luc Marion." *Il Cannocchiale. Rivista di studi filosopfici.* Rome, 2000/3.

Look, Brandon. Rev. of Marion, Jean-Luc. *Cartesian Questions: Method and Metaphysics.* Chicago, IL: University of Chicago Press, 1999. *The Review of Metaphysics* 54.1 (2000): 160–61.

Loparic, Z. "A propos du cartésianisme gris de J.-L. Marion." *Manuscripto* 11.2 (1988).

Loughlin, Gerard. "Transubstantiation: Eucharist as Pure Gift." *Christ.* London: SPCK, 1996. 123–41.

——. *Telling God's Story. Bible, Church and Narrative Theology.* Oxford: Oxford University Press, 1997.

Lowe, Walter. "Second Thoughts About Transcendence." *The Religious.* Ed. John D. Caputo. Oxford: Blackwell, 2002. 241–51.

Macann, Christopher. *Four Phenomenological Philosophers: Husserl, Heidegger, Sartre, Merleau-Ponty.* London: Routledge, 1994.

——, ed. *Critical Heidegger.* London: Routledge, 1996.

MacGregor, Lorie. "The Role of the Ego in Religious Experience." *Aporia* 12.2 (2002).

Mackinlay, Shane. "Eyes Wide Shut: A Response to Jean-Luc Marion's Account of the Journey to Emmaus." *Modern Theology* 20.3 (2004): 447–56.

——. "Phenomenality in the Middle. Marion, Romano, and the Hermeneutics of the Event." *Givenness and God: Questions of Jean-Luc Marion.* Eds. Eoin Cassidy and Ian Leask. New York: Fordham University Press, 2004. Forthcoming.

Macquarrie, John. Rev. of Jean-Luc Marion. *God Without Being.* Trans. Thomas A. Carlson. Chicago: University of Chicago Press, 1991. *The Journal of Religion* 73.1 (1992): 99–101.

——. "Postmodernism in Philosophy of Religion and Theology." *International Journal for Philosophy of Religion* 50 (2001): 9–27.

Maggiori, Robert. "Le sens de l'amour." March 27 2003. Internet. *Libération.* Available: http://www.liberation.com/page.php?Article=98845. April 14 2003.

Magnard, Pierre. *Le Dieu des philosophes.* Collection Philosophie Européenne. Ed. Henri Hude: MAME Éditions universitaires, 1992.

Makarian, Christian. "Aimer pour comprendre: La superbe réflexion philosophique de Jean-Luc Marion sur l'amour." April 14 2003. Internet. *L'Express Livres.* Available: http://livres.lexpress.fr/critique.asp/idC=6552/idR=12/idG=8. April 14 2003.

Manolopoulos, Mark. "If Creation is a Gift". Doctoral dissertation. Monash University, 2003.

Marshall, D. J. "J.-L. Marion: Werke zu Descartes." *Philosophische Rundschau* 31.1–2 (1984).

Martineau, Emmanuel. "L'ontologie de l'ordre." *Les Études Philosophiques* 81.4 (1976): 469–94.

Martis, John. "Postmodernism and God as Giver." *The Way* 36 (1996): 236–43.

——. "Thomistic *Esse*—Idol or Icon? Jean-Luc Marion's God Without Being." *Pacifica: Journal of the Melbourne College of Divinity* 9.1 (1996): 55–68.

Marty, F. "L'analogie perdue. La métaphysique sur les chemins de la science de Descartes à Kant." *Archives de Philosophie* 46.3 (1983).

Mason, Richard. *The God of Spinoza: A Philosophical Study.* Cambridge: Cambridge University Press, 1999.

Mattes, Mark Christopher. "Toward Divine Relationality: Eberhard Jungel's New

Trinitarian, Postmetaphysical Approach." Doctoral dissertation. The University of Chicago, 1995.

McCarthy, John C. Rev. of Jean-Luc Marion. *God Without Being.* Trans. Thomas A. Carlson. Chicago, IL: University of Chicago Press, 1991. *Review of Metaphysics* 46.3 (1993): 627–29.

—. "Amo Ergo Sum." Rev. of Jean-Luc Marion. *Prolegomena to Charity.* Trans. Stephen Lewis. New York: Fordham University Press, 2002. *Crisis: Politics, Culture, and the Church* (2002).

McKenna, Andrew J. "Derrida, Death, and Forgiveness." *First Things* 71 (1997): 34–37.

Mendez, A. F. "God and Alterity." *New Blackfriars* 80.946 (1999): 552–67.

Menn, Stephen. *Descartes and Augustine.* Cambridge: Cambridge University Press, 2002.

Mensch, James. "Givenness and Alterity." *Issues Confronting the Post-European World.* Eds. Chan-Fai Cheung, et al. Prague, Czech Republic, 2002. 1–8 of Essays in Celebration of the Founding of the Organization of Phenomenological Organizations.

Milbank, John. "Can a Gift be Given? Prolegomena to a Future Trinitarian Metaphysic." *Rethinking Metaphysics.* Eds. L. Gregory Jones and Stephen E. Fowl. Oxford: Blackwell, 1995. 119–61.

—. "Only Theology Overcomes Metaphysics." *New Blackfriars* 76.895 (1995): 325–42. *The Word Made Strange.* Oxford: Blackwell, 1997. 36–52.

—. "The Ethics of Self-Sacrifice." *First Things* 91 (1999): 33–38.

—. "The Soul of Reciprocity. Reciprocity Refused Part One." *Modern Theology* 17.3 (2001): 335–91.

—. *Being Reconciled: Ontology and Pardon.* London/New York: Routledge, 2003.

Milbank, John, and Catherine Pickstock. *Truth in Aquinas.* Radical Orthodoxy. London/New York: Routledge, 2001.

Monnoyer, Jean-Maurice. "Individualisme cartésien et sémantique externaliste." *Philosophie analytique et histoire de la philosophie.* Ed. Jean-Michel Vienne. Paris: J. Vrin, 1997. 167–69.

Moss, David. "Costly Giving: On Jean-Luc Marion's Theology of the Gift." *New Blackfriars* 74 (1993): 393–99.

Nadler, S. Rev. of Jean-Luc Marion. *Cartesian Questions: Method and Metaphysics.* Trans. Jeffrey L. Kosky, John Cottingham and Stephen Voss. Chicago, IL: University of Chicago Press, 1999. *Journal of the History of Philosophy* (2000).

Nawrocki, A. *Jean-Luc Marion. Nowe drogi w fenomenologii.* Varsovie, 2002.

Neamtu, M. "Le relief théologique de la pensée de Jean-Luc Marion." Thèse de license en Philosophie. Cluj-Napoca, Romanie, 2000a.

—. "Jean-Luc Marion—architectura unei gandiri." *Crucea vizibilului.* Deisis: Sibiu, 2000b. 135-173.

—. *Studia Phaenomenologica. Romanian Journal for Phenomenology* 1.3-4 (2001): 419-427.

Nemoianu, Virgil. "Literary Play and Religious Referentiality." *Play, Literature, and Religion*. Albany: State University of New York Press, 1992. 1–18.

Neutsch, M. "La révélation est un vrai phénomène." *La crois* septembre 1997.

Newman, L. "Descartes on Unknown Faculties and Our Knowledge of the Eternal World." *The Philosophical Review* 103.3 (1994): 489–531.

Nicolas, Jean-Hervé. "La suprême logique de l'amour et la théologie." *Revue Thomiste* LXXXIII.4 (1983): 639–59.

O'Donoghue, Noel Dermot. "In the Beginning was the Gift: A Marginal Note on *God Without Being*." *New Blackfriars* 76.895 (1995): 351–53.

O'Leary, Joseph S. *La vérité chrétienne à l'âge du pluralisme religieux*. Paris: Cerf, 1994. *Religious Pluralism and Christian Truth*. Edinburgh: Edinburgh University Press, 1996.

O'Rourke, F. *Pseudo-Dionysius and the Metaphysics of Aquinas*. Leiden: E. J. Brill, 1992.

Oliveros, Chris, and Frank King, eds. *Drawn & Quarterly*. Vol. 4: Drawn & Quarterly Publications, 2001.

Olivetti, Marco M. "Ueber J.-L. Marions Beitrag Zur Neueren Religionsphilosophie." *Archivio di Filosofia* LIV.1–3 (1986): 625–36.

——. "L'argomento ontologico." *Archivio di Filosofia* 1–3 (1990).

Olthuis, James H., ed. *Knowing Other-wise: Philosophy at the Threshold of Spirituality*. New York: Fordham University Press, 1997.

——, ed. *Religion With/Out Religion: The Prayers and Tears of John D. Caputo*. London/New York: Routledge, 2001.

Onimus, Jean. Rev. of Jean-Luc Marion. *L'idole et la distance*. Paris: Grasset, 1977. *Revue de Métaphysique et de Morale* 2 (1980): 280.

Overton, J. "See(k)ing God through the Icon: A Semiotic Analysis of Marion's *God Without Being*." *Semiotica* 110 (1996): 87–126.

Pagé, Jean-Guy. "Dieu et l'être." *Laval Théologique et Philosophique* XXXVII.1 (1981): 33–43.

Pedemonte Feu, Bonaventura. "Le sujet convoqué: à partir de la pensée de Buber, de Rosenzweig, de Lévinas, de Marion et de Ricoeur." Doctoral dissertation. Institut Catholique de Paris, 1995.

Pelluchon, Corine. Rev. of Jean-Luc Marion. *Le phénomène érotique*. Paris: Grasset, 2003c. *Religiologiques* 28 (2003).

——. *Commentaire* été 2003a.

——. *Esprit* juin 2003b.

Peperzak, Adriaan T. *Ethics As First Philosophy: The Significance of Emmanuel Lévinas for Philosophy, Literature and Religion*. London: Routledge, 1995.

Perl, E. *American Catholic Philosophical Quarterly* 68.4 (1994): 554–57.

Petit, P. *Marianne* 26 mai 2003.

Petrosino, S. "D'un livre à l'autre. *Totalité et l'infini-Autrement qu'être*." *Emmanuel Lévinas: Cahiers de la nuit surveillée*. Lagrasse: Verdier, 1984. 199ff.

Pickstock, Catherine. *After Writing: On the Liturgical Consummation of Philosophy*. Oxford: Blackwell, 1998.

Popkin, Richard Henry. *The History of Scepticism: From Savanorola to Bayle.* Oxford: Oxford University Press, 2003.

Power, David N. "Sacramental Theology: Postmodern Approaches." *Theological Studies* 55 (1994): 684–93.

——. "Roman Catholic Theologies of Eucharistic Communion: A Contribution to Ecumenical Conversation." *Theological Studies* 57.4 (1996): 587–610.

——. *Sacraments: The Language of God's Giving.* New York: Crossroad, 1999.

Prouvost, G. "La tension irrésolue." *Revue Thomiste* 98.1 (1998): 95–102.

Purcell, Michael. " 'This Is My Body' Which Is 'for you' ... Ethically speaking ..." *The Presence of Transcendence.* Eds. Lieven Boeve and John C. Ries. Leuven: Uitgeverij Peeters, 2001. 135–51.

Pyle, Andrew. *Malebranche.* London/New York: Routledge, 2003.

Rabouin, D. *Le magazine littéraire* mai 2003.

Reali, Nicola. *Fino all'abbandono: l'eucaristia nella fenomenologia di Jean-Luc Marion.* Roma: Città Nuova, 2001.

Reiter, J. *Philosophischer Literaturanzeiger* 32.4 (1979).

Renaut, Alain. *The Era of the Individual.* Trans. M. B. Debevoise and Franklin Philip. Princeton, NJ: Princeton University Press, 1999.

Ricard, Marie-Andrée. "La question de la donation chez Jean-Luc Marion." *Laval Théologique et Philosophique* 57.1 (2001): 83–94.

Ricci, R. "Da Heidegger a Marion: rifless sulla metafisica cartesiana come ontologia." *Discipline filosofiche* 1.1 (1991).

Richardson, William J. *Theological Studies* 54.3 (1993): 576.

Robbins, Jeffrey W. "Overcoming Overcoming: In Praise of Ontotheology." *Explorations in Contemporary Continental Philosophy of Religion.* Ed. Deane-Peter Baker. New York: Rodopi, 2003. 9–21.

Robert, Jean-Dominique. "Autour de *Dieu sans l'être* de Jean-Luc Marion." *Laval Théologique et Philosophique* 39.3 (1983): 341–47.

——. " 'Dieu sans l'être': À propos d'un livre récent." *Nouvelle Revue Théologique* 105.3 (1983): 406–10.

Rockmore, Tom. *Heidegger and French Philosophy: Humanism, Antihumanism and Being.* London: Routledge, 1994.

Röd, W. *Archiv für Geschichte der Philosophie* 75 (1993).

Rogozinski, J. "Remarques." *Hermeneutica. Annuario di filosofia e teologia.* Urbino, 2000.

Rolland, Jacques. *Parcours de l'autrement: lecture d'Emmanuel Lévinas.* Paris: Presses Universitaires de France, 2000.

Rolland, Jacques, and S. Petrosino. *La vérité nomade. Introduction à Emmanuel Lévinas.* Paris: Cerf, 1984.

Romano, C. "Remarques sur la méthode phénoménologique dans *Étant donné*." *Annales de Philosophie* 21. Bayreuth: Université Saint-Joseph, 2000.

Rosemann, Philipp W. "Der maskierte Philosoph. Die verborgene Theologie des Cartesianismus." *Frankfurter Allgemeine Zeitung* 2.3 (1992).

——. "Der Melancholiker sieht wie Gott. Aber weil er das Andere verweigert, blickt er ins Nichts: Jean-Luc Marion's negative Theologie." *Frankfurter Allgemeine Zeitung* 7.14 (1993).

——. "Penser l'Autre: théologie négative et 'postmodernité'." *Revue philosophique de Louvain* 91.90 (1993): 296–310.

——. *Understanding Scholastic Thought with Foucault.* Houndmills, Hampshire: Palgrave Macmillan, 1999.

Rostagno, Sergio. "La ragione teologica: Rassegna di teologia sistematica." *Protestantesimo* 53.1 (1998): 35–42.

Sacchi, M. E. "La fabulacion del horizonte del ser y la condeha du la metafisicaen nombre de ontoteologia. Replica a Jean-Luc Marion." *Philosophia* (1977). Reprinted in *Conquistas y Regresiones em Restauracion du la Velafiçica.* Rosario (Argentine), 2000.

Sanders, T. "The Otherness of God and the Bodies of Others." *Journal of Religion* 76 (1996): 572–87.

Sansonetti, G. "Distanza e differenza. A proposito del libro di Jean-Luc Marion." *Archives de Philosophie* 50.1 (1987).

Schlegel, Jean-Louis. "*Dieu sans l'être.* À propos de J.-L. Marion." *Esprit.* (1984): 26–36.

Schmitz, K. L. "The God of Love." *The Thomist* 57.3 (1993): 495–508.

Schmutz, J. Escaping the Aristotelian Bond; The Critique of Metaphysics in Twentieth-Century French Philosophy." *Dionysius,* XVII (1999).

Sebba, G. "Retroversion and the History of Ideas: J.-L. Marion's translation of the *Regulae* of Descartes." *Studia Cartesiana* 1 (1979).

Secher, Tobias. *Einen anderen Gott denken. Zum Verständnis der Alterität Gottes bei Jean-Luc Marion.* Frankfurt: Knecht, 2002.

Seubert, Xavier John. "A Discussion on the Eucharistic Theology in Jean-Luc Marion's *God Without Being.*" *The Catholic Theological Society of America – Proceedings of the Fifty-second Annual Convention.* Ed. Judith Dwyer. New York: CTSA, 1997. 111–12.

Shanks, Andrew. *God and Modernity: A New and Better Way to Do Theology.* London/New York: Routledge, 2000.

Shanley, Brian J. "Saint Thomas, Onto-theology, and Marion." *The Thomist* 60.4 (1996): 617–25.

Sichère, B. *Cinquante ans de philosophie française.* Paris: Ministère des Affaires Étrangères, 1998.

Smith, James K. A. "How to Avoid Not Speaking: Attestations." *Knowing Other-wise: Philosophy at the Threshold of Spirituality.* Ed. James H. Olthuis. Perspectives in Continental Philosophy. New York: Fordham University Press, 1997. 217–34.

——. "Respect and Donation: A Critique of Marion's Critique of Husserl." *American Catholic Philosophical Quarterly* 71.4 (1997): 523–38.

——. "How to Avoid Not Speaking: On the Phenomenological Possibility of Theology." Doctoral dissertation. Villanova University, 1999.

——. "Liberating Religion from Theology: Marion and Heidegger on the Possibility of a Phenomenology of Religion." *International Journal for Philosophy of Religion* 46.1 (1999): 17–33.

——. "Between Predication and Silence: Augustine on How (Not) to Speak of God." *Heythrop Journal* 41.1 (2000): 66–86.

——. *The Fall of Interpretation: Philosophical Foundations for a Creational Hermeneutic.* Downer Grove, IL: Intervarsity Press, 2000.

——. "How (Not) to Tell a Secret: Interiority and the Strategy of 'Confession'." *American Catholic Philosophical Quarterly* 74.1 (2000): 135–51.

——. *Speech and Theology: Language and the Logic of Incarnation.* Radical Orthodoxy. London: Routledge, 2002.

Sneller, Rico "Mysterie of incarnatie? Marion en Derrida." *Il Cannocchiale. Rivista di studi filosopfici.* Rome, 2000/3.

——. "Incarnation as a Prerequisite: Marion and Derrida." *Bijdragen* 65.1 (2004): 38–54.

Sommavilla, G. "La nuova teologia di Marion e la sua logica." *Rasegna di teologia* 3 (1979).

Specker, T. *Einen anderen Gott denken? Zum Verständnis der alterität Gottes bei Jean-Luc Marion.* Frankfurt a./M, Knecht.

Steinbock, A. "Saturated Intentionality." *Resituating Merleau-Ponty.* Atlanti Highlands, NJ: Humanities Press, 1995.

Stout, Jeffrey. *Democracy and Tradition.* Princeton, NJ: Princeton University Press, 2003.

Svenungsson, Jayne. "Guds aterkomst. En studie av gudsbegreppet inom postmodern filosofi." Doctoral thesis. Lund University, 2002.

Sweetman, Brendan. *New Oxford Review.* (1993).

Tarnowski, K. "God After Metaphysics?" *Kwartalnik Filozof* 24.1 (1996): 31–47.

Taylor, Victor E., and Charles E. Winquist, eds. *Encyclopedia of Postmodernism.* London/New York: Routledge, 2001.

Tilliette, Xavier. Rev. of Jean-Luc Marion. *Étant donné.* Paris: Presses Universitaires de France, 1997. *Archives de Philosophie* 61.4 (1998): 759–63.

——. *Etudes* septembre 2003.

Tracy, David. "Foreword." *God Without Being.* Chicago, IL: University of Chicago Press, 1991. ix–xv.

Valadier, Paul. *Jésus-Christ ou Dionysos: La foi chrétienne en confrontation avec Nietzsche.* Paris: Desclée, 1979.

Van den Bossche, Stijn. "God verschijnt toch in de immanentie. De fenomenologische neerlegging van de theologie in Jean-Luc Marion's *Étant donné.*" *God en het Denken. Over de filosofie van Jean-Luc Marion.* Ed. Ruud Welten. Nijmegen: Annalen van het Thijmgenootschap 88.2, 2000. 128–53.

——. "God Does Appear in Immanence After All: Jean-Luc Marion's Phenomenology as a New First Philosophy for Theology." *Sacramental Presence in a Postmodern Context.* Leuven: Peeters, 2001. 325–46.

——. "Twee verschillende kijkwijzen. Jean-Luc Marion over idool en icoon." *God ondergronds. Opstellen voor een theologisch vrijdenker.* Eds. L. Boeve and J. Averbode, 2001. 339–356.

——. "Gott ist ganz anders." *Philokles. Zeitschrift für populäre Philosophie* 1 (2001): 35–38.

——. Rev. of Marion, Jean-Luc, and Josef Wolmuth. *Ruf und Gabe. Zum Verhältnis von Phänomenologie und Theologie*. Bonn: Borengässer, 2000. *Bijdragen* 62.2 (2001): 239–40.

——. "A Possible Present for Theology." *Bijdragen* 65.1 (2004): 55–78.

Van den Bossche, Stijn, and Ruud Welten. "Preface." *Bijdragen* 65.1 (2004): 3–4.

Van den Hoogen, T. "Theo-logie tussen verzwijgen en stilte. Marions voorstel om over God te zwijgen." *Il Cannocchiale. Rivista di studi filosopfici*. Rome, 2000/3.

Van Maas, Sander. "On Preferring Mozart." *Bijdragen* 65.1 (2004): 97–110.

Vanhoozer, Kevin J. *First Theology: God, Scriptures and Hermeneutics*. Downers Grove, IL: Intervarsity Press, 2002.

——, ed. *The Cambridge Companion to Postmodern Theology*. Cambridge: Cambridge University Press, 2003.

Verneaux, Roger. *Étude critique du livre "Dieu sans l'être."* Paris: Téqui, 1986.

Vienne, Jean-Michel. *Philosophie analytique et histoire de la philosophie*. Paris: J. Vrin, 1997.

Villela-Petit, M. "Heidegger est-il idolâtre?" *Heidegger et la question de Dieu*. Eds. Richard Kearney and Joseph S. O'Leary. Paris: B. Grasset, 1980. 75–102.

Virgoulay, René. "Dieu ou l'être? Relecture de Heidegger en marge de J.-L. Marion, *Dieu sans l'être*." *Recherches de Science Religieuse* 72.2 (1984): 163–98.

Vogel, Arthur A. "Catching Up With Jean-Luc Marion." *Anglican Theological Review* 82.4 (2000): 803–11.

Vries, Hent de. "Theotopographies: Nancy, Hölderlin, Heidegger." *MLN* 109.3 (1994): 445–77.

——. *Philosophy & the Turn to Religion*. Baltimore, MD: Johns Hopkins University Press, 1999

——. *Religion and Violence: Philosophical Perspectives from Kant to Derrida*. Baltimore, MD: Johns Hopkins University Press, 2002.

Wall, John, William Schweiker, and W. David Hall, eds. *Paul Ricoeur and Contemporary Moral Thought*. London/New York: Routledge, 2002.

Ward, Graham. "Introducing Jean-Luc Marion." *New Blackfriars* 76.895 (1995): 317–24.

——. "Theology and the Crisis of Representation." *Literature and Theology at Century's End*. Atlanta, GA: Scholar's Press, 1995. 131–58.

——. "Between Postmodernism and Postmodernity: The Theology of Jean-Luc Marion." *Postmodernity, Sociology and Religion*. Eds. Kieran Flanagan and Peter C. Jupp. London: Macmillan, 1996. 190–205.

——. "Introduction." *The Postmodern God*. Ed. Graham Ward. Oxford: Blackwell, 1997. xv–xlvii.

——. "The Theological Project of Jean-Luc Marion." *Post-Secular Philosophy: Between Philosophy and Theology*. Ed. Philip Blond. London: Routledge, 1998. 67–106.

——. *Cities of God*. London/New York: Routledge, 2000.

Webb, S. H. *The Gifting God*. Oxford/NewYork: Oxford University Press, 1996.

Weinstein, Idit Dobbs. *Maimonides and St. Thomas on the Limits of Reason.* Albany: State University of New York, 1995.

Welten, Ruud. "Het andere ego van Descartes." *Tijdschrift voor Filosofie* 60.3 (1998): 572–79.

——, ed. *God en het Denken. Over de filosofie van Jean-Luc Marion.* Nijmegen: Annalen van het Thijmgenootschap 88.2, 2000.

——. *Fenomenologie en Beeldverbod bij Emmanuel Levinas en Jean-Luc Marion.* Damon: Budel, 2001.

——. "Saturation and Disappointment. Marion According to Husserl." *Bijdragen* 65.1 (2004): 79–96.

Westphal, Merold. "Postmodernism and Religious Reflection." *International Journal for Philosophy of Religion* 38 (1995): 127–43.

——, ed. *Postmodern Philosophy and Christian Thought.* Bloomington: Indiana University Press, 1999.

——. *Overcoming Onto-theology.* Perspectives in Continental Philosophy. Ed. John D. Caputo. New York: Fordham University Press, 2001.

——. "Divine Excess: The God Who Comes After." *The Religious.* Ed. John D. Caputo. Oxford: Blackwell, 2002. 259–76.

——. "Transfiguration as Saturated Phenomenon." *Journal of Philosophy and Scripture* 1.1 (2003): 1–10.

——. *Transcendence and Self-transcendence.* Bloomington, Indiana University Press, 2004.

Winkler, K. "Descartes and the Three Names of God." *American Catholic Philosophical Quarterly* 67.4 (1993): 451–65.

Wirzba, Norman. Rev. of Jean-Luc Marion. *God Without Being.* Trans. Thomas A. Carlson. Chicago, IL: University of Chicago Press, 1991. *Christian Century* 109.15 (1992): 458.

Wolf, K. *Religionsphilosophie in Frankreich.* Munich, 1999. 153–164.

Wolmuth, Josef. *Ruf und Gabe. Zum Verhältnis von Phänomenologie und Theologie.* Bonn: Borengässer, 2000.

Wood, John. *The Virtual Embodied: Presence/Practice/Technology.* London/New York: Routledge, 1998.

Wright, John P., and Paul Potter, eds. *Psyche and Soma: Physicians and Metaphysicians on the Mind–Body Problem from Antiquity to Enlightenment.* Oxford: Oxford University Press, 2003.

Wyschogrod, Edith. *Emmanuel Lévinas: The Problem of Ethical Metaphysics.* Perspectives in Continental Philosophy. Ed. John D. Caputo. New York: Fordham University Press, 2000.

Wyschogrod, Edith, and John D. Caputo. "Postmodernism and the Desire for God." *Cross Currents* 48.3 (1998).

Yovel, Yirmiyahu. *Spinoza and Other Heretics.* Reprint ed. Vol. 1. Princeton, NJ: Princeton University Press, 1992.

Yun, W.-J. "The 'Gift' With/Of No-Return: A Christian (De)Constructive Ethic of Alterity." Doctoral dissertation. Southwestern Baptist Theological Seminary, 1999.

Zhang, Ellen Y. "Icon Without Logos; Theology Without Ontology." Rev. of Jean-Luc Marion. *God Without Being: Hors-Texte*. Chicago, IL: University of Chicago Press, 1991. *Cross Currents* (1993): 273–77.

Ziarek, K. "The Language of Praise: Lévinas and Marion." *Religion and Literature* 22 (1990): 93–107.

Appendix 3

Excerpts from Selected Texts

Excerpt 1. The Intentionality of Love*

The Crossing of the Gazes

The unconsciousness that we are seeking can therefore be reached. It is not a matter of an unconsciousness wherein the process of a likely love is clouded over with illusory ambiguities; nor is it a matter of simple inversion of the axis of the gaze, where the function of the *I* simply displaces itself from one to the other of the terms at play, thereby reinforcing all the more its validity. Instead, it is a matter of a consciousness that exerts itself on my consciousness, without following it into polarization in terms of the *I*—a consciousness against the grain of the *I*. The moral injunction (*Gewissen*) brings to bear the consciousness of an obligation that imposes itself on the *I* and thus destroys it as originary pole. Still consciousness is not closed up (*Bewusstsein*) in the indistinctness of the id. The *I* reduced to the *me* retains consciousness, precisely so as to see that it no longer becomes conscious of *itself*, but of an obligation that links it, despite itself, to the anterior other. The moral consciousness forbids the transcendental consciousness to fold itself back over and into an *I* and enjoins it to see itself as consciousness, in itself, of the other than self. The moral consciousness contradicts self-consciousness by counterbalancing the intentionality exerted by the *I*, thanks to the injunction summoning *me*. The injunction constrains and contains intentionality; intentionality objectifies the other on the basis of the *I*, but all the same, the injunction summons me on the basis and in the name of the invisible other. The invisibility passes from one extreme to the other, the means alone remaining visible to the corresponding aim. Whence comes what we will from now on consider the phenomenological determination of love: two definitively invisible gazes (intentionality and the injunction) cross one another, and thus together trace a cross that is invisible to every gaze other than theirs alone. Each of the two gazes renounces seeing visibly the other gaze—the object alone can be seen, the eye's corpse—in order to expose its own invisible intention to the invisible impact of the other intention. Two gazes, definitively invisible, cross and, in this crossing, renounce their invisibility. They consent to let themselves be seen without seeing and invert the original disposition of every (de)nominative gaze—to see without being seen. To love would thus be defined as seeing the definitively invisible aim of my gaze nonetheless exposed by the aim of

---

* This excerpt is taken from Jean-Luc Marion, *Prolegomena to Charity*, trans. Stephen Lewis (New York: Fordham University Press, 2002) 86–101. Reproduced with kind permission.

another invisible gaze; the two gazes, invisible forever, expose themselves each to the other in the crossing of their reciprocal aims. Loving no longer consists trivially in seeing or in being seen, nor in desiring or inciting desire, but in experiencing the crossing of the gazes within, first the crossing of aims.

Lived Experience Crossed

Determining love as the crossing of aims gives rise to a clear-cut difficulty: does the crossing itself remain invisible or does it give rise to visibility? Put another way, does it become an object, which can actually be seen as a lived experience of consciousness? We will try to argue that the crossing of the invisible gazes becomes visible only for the parties involved, because they alone undergo an experience without recognizing an object in that experience. The intentional gaze, if it crosses the moral injunction, experiences an interdiction, an obligation, or a provocation. It matters little whether it respects them or transgresses them, for in both cases this intentional gaze will actually feel the weight of a counter aim, a weight that is all the more objective in that, in order to pass beyond, the intentional gaze will require the imbalance of a higher weighing—which would thus be more highly actual. The ethical counter aim makes its weight felt with the same force whether I transgress it or subscribe to it, whether I resist it or consent to it. But if gazes that are foreign to one another see nothing of the crossing of two invisible gazes, in short if this non-objective crossing remains decidedly invisible to them, too, things are not the same for each of the two concerned gazes—the two gazes concerned each by the other. The intentionality of the *I* and the obligation to the other (which opposes *me* to him) cross, in that they experience each other; they experience each other in the common lived experience of their two efforts, constrained each to the other, buttressed by their contradictory and thus convergent impetuses. Intentionality and the injunction exchange nothing, especially not two (objectified) lived experiences; yet they come together in a lived experience which can only be experienced in common, since it consists in the balanced resistance of two intentional impetuses. This common lived experience results from the crossed conflict of two invisibles: without one, without the other, without both the one and the other in strict equality, the lived experience either would not be fixed or else would not remain in a lasting equilibrium. The two gazes are balanced in a common lived experience, which does not touch them in their respective origins, but summons them and finally blocks them in their mutual impetuses, to the point of balance in their crossing. With the two invisible aims, this crossing traces a cross, still invisible except to those who suffer its weight in a common lived experience. Thus, in crossing swords, duelists experience something like a single lived experience that communicates a common tension—the pressure that my weapon, and thus my arm, and thus my whole body imposes, contains and renders to the opposed pressure. Whence I infer an arm out-stretched and an entire fighting body, which exerts against me the intention that I exert against it. Arm wrestling, where the two arms cross and where the impetuses of each of the two bodies are immobilized, brings together, face to face, the two fleshly faces. What then do each of these two invisibles see of the other? Nothing objective, nor visible (the two adversaries still remain nondead, nonvisible, because not cadavers). However they see their encounter, for they experience the weight of each impetus against the other, a unique and common weight, balanced and shared. They see, with their always-invisible gazes, the lived experience of their tensions. The crossing of gazes here imitates the crossing of swords—what they each see of the other consists in the balanced tension of aims, like two weapons crossed. The crossed encounter is made to stand as a lived experience of the invisible; however, the experienced vision of the lived experience never results in the visibility of an object. The crossing of invisible gazes draws near to being quasi-visible only for the two aims that experience, like a heavy weight falling on the shoulders all at once, the balance of their two impetuses buttressed at full force. Neither the lover nor the beloved encounter each other in passing, dreamily, each in the other. They experience one another in the commonality of the lived experience of their unique tension—the weight of one gaze on the other, crushed by experiencing itself seen, crushing by seeing itself experienced. Two gazes, which seek each other, seek not the invisible site of the other gaze, but the point of equilibrium between my tension and his or her own. The sudden fixity of their common level, like water equilibrated in a lock, does not arouse in them any less inexpressible pleasure than bodily pleasure. For bodily pleasure, perhaps, comes down to generalizing for all flesh the balance of aims, where each attests to its humanity by honouring itself with invisibility—as if with glory. Whence the inverse consequence, that pleasure can answer to the high name of love only as a common lived experience, where two invisibles balance each other; if they fail, the pleasure sinks into insignificance, or, if it claims to overcome insignificance, it sets itself up as an unforgivable posturing as the invisible—an obscene incarnation of the gaze's corpse. The pleasure of the eyes disfigures the pleasure of the gazes, wherein no object—especially not a heart or a face—can bring climax, for climax (*la jouissance*) is born from the inobjectivity that only the tension of the gazes governs. A visible jubilation of invisibles, without any visible object, yet in balance, through the crossing of aims: let this situation count, here, as the sketch of a definition of love.

Originary Alterity

To define love as the crossed lived experience of invisible gazes implies, at the very least, that the gaze of the other reaches me and weighs upon my own gaze. We have admitted under the name injunction the advent of a gaze other than that of my own intentionality. The injunction benefits from a noteworthy privilege: it is a lived experience of mine in that it greatly affects my consciousness; I experience the obligation that imposes itself on me and compels me, whether I admit it or not; the obligation affects me directly, inevitably to the point that I cannot release myself from it by handing it off to someone else, nor even make him experience it (except if he directly experiences a parallel obligation). For the injunction is not received by derived appresentation, in which the originary presence would reside in the other. The injunction does not enjoin the other to me simply because it might come from him; it does not result from a disposition of the other, wherein it would reside first and actually, so as then to pass from an originary presence to a derived presence. The injunction does not come from the other toward me, by an inverted intentionality of the other consciousness acting against my own. It actually arises in me, as one of my lived experiences, which an originary presence assures to my consciousness; yet as a lived experience of my consciousness, the injunction imposes on my consciousness, without the least bit of intentionality (neither its own, nor another's), the first coming of the other. From the beginning I experience the rights of the other over me, as more original to me than myself. The injunction makes another gaze weigh on my own, another gaze of which the other knows nothing and, literally, of which he has no idea. In the best of cases, the physical gaze of the other furnishes only the schema of the injunction; or rather, I can regard the other as an invisible gaze (and not see him as an object) only because first of all the injunction imposes him on me, designates him to me and leads me to him—despite myself, but also despite him. The injunction does not come to me from the other, nor does it push me toward him; it makes me experience, in and through myself, the advent of the other; I experience myself, in myself and as such, obliged to an other who can be entirely ignorant of this obligation. The obligation toward the other is born in me, though it is not born of me; it is born for him though it is not born through him. The obligation, really and truly mine, makes the original weight of a gaze that the other does not even have to produce weigh upon me; or rather, the invisible gaze of the other can come to bear on my own gaze only to the degree that the injunction in me precedes it and welcomes it—contrary to all intentionality.

The Means of the Universal

The privilege and the paradox of the injunction alone make possible a phenomenological sketch of love. But in this direction a difficulty also appears; the injunction certainly incites me toward the other, but without my having to or being able to discern love there. If the injunction enjoins to any other whatsoever, indeed to every possible other, simply inasmuch as it offers the face of man, it does not permit the election of such a one, precisely because it enjoins rendering to the other as other what I owe him. The injunction gives rise not so much to love as to duty, for, like duty, the injunction concerns every other, universally. The injunction addresses me to the other in order that I offer him the recognition that he deserves as end, and not as means, or, which amounts to the same thing, the continuation of the particular maxim guiding my action into the universality of a law. The formal universality that determines my behaviour toward the other does not in any way depend upon the particular identity of this or that other. The formal universality of the obligation becomes thinkable only once persons have been abstracted from it, such that the other opened by the injunction can be played by anyone: the other thus passes from one face to the other according to the radical substitution that universality imposes. That the particular face here holds the role of the other, without incarnating him definitively, that this face occasionally lends its gaze to the universal injunction, in short that this other remains only the lieutenant of the other (*l'autrui*), finds its confirmation in respect. Without a doubt, the injunction of the law moves me to respect, whether I transgress it or obey it, and thus becomes as particular as my sensibility. But it is precisely this respect, which I experience in particularity, that I do not feel for *this* other, *this* face, *this* individual, but rather for the universal law alone. My individuality submits to affection for the universal, and never for the other who accidentally lends his face to it. Far from my individuality feeling for another, individually unsubstitutable by the mediation of respect for the universal of the law, my individuality instead lets itself be moved by the accidental and substitutable mediation of any individual face in favour of the universal of the law (to the point of becoming, like a free noumenon, itself universal). Accordingly, and paradoxically, the moral law—which states that the other man must always count as end and not as means—never uses the face of an individualized other except as a means for accomplishing the universal. The injunction of obligation toward the other (*autrui*) leads, in reality, to the neutralization of the other as such. The other is neutralized as other, for another can always be substituted who can offer the face of the other (*d'autrui*) that the universal moral law requires; no face can claim to be irreplaceable because, if it in fact became so, at once by right, the act accomplished in regard to him would cease to satisfy the universality of the law. The other as such therefore undergoes a second neutralization: to the substitution that is, on principle, always possible, there is added the always required gap between the law and *every* singular individual. Between the letters of the law all possible individuals can and must parade, with equal dignity—which is to say, without any dignity, except borrowed, lent by the law itself. The injunction does not lead to loving *this* other, if only the universality of the law pronounces it; rather it leads to the law itself, while neutralizing the other in particular (*comme un tel*).

That Face

The injunction must therefore be singularized for my gaze to cross an individually irreducible gaze. It attains this singularization in passing from obligation to responsibility: "it is my responsibility before the face looking at me as absolutely foreign ... that constitutes the original fact of fraternity."[1] Responsibility inverts the legal arrangement of end and means: I am responsible not in front of the law by means of the other, but directly for the other by means of the injunction itself; the death of the other, or his life, depends directly on my regard for his open face; the other unreservedly constitutes the sole stake of my responsibility; nothing surpasses him, surprises him, or utilizes him. The suspicion of neutralization does not disappear, however. For I am responsible standing before every other, provided that his face exposes itself to my gaze; and it is precisely this provision that enables substitution to remain possible: each of the visible faces enjoins upon me a responsibility which at once prompts and orients my own intention; in order to

---

[1] Lévinas, *Totalité et infini*, p.189; tr. Lingis, p.214.

compel my responsibility, a face suffices, every face, each face, indeed, any face, so long as it opens in an invisible gaze. The unconditioned nature of responsibility implies its universality, from face to face, up until the last, whoever that might be. The neutrality persists because a substitution persists. To be sure, the Neuter, *here*, owes nothing to the Neuter that Lévinas stigmatizes in the primacy of the ontological difference; it is not a question of neutralizing the face, nor a being, nor being in its variance with Being; but the face itself neutralizes unsubstitutable individuality; I do not find myself responsible before *such a one* as much as *this such a one* admits of being reduced to *a* face in general, addressee of my gaze, and conjuring of its aim. Now, recourse to a face in general leaves two difficulties unbroached: (1) Where will things stand with the disfigured face? No doubt, it is in just such an undone face (*un tel visage defait*) that the essence of every face must be squarely faced. It nonetheless remains the case that to approach this disfiguration as to a face, one needs to employ a gaze that recognizes and knows how to envisage; not every gaze, even those already affected by responsibility, succeeds. What gap, then, separates the recognition of the disfigured face from its nonrecognition? Responsibility, doubtless, is not enough, not excluding its eventual and explicit deepening. (2) Can the other designated to me by a face, individualize himself to the point of becoming unsubstitutable for every other other? This question opens out into another question: why am I enjoined by this other and not that one? And if the reason for this should not be sought, we must then acknowledge that the injunction concerns alterity in its universality, as indifferent as possible to *such* or *such*. No doubt, ethical responsibility cannot and even must not make distinctions between faces, such that, *with regard to responsibility*, the universality of the injunction implies no return whatsoever of the Neuter. But, if we are seeking to define love as it is distinguished from respect and responsibility, then the possibility of substituting one face for the other constitutes a final obstacle, all the more fearsome because it results directly from love's most advanced approach.

That to Which I Enjoin Myself

In order to bring love back to its conceptual determination, we were obliged to subtract it from representation, even intentional representation, so as to substitute for it the injunction. The injunction itself now remains to be determined, so that it will not settle into any figure of the Neuter. If we want to secure responsibility all the way to the point of love, then the injunction must designate not only the other as such, but *just such* an other as the invisible gaze that crosses my own. That *just such* an other enjoins me implies that he sets himself up as unsubstitutable and strictly irreplaceable. Not only would "The other ... no longer be now, where I respond for him, the first-come (*le premier venu*)—he would be an old acquaintance"[2]: but he would also no longer be something known at all, if science bears only on the

---

[2] Emmanuel Lévinas, *De Dieu qui vient à l'idée* (Paris: J. Vrin, 1982), p. 250; *Of God Who Comes to Mind*, tr. Bettina Bergo (Stanford: Stanford University Press, 1998), p.166. It could even be that the other, neither known nor replaceable, belongs, more than to the past and the present, to the future—no matter what happens, the other will always be just such (*tel*).

universal, or at least on the repeatable. The other as *such* redoubles his invisibility with a particularity unknowable in itself. Love passes beyond responsibility only if the injunction reaches atomic particularity: love requires nothing less than *haecceitas*, which is also situated beyond essence (unless we must say on the hither side of essence). *Haecceitas* passes beyond beingness (*l'étantité*) in general, but also beyond that which, in the injunction and responsibility, falls under the universal, and thus the Neuter. It pierces all the way through to the unique, which no fellow will ever be able to approach, nor replace. The other as such asserts itself as the other of all the others, and does not reside in itself alone except insofar as it separates from everyone else. *Haecceitas* decides for an absolute separation from every similitude, to the point of provoking the holiness of the other. The other alone singles out himself.

Such a claim immediately gives rise to an objection. Does the singular particularity of the other as *just such* an other—as the sole and unique one—not reproduce, displaced from the one (the I) to the other (the other as such), the fundamental injustice of every self: to insist upon oneself as a basis, which, under the heading of irreplaceable center, centralizes the world into so many interests, to the point of including, as if these interests were reducible to the Same, men to whom this self denies any face? Does not the other win its *haecceitas* as an ultimate and full proprietorship that appropriates the other, starting with my own gaze, which he claims from me with injunction? In short, does not *haecceitas* as unsubstitutable center and appropriating proprietorship, repeat what Emmanuel Lévinas denounced as "mineness," the characteristic of *Dasein* that disqualifies it ethically? This characteristic of the self appropriating itself to itself in the experience of its nonsubstitutability—the egoity of *Dasein*[3]—reappears in the injunction of the other as such, since the *as such* is fulfilled finally (and ever since Leibniz)[4] only in the *I*. The other as such would only open onto an *alter ego*, an alterity still under the figure

---

[3] Criticism (for example in *De Dieu qui vient à l'idée*, pp.81–83, 145–148) of Heidegger, *Sein und Zeit*, §9:"The Being of this entity is *in each case mine*. This entity, in its Being, comports itself toward its Being. As entity of this Being, it is delivered over to its own Being. Being is that which is an issue for this entity each time" (*Being and Time*, tr. Macquarrie and Robinson [New York: Harper and Row, 1962], p.67 [translation modified]). *Jemeiningkeit* compels *Dasein* to personalize with a pronoun the verb to be only on the basis of its radical claim *(Anspruch)* by Being. Whence Lévinas's attempt to institute a claim prior to that of Being (*De Dieu*, p.245, 265; see *Le Temps et l'autre*, 2d ed. [Montpelier: Fata Morgana, 1979], p.133ff.).

[4] "Because it is necessarily the case that in corporeal nature we find true unities, without which there would be absolutely no multitudes nor collection, it must be that that which makes corporeal substance would be something which responds to that which I call the self [*moy*] in us, which is indivisible and yet acting" (G. W. Leibniz, *Système nouveau pour expliquer la nature des substances* … , in *Die philosophischen Schriften*, ed. Gerhardt, IV, p.473). As a result, on the basis of the I, and without ever contesting it, every other other can be reached: "The reflexive acts, which enable us to think of that which is called *I* … and it is thus that in thinking of ourselves we think of Being, of Substance, of the simple and compound, of the immaterial, and of God himself" (*Monadologie*, §30; *G. W. Leibniz's Monodology: An Edition for Students*, ed. Nicholas Rescher [Pittsburgh, PA: University of

of the *ego*, and thus an alterity reduced to the Same: this other amounts to the same as me, since we both come back to the figure of the *I*. An *I* displaced still remains an *I*, radically foreign to all alterity as such. And to accede to such an other simply a displaced *I*, neither love nor ethics would be required—a simple knowledge through analogical appresentation of one monadic ego by another would be enough. In claiming to pass beyond ethics through love, we would only have regressed to ordinary intentionality of consciousness. The objection, however, is less forceful than it appears: it proceeds as if the unsubstitutable other could be understood as a displaced *I*; or more precisely, as if a displaced *I* still remained, rightfully, an *I*; and therefore as if the unsubstitutable character of the other (what makes him *just such* this other) could be reduced to the egoity of the *I*. But of course a capital difference opposes them: I impose my egoity (or impose myself through it), while the unsubstitutability of the other is not imposed on me by him, but indeed by I who seek it as such (or seek him as *just such* within that unsubstitutability). The other requires his *haecceitas* not because he imposes it on me as his rule, but because *it is necessary for me* that it be imposed in order that the injunction allow me to experience his gaze as such. Inversely, I can and even must renounce my own, my proprietorship of egoity, for the sake of exposing myself to alterity; but I cannot— for that very reason—renounce proprietorship, what is proper to the other, if I want to encounter the injunction of his gaze as such. *Haecceitas* does not reproduce, as a symmetrical reply, the egoity of an I; it reverses it. The other resolves himself in the crossing of gazes on the condition of entering this crossing as unsubstitutable, while I enter it only on condition of leaving myself destitute of all intentionality, and thus of all egoity. What is more, intentionality directly contradicts unsubstitutable particularity, because it has as its unique function to permit consciousness to substitute itself for every thing; consciousness is intentionally every thing, thus it itself is counted among none of these things; the unreality of consciousness results from its intentionality and dispenses from identifying itself among things. *Haecceitas* thus marks the renunciation of intentionality and egoity, and thus stigmatizes the precise act by which the other enters into play as *such*—namely as stranger to an *I*. The injunction that would finally put into play the other as such would, thus, also accomplish the transgression of the intentionality by love.

The Invisible Unsubstitutable

But a conditional will weaken this confirmation, as long as we have not established that an injunction actually imposes upon me the gaze of the other as *such*. Can such confirmation ever emerge? Perhaps, if one considers further the injunction itself. (1) The injunction asserts itself upon my gaze because it weighs upon it with the weight

---

Pittsburgh Press, 1991] p.21). Whence the perfect diagnosis offered by Nietzsche (14 [79]): "We have borrowed the concept of unity from our 'I' concept—our oldest article of faith" (Nietzsche, *Werke*, ed. Collis and Montinari [Berlin: Walter de Gruyter, 1972], vol III/3, p.50; *The Will to Power*, tr. Walter Kaufman [New York: Viking Press, 1962], p.338).

of another gaze. Why does this gaze itself weigh in with all of its weight? Because the other person exposes himself to it. Why then does he lay himself open to it to the point of imposing on me? Because, as we have just seen, the other only becomes absolutely "just such" an other (*tel*) by becoming unsubstitutable for every other other. The other accedes to himself by coming forward in his irreplaceable *haecceitas*; he is thrown off balance, so to speak, by jumping into his alterity with a step that throws him into the final singularity. The other poses his gaze as inescapable injunction only insofar as he weighs into it with all his weight; and he weighs with all the weight of alterity only insofar as he throws himself madly into his alterity. But *haecceitas* is not accomplished as such (does not reach the end of its individuality) unless the other as such becomes unreservedly ecstatic. Now ecstasy, understood in the sense of the Aristotelian ecstasy of time, is summed up in the gaze, which weighs with the weight of *haecceitas* only insofar as *haecceitas* surpasses itself and comes to die in the gaze, as though in a final impetus. The alterity of the other as *such* attains its final individuality because it moves ecstatically through its *haecceitas*, into a gaze: the other passes completely into his gaze, and will never have a more complete manifestation. Whence a twofold consequence: finally, only the gaze can be called unsubstitutable, and thus gaze is simply one with the injunction, since the injunction enjoins for the sake of the other as such. (2) If the injunction that I receive gives me, in a gaze, the last possible ecstasy of the other, it delivers the other to me, without remainder, without reserve or defense, the perfect operative of the unsubstitutable in him. The injunction thus enjoins me to support, with my own gaze, the unsubstitutable alterity of the gaze of the other as such. To support a gaze means to support the invisible unsubstitutable within it. That it can only be an invisible gaze is newly confirmed in the impossibility of an unsubstitutable objectivity—the object is seen, is defined and is therefore repeatable. The unsubstitutable is fulfilled only in a gaze (ceaselessly other), because it is the operative of alterity itself. The gaze wherein the other is exposed as such can, in weighing on my own, only enjoin him to expose himself in turn to unsubstitutable individuality. The gaze that accomplishes in itself the unsubstitutable can enjoin me to accomplish, in projecting myself within a gaze, my unsubstitutable. If in his gaze the other risks himself in his last individuality, he can only enjoin me to risk myself, in return, in my ultimate individuality—to risk rendering the unsubstitutable to the unsubstitutable. Note that it is not a matter of re-establishing two self–possessors, and thus two *I*'s. Rather it is up to each one to let himself be summoned, by another's injunction, to his own individuality, entirely completed in the ecstasy of the gaze—not for the purpose of retaking possession of self by reintegrating what is proper to him, but in order to expose himself in person to the final ecstasy of the other. I owe the other for making me, under his absolutely unsubstitutable gaze to the point of nakedness, also unsubstitutable, individualized, and naked. The other's exposition enjoins me to expose myself, too, in order to shelter it, to maintain it, and to protect it. I receive my unsubstitutable individuality from the advance of the other in his gaze; I receive myself, then, unsubstitutable from his own ecstasy. I receive it as *such* because it provokes me to make myself an *as such*. The injunction imposes upon me the gaze of the other as such, since it imposes upon me to expose myself there, in person, *as such*, by myself moving ecstatically into my unsubstitutable gaze. The other comes upon me as such, because he renders me indispensable—the injunction exerts itself as a summons.

Freed from intentionality,[5] love in the end would be defined, still within the field of phenomenology, as the act of a gaze that renders itself back to another gaze in a common unsubstitutable. To render oneself back to a gaze means, for another gaze, to return there, as to a place for rendezvous, but above all to render oneself there in an unconditional surrender: to render oneself to the unsubstitutable other, as a summons to my own unsubstitutability—no other than me will be able to play the other that the other requires, no other gaze than my own must respond to the ecstasy of this particular other exposed in his gaze.

But to render oneself other, to surrender this gaze to the gaze of the other who crosses me, requires faith.

Excerpt 2. §24 to Give Itself, to Reveal Itself*

The Last Possibility—The Phenomenon Of Revelation

Arranging the topics of the saturated phenomenon, I noted that the last type—the Other showing himself as icon—gathered within it the modes of saturation of the three other types (the historical event, the idol and the flesh). One cannot help but conclude that, be it only within the privileged region of saturation, not all phenomena, saturated though they are, offer the same degree of givenness. The question of determining the degree to which saturation can be deployed thus presents itself. Does it attain a maximum or does it, by hypothesis, always transgress it—but also is there any sense in envisaging a phenomenon that gives (itself) according to a maximum of phenomenality? This question arises inevitably from the mere fact that it alone permits all dimensions of phenomenality to be glimpsed, explores the region of saturated givenness, thoroughly inventories it, and

---

[5] Lévinas's critique of intentionality admits different degrees; sometimes, it is only a question of freeing intentionality from the pair subject/object (*En découvrant l'existence*, p.139) or from the couple noesis/noema (*Totalité et infini*, p.271); other times, it is more radically a question of attaining "a non-intentional thought whose devotion can be translated by no preposition in our language—not even the *to* which we use" (*De Dieu*, p.250, see pp. 184, 243, 261; *Of God Who Comes to Mind*, tr. Bergo, modified, p.166). No doubt, today, its author would no longer subscribe completely to the thematization that he gave of love in terms of intentionality: "The act of love has a sense ... The characteristic of the loved object is precisely to be given in a *love intention*, an intention which is irreducible to a purely theoretical representation" (*La théorie de l'intuition dans la phénoménologie de Husserl* [Paris: Alcan, 1930], p.75; *The Theory of Intuition in Husserl's Phenomenology,* tr. André Orianne [Evanston: Northwestern University Press, 1973], pp.44–45); the meaning of the act of love (if it is still a matter of an act) exempts love not only from "purely theoretical representation," but even more from every intention, because from all intentionality.

* This excerpt is taken from Jean-Luc Marion, *Being Given: Toward a Phenomenology of Givenness*, trans. Jeffrey L. Kosky (Stanford, CA: Stanford University Press, 2002) 234–47. Reproduced with kind permission.

cannot be dodged. This constraint, however, is most often not enough to block its pure and simple denegation. Why is it challenged? Obviously not for a theoretical (phenomenological or not) reason, at least not at first, but out of a more banal, ideological fear: that the question of God might again arise. As we know, theology contradicts logic. We would therefore preserve rationality by banishing the question of a maximum point of phenomenality. The argument is so lacking in rigor and precision that, for now, I will not examine it as such. With the question of a phenomenon taking saturation to its maximum, it is not straightaway or always a question of debating the status of the theological in phenomenology, but at the outset and in the first place of a possible figure of phenomenality as such.

A possible figure of phenomenality—my entire project has been directed to liberating possibility in phenomenality, to unbinding the phenomenon from the supposed equivalencies that limit its deployment (the object, the being, common-law adequation, poverty of intuition). What remains is to determine just how far such a possibility goes and if we can assign a maximum to it. To be deployed without contradiction, this possibility posits two requirements: (i) the potential maximum must remain a phenomenon; that is to say, it must be inscribed within the already acquired definition of phenomenality (determinations in general, saturation in particular), as a variation of this one and only definition; (ii) the maximum must also remain a possibility, in the twofold sense of transgressing itself permanently without being fixed in a definite figure and also designing itself independently of all actual and worldly accomplishment of this maximum. The maximum of saturated phenomenality must remain an ultimate possibility of the phenomenon—the last, but still under the heading of possibility. This twofold and at first contradictory requirement is carried out with what I will now call the phenomenon of *revelation*. In effect, (i) it is a question of the last possible variation of the phenomenality of the phenomenon inasmuch as given. The phenomenon of revelation not only falls into the category of saturation (paradox in general), but it concentrates the four types of saturated phenomena and is given at once as historic event, idol, flesh and icon (face). This concerns a fifth type of saturation, not that it adds a new one (arbitrarily invented in order to do right by the supposed right of the "divine") to the first four (the sole describable ones), but because, by confounding them in it, it saturates phenomenality to the second degree, by saturation of saturation. From the common-law phenomenon there followed, through a variation of intuitive possibility, the saturated phenomenon or paradox; likewise from the latter, there follows, as an ultimate variation on saturation, the *paradoxōtaton*, the paradox to the second degree and par excellence, which encompasses all types of paradox.[6] Nevertheless, (ii) the phenomenon of revelation remains a mere possibility. I am going to describe it without presupposing its actuality, and yet all the while propose a precise figure

---

[6] This superlative, attested by the Septuagint in Wisdom 16:17, is used, rarely, it is true, by Athanasius (PG 25 696 *d*), Gregory of Nyssa (*Life of Moses*, §24, p.44, 406 *c*), and Evagrius (p.86, 2753 *B*). See, even if he uses *paradoxōtaton* only in common usage, the occurrences of *paradoxon* in Cyril of Alexandria: M. O. Boulnois, *Le paradoxe trinitaire chez Cyrille d'Alexandrie: Herméneutique, analyses philosophiques et argumentation théologique* (Paris, 1994), pp.574ff and 696ff.

for it. I will say only: if an actual revelation must, can or could have been given in phenomenal apparition, it could have, can or will be able to do so only by giving itself according to the type of the paradox par excellence—such as I will describe it. Phenomenology cannot decide if a revelation can or should ever give itself, but it (and it alone) can determine that, in case it does, such a phenomenon of revelation should assume the figure of the paradox of paradoxes. If revelation there must be (and phenomenology has no authority to decide this), then it will assume, assumes or assumed the figure of paradox of paradoxes, according to an essential law of phenomenality. In this sense, since revelation remains a variation of saturation, itself a variation of phenomenality of the phenomenon inasmuch as given, it still remains inscribed within the transcendental conditions of possibility. Would I have come all this way only to recover precisely what I wanted to destroy—conditions preceding possibility and delimiting it a priori? Better, wouldn't I have recovered precisely, in regard to revelation, the very type of phenomenon that neither can nor should submit to them? In fact, it's nothing like this—here (as in §1), the condition of possibility does not consist in rendering the phenomenon possible by delimiting it a priori from the impossibilities, but in freeing its possibility by destroying all prerequisite conditions for phenomenality, therefore by suspending all so-called impossibilities, indeed by admitting the possibility of certain ones among them. The phenomenon of revelation would be defined, it too, as the possibility of the impossibility—on condition of no longer understanding impossibility confiscating possibility (being toward death), but possibility assimilating impossibility (incident, fait accompli). Simply put, this feeling of possibility as revelation and through revelation is always deployed solely as a means of a second variation (paradox of paradoxes) on a first variation (saturated phenomenon) of the initial determination of the phenomenon as what shows itself only insofar as it gives itself. The phenomenon of revelation is therefore officially inscribed within the one and only figure of the phenomenon that, ever since the beginning and without interruption, I have been seeking—the given. In this sense, formally, the paradox of paradoxes offers no extraordinary phenomenological trait. Though exceeding the common-law phenomenon, it does not make an exception to the original determination of what shows itself: it gives itself—and without common measure.

The phenomenon of revelation (§24) is therefore defined as a phenomenon that concentrates in itself the four senses of the saturated phenomenon (§23), where each alone sufficed to pass beyond the common-law phenomenon (§§21–22). I am obliged *here*—in phenomenology, where possibility remains the norm, and not actuality—only to describe it in its pure possibility and in the reduced immanence of givenness. I do not *here* have to judge its actual manifestation or ontic status, which remain the business proper to revealed theology.[7] If I therefore privilege the

---

[7] Phenomenology describes possibilities and never considers the phenomenon of revelation except as a possibility of phenomenality, one that it would formulate in this way: If God were to manifest himself (or manifested himself), he would use a paradox to the second degree. Revelation (of God by himself, *theo*-logical), if it takes place, will assume the phenomenal figure of the phenomenon of revelation, of the paradox of paradoxes, of saturation to the second degree. To be sure, *R*evelation (as actuality) is never confounded

manifestation of Jesus Christ as it is described in the New Testament (and in conformity with the paradigms of the theophanies of the old), as an example of a phenomenon of revelation, I am nevertheless proceeding as a phenomenologist—describing a given phenomenological possibility—and as a philosopher—confronting the visible Christ with his possible conceptual role (as Spinoza, Kant, Hegel or Schelling dared to do), with an eye toward establishing it as paradigm. The manifestation of Christ counts as paradigm of the phenomenon of revelation according to the paradox's four modes of saturation. According to quantity, the phenomenon of Christ gives itself intuitively as an event that is perfectly unforeseeable because radically heterogeneous to what it nevertheless completes (the prophecies). It arises "as the lightning comes from the East and shows itself [*phainetai*] as far as the West" (Matthew 24:27), saturating the visible at one fell swoop. This character of event that happens is not added extrinsically to the figure Christ assumes, but by contrast determines its first aspect, since he becomes intrinsically as "he who must come [*ho erkhomenos*]" (John 1:15 or 27). He arrives under the banner of an advent and advances only with his own advance, which counts as one of his names. The coming, according to which he comes forward, defines him so essentially that it embraces him and precedes him—he himself depends on it without determining it; and he arises from this eventfulness because it attests that he does not come forward from himself ("I have not come of my own" John 8:43) but at the bidding of the Father ("You have sent me," John 17:18, 23). Christ therefore submits his own unforeseeable eventfulness, in the same sense that he submits to the Father. As a result, the end of the world is unforeseen by him, by him the Son, as his own coming as the Christ surprises those who inhabit this same world. The unforeseeability comes to an end only for the Father. "As for the day and the hour, no-one knows them, neither the angels in heaven, nor [even] the Son, except the Father" (Mark 13:33), "except the father alone" (Matthew 24:36). And this is why, for the men of the world, the impossibility of knowing the hour, therefore of foreseeing (the end of time and the coming of Christ, which in fact are one), demands renouncing the anticipatory calculation that would allow them to appropriate this event par excellence; they must instead await it insofar as it remains unforeseeable, that is to say, as if each moment was and was not the right one. This expectation without foresight, characteristic of the unpredictable landing, defines the phenomenological attitude appropriate to the event—vigilance: "Open your

---

with *r*evelation (as possible phenomenon). I will scrupulously respect this conceptual difference by its graphic translation. But phenomenology, which owes it to phenomenality to go this far, does not go beyond and should never pretend to decide the fact of Revelation, its historicity, its actuality, or its meaning. It should not do so, not only out of concern for distinguishing the sciences and their respective regions, but first of all, because it does not have the means to do so. The fact (if there is one) of Revelation exceeds the scope of all science, including that of phenomenology. Only a theology, and on condition of constructing itself on the basis of this fact alone (Karl Barth or Hans Urs von Balthasar, no doubt more than Rudolf Bultmann or Karl Rahner), could reach it. Even if it had the desire to do so (and, of course, this would never be the case), phenomenology would not have the power to turn into theology. And one has to be completely ignorant of theology, its procedures, and its problematic not to imagine this unlikeness.

eyes, be vigilant, for you do not know when the [right] moment [*kairos*] will come" (Mark 13:33), "Be vigilant, for you do not know the day when your Master will come" (Matthew 24:42). Vigilance and expectation invert foresight; thus the event itself escapes all prepatory anticipation in the past, is concentrated in its pure *fait accompli*, arises without genealogy and can even be established after the fact as a new beginning: "He who must come after me is before me"(John 1:15). The past now comes after (and not before) the event, which happens solely in terms of its arising: "Before Abraham was born, I am" (John 8:58). The figure of Christ therefore offers the characteristic of a paradox that is perfectly unforeseeable because intuition saturates every prior concept quantitively. It is a case par excellence of the event.

In terms of quality, the figure of Christ obviously attests its paradoxical character because the intuition that saturates it reaches and most often overcomes what the phenomenological gaze can bear. Does he not say to his own: "I still have many things to say to you, but you do not yet have the power to bear them [*ou dunasthe bastazein*]" (John 16:12)? But what is to be borne? The visible and its excess, like the whiteness that absorbs the entire prism of colors and is excepted form the world of objects: "He was transformed before them, and his clothes became resplendent, excessively white [*leuka lian*], the likes of which no fuller on earth could bleach" (Mark 9:3). And also the voice from beyond the world, which comes from the heavens and does not belong to space, and which therefore terrifies: "A cloud came and overshadowed them: as they entered it, they were afraid. And a voice came out of the cloud saying 'This is my beloved Son, listen to him'" (Luke 9:34–35; see Matthew 7:5–7). In fact, the unbearable stems from nothing less than the pure and simple recognition of Christ as such. For example, when he declines his identity and pronounces his name before those who come to arrest him, he becomes visible to them as Christ and therefore unbearable in all senses; they therefore collapse: "When he said to them: 'It is me (I am),'[8] they recoiled and fell to the ground" (John 18:6–7). The unbearable therefore suspends perception in general, beyond the difference between hearing and sight, because it results from the thorough saturation of the figure of Christ. And this paradox culminates in the resurrection itself; for, since it by definition passes beyond what this world can receive, contain or embrace, it can let itself be perceived only by terrifying, to the point that this terror sometimes suffices to designate it by denegation: "[The women in the tomb] said nothing to anybody; for they were terrified" (Mark 16:6). This terror implies neither refusal nor flight. It is allied with its opposite, joy ("They left the tomb with

---

[8] A magnificently untranslatable text. In effect, the formulation *egō eimi* means first: "It is me!" in answer to the question "Who are you looking for?—Jesus of Nazareth." But more radically, it means literally "I am," through a phrase that declines the very identity that Jesus claims in John 8; but these two translations can be added to one another in a subtle and secret dialogue: Who are you looking for? Jesus of Nazareth./It is me./But it is me because I am "I am."/By this redoubling, Here I am, the one who is always there for you to take ("Here I am")/and to take me for what I am, namely "I am." Whence the last meaning: "I am" equals, in the dialogue at Gethsemane, "I am he who says I am," therefore I am He from Exodus 3:14; and it is precisely on account of this claim (a blasphemy according to Matthew 26:65) that he will be put to death.

terror and joy," Matthew 28:8), in marking two registers of the same intuitive saturation—beyond terror and joy, as well as beyond touch ("Put out your finger ... put out your hand," John 20:27) and the avoidance of touch ("Do not touch me," John 20:17) beyond union ("and behold I will be with you for all days until the consummation of time," Matthew 28:20) and separation ("And it happened that while blessing them, he parted from them," Luke 24:51). Christ thus accomplishes the paradox of the idol as well: saturation of the gaze by excess of intuition renders its phenomenon unbearable; vision—fulfilled—no longer sees by dint of seeing.

In terms of relation, Christ appears as an absolute phenomenon, one that annuls all relation because it saturates every possible horizon into which relation would introduce it. It saturates every possible horizon not only because its "moment" escapes the time of the world (saturation in terms of the unforeseeable event) and its figure the space of the "earth" (saturation in terms of the unbearable), but because "his kingdom is not of this world" (John 18:36). The world of common-law phenomenality is not for him and eventually would turn against him and condemn him to not appear in it or to appear in it only disfigured (which was indeed the case). From this principal characteristic, we can draw two arguments establishing that this is a question of saturation pertaining to the flesh. (i) The death of Christ offers the apex of his visibility—"Truly this was the son of God!" (Matthew 27:54), "They shall look upon him whom they have pierced" (John 19:7, citing Zechariah 12:10)—and of his visibility as royal (John 19:19–22). This paradox would remain unintelligible if we did not see in it the flesh that is all the more manifest as such as it auto-affects itself more radically in its agony. Only the flesh suffers, dies and therefore can live. (ii) If the paradox of the flesh consists in the fact that it affects itself by itself, it also manifests itself without having to be inscribed in any relation, therefore in an absolute mode, outside or beyond any horizon. It follows that the saturated phenomenon of Christ assumes the paradox of the flesh by always subverting the supposedly unique horizon of phenomenality, thereby demanding a never definite plurality of horizons. This is indicated perfectly by a similar formulation in the two final chapters of John: "Jesus did still more signs and others in the sight of his disciples, but these are not written in this book" (20:30–31); "There are also many other things Jesus did; but if it were necessary to write every one of them, I do not know if the world itself could receive all the books to be written" (21:25). The world cannot welcome the writing that would describe what Christ did; it is clear that the acts of Christ, even reduced to writings, exceed the horizon of this world, are not of this world, demand other horizons and other worlds. This principle of the plurality of worlds, or rather horizons, governs all dimensions of the phenomenality of Christ's flesh. His royal character, which is not of this world, is therefore spoken in three tongues, not just one (Luke 23:38; John 19:20). The writers who attempt to offer witness to the paradox they have seen are at least four and necessarily in partial disagreement on account of the finite aspect and horizon that each was able to take into view and put into operation. Scripture itself traditionally admits four concurrent meanings, something that recent exegesis confirms by according it an unlimited number of different literary genres, each of which in fact offers a new horizon in order to welcome a new aspect of the one and only paradox. In this context, the fact that Christ can receive a plurality of names, none of which says his essence, does nothing more than reproduce the property of God himself of admitting all names and refusing each of them (*poluonumon kai anonumon*)—the property of summoning an infinity of nominative horizons in order to denominate he who saturates not only each horizon, but the incommensurable sum of the horizons. Consequently the absolute marked by the paradox of Christ's flesh can be deployed in the limited visibility of worldly horizons only by their indefinite temporal and spatial proliferation in so many fragmented and provisional approaches to the same bursting absolutely without compare, common measure, or analogy. It could even be that history (in the case of time), civilizations (in the case of space) and spiritualities, literatures, cultures (in the case of horizons) are set forth only to decline, unfurl, and discover the paradox of Christ, which his absoluteness renders inaccessible as such to all sight, contact and speech.

In terms of modality, finally Christ appears as an irregardable phenomenon precisely because as icon he regards me in such a way that He constitutes me as his witness rather than some transcendental I constituting Him to his own liking. The inversion of the gaze lacks no textual references. In effect, the I loses primacy as soon as "the servant is not greater than his master" (John 15:19). Next, Christ constitutes his disciples as witnesses by electing them: he can do this legitimately only because he sees them first—before they see themselves ("He saw two brothers," Matthew 4:18)—and foresees them "from afar" (Luke 14:20). He therefore names them with a borrowed proper name (John 1:42) and can dispatch them as witnesses (Matthew 28:18). A text illustrates perfectly how the inversion of the gaze produces saturation (Mark 10:17–22). Consider a rich young man. He "runs and kneels before" Christ, that is to say, exposes himself to his gaze and implicitly recognizes his primacy. He asks him, in the name of his "goodness," to teach him access to eternal life—that is to say, to perfection, therefore to a, indeed the, saturated phenomenon par excellence. Christ answers him by denying goodness for himself and referring it to his Father, then by enumerating the known commandments of the Law, at least all those that demand respect for the Other inasmuch as Other (do not commit adultery, do not kill, do not steal, do not give false testimony, honor your father and mother). Thus the saturated phenomenon comes from the counter-gaze of the Other (Christ) such that it constitutes me its witness. The young man acknowledges this phenomenon as saturated: he lets himself be measured with neither reserve nor dissimulation by the requirements of the gaze of the Other, and he conforms to this icon: "Master, all this I have observed from my youth." Now it is precisely at this point, where the saturated phenomenon is acknowledged and admitted, that two essential characteristics are accentuated. (i) First, the irregardable paradox provokes and identifies its witness by the gaze it casts over him: "Jesus gazed upon [*emblepsas, intuitus*] him and loved him"—to gaze upon is of course not equivalent to just casting one's gaze (otherwise the text would have said nothing at all), but to instituting what one gazes upon. In effect, the gaze is not cast indifferently on just anyone, but differently on this one or that one, each time another Other. The gaze recognizes, establishes and individualizes what it thus takes under its wing; and for all that, this electing gaze does not objectify or reify since it ends up loving, therefore letting what it has just posited be set forth by its own withdrawal. The irreducible saturated phenomenon therefore transforms the I into a witness, into its witness. (ii) Accordingly, the paradox, far from being spread thin, will be redoubled. To the first saturation (accomplishing the commandments of the Law concerning the Other), the irregardable gaze adds a saturation of saturation—sell your goods "whatever they might be" and "give [the proceeds] to the poor." The last type of saturation implies its redoubling: one must not only respect the gaze of the poor (not objectify them but recognize their *originarity*), and, doing that, come to stand before the irregardable gaze of Christ; one must also annul all possession and all originarity in order to "give [oneself] to the poor," therefore to the first among them. Thus, when the young man decides to stay rich, he confesses to remaining stuck between two states of the paradox: intuitive saturation and saturation beyond itself, saturation to the second degree. We therefore recover, in the figure of Christ, not only the four types of paradox, but the redoubling of saturation that defines the last among them.

Either ... Or

The saturated phenomenon therefore culminates in the type of paradox I call revelation, one that concentrates in itself—as the figure of Christ establishes its possibility—an event, an idol, a flesh and an icon, all at the same time. Saturation passes beyond itself, exceeds the very concept of maximum, and finally gives its phenomenon without remainder or reserve. We thus possess for the first time a model of phenomenality appropriate to phenomena that are neither poor nor common. In effect, when these phenomena appear fully, that is to say, when they are given without reserve, they do so neither according to the Cartesian evidence that applies solely to objects, nor according to the manifested being (*geoffenbart sein*) of the concept (to which Hegel, without reason, reduced revelation, *Offenbarung*), nor according to the opening with withdrawal of the *Ereignis* (to which Heidegger pretends to confide the advent of a possible "god"). If the Revelation of God as showing himself starting from himself alone can in fact ever take place, phenomenology must redefine its own limits and learn to pass beyond them following clear cut and rigorous procedures. That is to say, it must design one of its possible figures as a paradox of paradoxes, saturated with intuition to the second degree, in a word, a phenomenon of revelation. Otherwise, it will repeat the absurd denegation on which metaphysics and the "question of Being" stubbornly insist: better to erase or disfigure the possibility of Revelation than redefine the transcendental conditions of manifestation in order to admit the mere possibility of a phenomenon of revelation. The debate is summed up in a simple alternative: is it necessary to confine the possibility of the appearing of God to the uninterrogated and supposedly untouchable limits of one or the other figure of philosophy and phenomenology, or should we broaden phenomenological possibility to the measure of the possibility of manifestation demanded by the question of God? One should not, once again, pose as an objection to the phenomenon of revelation the argument that the transcendence of God is bracketed by Husserl. Though apparently incontestable, it does not stand up for the following reasons: (a) Husserl submits what he names "God" to the reduction only insofar as he defines it by transcendence (and insofar as he compares this particular transcendence with that, in fact quite different, of the object in the natural attitude); and yet in Revelation and *theo*-logy, God is likewise, indeed especially, characterized by radical immanence to consciousness, and in this sense would be confirmed by a reduction. (b) Husserl aims to reduce the transcendent "God" only by identifying him with a " 'ground,' *Grund*"; and yet this metaphysical domination par excellence would not concern the *theo*-logical names of God, to which the phenomenon of revelation means to do justice.[9] (c) Here it is a matter of admitting only the *possibility* of the phenomenon of revelation (and not, once again, the *fact* of a Revelation), and yet this possibility does not put the reduction into question, since it is designed entirely within and on the basis of the radical immanence of the phenomenon. Not only does the phenomenon of revelation show itself only insofar as it is given, but it owes the excellence of its visibility to the givenness beyond the common (law) that its saturation of saturation ensures to it. In other words, as paradox of paradoxes, the phenomenon of revelation does nothing more than accomplish the immanence of the given phenomenon by carrying it first to saturation and then to saturation redoubled. It thus does no less than produce the ultimate variation of the one and only figure of the given phenomenon, all of whose determinations it maintains (anamorphosis, unpredictable landing, fait accompli, incident, event) carries to saturation (historical event, idol, flesh, icon) and gathers into one single apparition. (d) If danger there must be here, it would reside more in the formal and, in a sense, still transcendental phenomenalization of the question of God than in some sort of theologization of phenomenality. It could be that the fact of Revelation provokes and evokes figures and strategies of manifestation and revelation that are much more powerful and more subtle than what phenomenology, even pushed as far as the phenomenon of revelation (paradox of paradoxes), could ever let us divine. Whatever the case might be, there is nothing astonishing in the fact that one inquires after God's right to inscribe himself within phenomenality. What is astonishing is that one should be stubborn—and without conceptual reason—about denying him this right, or rather that one is no longer even surprised by this pigheaded refusal.

But another objection arises, one that is much more serious because less polemic and better focused on what is at stake. It distinguishes a contradiction between, on the one hand, the description of the phenomenon of revelation according to intuitive saturation and, on the other, the ongoing tradition of apophaticism in which God is known only as unknown, in the "night" of the senses and concepts, therefore in a radical intuitive shortage.[10] The response to this objection will also permit me to

---

[9] Husserl, *Ideen I*, §58, Hua. III, p.139 [English trans., pp.133–34] (cited *supra*, Book 2, §7).

[10] A position that we had assumed in *God Without Being*. We owe this objection, in comparable terms, to Didier Franck and Thomas Carlson. See Carlson's *Indiscretion: Finitude and the Naming of God* (Chicago: University of Chicago Press, 1999); especially pp.232–36.

explain the saturation of saturation in more detail. (a) First, a saturated phenomenon cannot by definition be seen according to a definite intuition that would be simply lacking or sufficient. The saturating intuition cannot not bedazzle and give to see, at first, only its bedazzlement rather than some certain spectacle (§22). Hence, intuitive saturation can be perfectly translated by the (at least provisional) impossibility of seeing some *thing*, and so appears as a lack of intuition. To stick with just one of the paradigms of the saturated phenomenon (without going so far as its redoubling), let us consider the face. It uncontestably saturates phenomenality, since it reverses intentionality and submerges my gaze with its own; and yet this counter-gaze comes to meet me only while remaining invisible, at least as object or being—strictly speaking, there is nothing to see. And this, for that matter, is why the majority of the time I do not see the face of the Other as the face of the Other: the invisible of his gaze escapes me. As soon as this invisible has disappeared, I can once again begin to see his face as a simple object and a being available in visibility (a face that is beautiful or ugly, desirable, contemptible, etc.). The same paradox can be found in the historical event, the painting (the idol), and the flesh. There is, properly speaking, nothing to see when they give themselves as such. In effect intuitive saturation is never equivalent to giving a great (or too great) quantity of intuition for the purpose of simply fulfilling a concept that lets us better perceive an object, for this first degree of excess can still define a common-law phenomenon in which objectivity would be simply blurred but not overcome. By contrast, if saturation gives too much intuition, it therefore gives even less objectivity. From the perspective of objectivity, one can and should say—without any contradiction—that the saturated phenomenon gives nothing to see. (b) Next, it will be observed that the deception of the senses and of the understanding obviously indicates that there is nothing (no thing) to perceive, but not that intuition is lacking. Simply the paradox and, especially, the phenomenon of revelation are never used to construct an object, but always to provoke the unforeseeable, the excess, the absolute or the assignation to witness—in short, to affect the flesh and to saturate it with intuition. The moments and movements of this nonobjectifying saturation become, to different degrees, the affair of mystical theology, as well as novels or the analytic cure—in all these cases, intuitive saturation in no way concerns objectness, or rather, in no way concerns the object, and therefore is equivalent to its lack. But the lack of an object is not equivalent to a shortage of givenness, for saturated givenness gives much more (and better) than objects. (c) Finally, it will be observed that if shortage (thus understood as a shortage of objects) was absent and lack was lacking, manifestation would not only not increase—it would decrease. What is at issue here is the possibility of the phenomenon of revelation, in which an excess of intuition is redoubled in a paradox of paradoxes. It is therefore a question of letting a phenomenon come to manifestation, which is given in such a way that nothing more manifest can be given—*id quo nihil manifestius donari potest*. So I ask: Does the moment of denegation that the redoubled excess of intuition imposes diminish *this* phenomenon, confirm it, or even add to it? If the *phenomenon* of revelation could be seen without lack, indeterminacy, or bedazzlement, would it be manifest more perfectly as phenomenon of *revelation* or, on the contrary, would it be disqualified?

Doesn't it belong essentially to the paradox and its apparition to contradict the course of apparition in general, to give itself as *para*-dox and not only as a para-*dox*? Here finally it is necessary that we no longer define the saturated phenomenon simply by the inversion of the determinations of the common-law phenomenon. With the phenomenon of revelation, we come to the point where it is necessary to free ourselves not only from these (metaphysical or phenomenological) determinations, but even from their destruction. The paradox of paradoxes does not have to choose between cataphasis and apophasis any more than between saturation and shortage of intuition; it uses them all in order to push to its end the phenomenality of what shows itself only insofar as it gives itself.

The Given Without Intuition—A Question

Now I can confront a difficulty that, since the opening of our study, I have continually run up against and dodged at the same time. It can be put in this way: if the privilege of intuition stems from its character of givenness (§20), how are we to explain that givenness is often accomplished without intuition?[11] The response is deduced from the principle just laid out—when givenness no longer gives an object or a being, but rather a pure given, it is no longer carried out by pure intuition; or rather, the alternative between a shortage and a saturation of intuition becomes undecidable. Among these pure givens, at once empty of and saturated with intuition, we can distinguish three types. (a) The cases where givenness brings it about that phenomena show themselves that are by definition non-objectifiable, therefore without intuition fulfilling an intentional aim of an object. For example, "giving time" gives nothing (no thing, no object), therefore mobilizes no intuition; and yet, in giving the non-object par excellence, time, givenness grants to all the things that benefit from it the possibility of giving and re-giving themselves. To give time amounts to giving non-actuality itself, which is not nothing since it ensures possibility to all that is. Likewise "to give life" in fact gives nothing, since the flesh intrinsically avails itself of its power to live and "life" remains what is absent par excellence from all biological science; and yet this "nothing" does not say nothing. He to whom it was given, and for as long as he receives it, keeps the possibility of living in and for himself; life never has objective status, and so it must give itself without intuitive fulfilment (or a concept to be fulfilled); but in this way it appears all the more as a pure given possibility, since it itself gives possibility to objective and being phenomena. Givenness without intuition by default. (b) Next, there are cases where givenness brings it about that phenomena of nonbeings, of what by definition should not be, show themselves, phenomena which can appear only insofar as they give themselves outside Being. For example "the gift of death" amounts to giving not only no being, but to the state of no longer Being, since death itself cannot be any more than it can let Be what it reaches. It is not merely a matter of giving the impossibility of being, but giving impossibility itself as directly nonbeing. Similarly "to give one's life" (which sometimes strangely equals "giving

---

[11] See *supra*, Book I, §§4–5, and Book 2, §11.

death," "giving oneself death") for the Other (whether it be individual, collective, abstract, finite or infinite) implies giving to him (therefore giving oneself to him as) a nonbeing. Givenness conflicts precisely and explicitly in this disappearance of all beingness, and it would in turn be annulled if "death" or "my life" recovered an ontic positivity. Givenness without intuition by definition. (c) Finally, cases present themselves in which givenness lets phenomena that exceed, and therefore include, all beingness and objectness show themselves. For example, "to give one's word" indicates a gift always still to come, all the more still to come as it has already been accomplished for a long time. The soldier or the lover, equally engaged in risking their life in a hard struggle, should stick to their word even more as they have already not only given, but maintained it. The more they realize it, the less they are dismissed from keeping it. The more it was, the less it is ensured of still being. In effect, it bears on no object, nor any being, but on the very temporality of what shows itself thanks to the given word. The same is true when one "gives peace," "gives meaning (*Sinngebung*)," or "gives a face to ..." Givenness without intuition by excess. All these givennesses succeed in giving paradoxes saturated phenomena without intuition or without one being able to decide between excess and shortage. I will name the phenomena of revelation (saturation of saturation), where the excess of the gift assumes the character of shortage, with the name the *abandoned* [*l'abandonné*].[12]

Thus I have not only set out a topics of the phenomenon in general. I have above all broadened it to the point of doing justice to a heretofore repressed or denied type: the paradox, or the saturated phenomenon, including even its most complex figure, the phenomenon of revelation. The principal result of this broadening is not that we can now accord a phenomenological possibility to the possible fact of revelation (though this is indeed a remarkable advance in relation to metaphysics). Rather, its essential effect is to extend the previously won definition of the phenomenon— what shows itself in the measure to which it is given (Book I, §6)—to its fullest extent, so that we end up at this last definition: what gives itself in the measure to which it reveals itself. To be sure, this radicalization does not count for every given phenomenon (Book 3), nor even for every saturated phenomenon (paradox, Book 4, §§20–22), but only for phenomena saturated to the second degree (paradox of paradoxes, §24). And yet, this exceptional phenomenon is inscribed within the general definition of the phenomenon as given, under the heading of a simple though remarkable variation of the originary phenomenological givenness. It accomplishes it, but because it comes from it.

---

[12] See *supra*, Book 5, §30.

Excerpt 3. In the Name; How to Avoid Speaking of it*

The Privilege of the Unknowable

... the Name does not name God as an essence; it designates what passes beyond every name. The Name designates what one does not name and says that one does not name it. There is nothing surprising, then, in the fact that in Judaism the term "Name" replaces the Tetragrammaton which must and can never be pronounced as a proper name, nor that, amounting to the same thing, in Christianity it names the fortunate and necessary "absence of divine names" (Hölderlin). For the Name no longer functions by inscribing God within the theoretical horizon of our predication, but by inscribing us, according to a radically new praxis, in the very horizon of God. This is exactly what baptism accomplishes exactly when far from our attributing to God a name that is intelligible to us, we enter *into* God's unpronounceable Name, with the additional result that we receive our own. This pragmatic theology is deployed, in fact, under the figure of the liturgy (which begins with baptism), where it is never a matter of speaking *of* God, but always of speaking *to* God in the words of the Word. The Name above all names therefore de-nominates God perfectly, by excepting God from predication, so as to include us in it and allow us to name on the basis of its essential anonymity. The Name does not serve knowledge by naming, but by including us in the place de-nomination clears out. The basket never overflows except with bread that first was lacking. In this way, mystical theology no longer has its goal to find a name for God, but to make us receive our own from the unsayable Name. Concerning God, this shift from the theoretical use of language to its pragmatic use is achieved in the finally liturgical function of all *theo*-logical discourse.

Whence this absolute rule of the pragmatic theology of absence, by which it is opposed to the "metaphysics of presence" at least as much as deconstruction is: "our best theologian is not he who has discovered the whole, for our present chain does not allow of our seeing the whole, but he who has better pictured or represented in himself the image of the Truth, *or its shadow or whatever we may call it.*"[13] Or: "... God as such cannot be spoken. The perfect knowledge of God is so to know him that we are sure we must not be ignorant of Him, yet cannot describe Him."[14] The theologian's job is to silence the Name and in this way let it give us one—while the metaphysician is obsessed with reducing the Name to presence, and so defeating the Name. The dividing line has been established by an inescapable formulation:

---

* This excerpt is taken from Jean-Luc Marion, *In Excess: Studies of Saturated Phenomena*, trans. Robyn Horner and Vincent Berraud (New York: Fordham University Press, 2002) 157–62. Latin and Greek quotes that have been translated are omitted. Reproduced with kind permission. The translation is based on a version by Jeffrey L. Kosky.

[13] Gregory of Nazianzus, *Fourth Theological Oration* 30, 17, PG 36, 125c [*Nicene and Post-Nicene Fathers*, vol. 7 (Grand Rapids: Wm. B. Eerdmans Publishing Co., 1983) p. 316 (modified)].

[14] Hilary of Poitiers, *De Trinitate*, II, 7, PL 10, 36 [*Nicene and Post-Nicene Fathers*, vol. 9, Grand Rapids: Wm. B. Eerdmans Publishing Co., 1981].

"... between creator and creature no likeness can be recognized which would be greater than the unlikeness that is to be recognized between them."[15]

VI. The Saturated Phenomenon *Par Excellence*

We have thus wound up with a complete reversal of the initial problematic. But to observe this by examining the theological tradition of mystical theology and reconstructing its logic is one thing. It is quite a different matter to describe the phenomenon to which it is trying to do justice. The remaining task, then, is to conceive the formal possibility of the phenomenon that seems to demand an "absence of divine names" and our entering *into* the Name. It is a matter of conceiving its formal possibility—but nothing more, since phenomenology cannot and therefore must not venture to make any decisions about the actuality of such a phenomenon—this is a question entirely beyond its scope. Phenomenology is to make decisions only about the type of phenomenality that would render this phenomenon thinkable.[16] The question is to be formulated in this way: if that with which the third way of mystical theology deals in fact is revealed, how should the phenomenon be described, such that we do justice to its possibility?

Let us suggest a response. If one admits, with Husserl, that the phenomenon is defined by the inescapable duality of appearing and what appears [*l'apparaître et l'apparaissant*] and that this duality is deployed in terms of the pairs signification/fulfillment, intention/intuition, or noesis/noema, one can imagine three possible relationships between the terms at issue: (i) The intention finds itself confirmed, at least partially, by the intuition, and this tangential equality defines adequation, therefore the evidence of truth. (ii) In contrast, the intention can exceed all intuitive fulfillment, and in this case the phenomenon does not deliver objective knowledge on account of a lack. The first case would correspond to the first way, kataphasis, which proceeds through a conceptual affirmation that justifies an intuition. The second would correspond to the second way, apophasis, which proceeds by negating the concept because of an insufficiency in intuition. Husserl (in this following Kant) admits only these two hypotheses and thus remains stuck within the horizon of predication, and therefore of a possible "metaphysics of presence." But, a third possibility still remains. (iii) The intention (the concept or the signification) can never reach adequation with the intuition (fulfillment), not because the latter is lacking but because it exceeds what the concept can receive, expose, and comprehend. This is what we have elsewhere called the saturated

---

[15] Fourth Lateran Council (1215) in H. Denzinger, *Enchiridion Symbolorum* §432. Despite its title, the work of Erich Przywara, *Analogia entis* (Einsiedeln: Johannes Verlag, 1962), has indicated this in an exceptionally strong fashion.

[16] Concerning this distinction, see "Métaphysique et phénoménologie. Une relève pour la théologie," "Metaphysics and phenomenology: a Relief for Theology," and *Etant Donné*, §24, only speaking here of Revelation as a " ... possible figure of phenomenology as such" (p.326).

phenomenon.[17] According to this hypothesis, the impossibility of attaining knowledge of an object, comprehension in the strict sense does not come from a deficiency in the giving intuition, but from its *excess*, which neither concept, signification, nor intention can foresee, organize, or contain. This third relation between the two inseparable facets of the phenomenon—in the occurrence of the saturated phenomenon—can perhaps allow us to determine the third way, where mystical theology is accomplished. In this third way, no predication or naming any longer appears possible, as in the second way, but now this is so for the opposite reason: not because the giving intuition would be lacking (in which case one could certainly make a favorable comparison between "negative theology" and atheism or establish a rivalry between it and deconstruction), but because the excess of intuition overcomes, submerges, exceeds, in short, saturates, the measure of each and every concept. What is given disqualifies every concept. Denys states this to the letter: "It is stronger than all discourse and all knowledge and therefore surpasses comprehension in general and therefore [is also excepted from] essence."[18] Indeed it is precisely by means of this undoing of the concept and intentionality that the theologians reach de-nomination. For example, Athenagoras: "On account of his glory, he cannot be received; on account of his greatness, he cannot be comprehended; on account of his sublimity, he cannot be conceived; on account of his strength, he cannot be compared; on account of his wisdom, he can be referred to nothing at all; on account of his goodness, he cannot be imitated; on account of his goodwill, he cannot be described."[19] The undoing of knowledge here arises explicitly from an excess, not from a lack. Likewise, John Chrysostom: "We therefore call him … the unutterable, the inconceivable, the invisible, and the incomprehensible, he who conquers the power of human language and goes beyond the comprehension of human thought."[20] Excess conquers comprehension and what language can say. We have already heard from Gregory of Nyssa: "... the uncreated nature surpasses all signification that a name could express."[21] This text describes a shortcoming and a shortcoming that results from a lack of utterable signification, not of intuition. In short, God remains incomprehensible, not imperceptible— without adequate concept, not without giving intuition. The infinite proliferation of names does indeed suggest that they are still there, but it also flags as insufficient the concepts that they put in play and thereby does justice to what constantly subverts them. Consequently, the third way cannot be confused with the sufficiency of the concept in the first way, or with the insufficiency of intuition in the second; rather, it registers the ineradicable insufficiency of the concept in general. The de-

---

[17] See *Étant donné,* §§24–25.

[18] *Divine Names,* I, 5, 593a.

[19] *To Autolycos,* I, 3, PG 6, 1028c.

[20] *On the Incomprehensible Nature of God,* III, PG 48, 720 (see also, among other examples, III, p. 713 and 723). Likewise, "The invisible, the incomprehensible he who surpasses all understanding and conquers every concept." (*Sermon "Father, if it is possible...,"* 3, PG 51, 37).

[21] *Against Eunomius,* II, §15, ed. W. Jaeger, t. 2, p. 302 = PG 45, 473b.

nomination that puts us *in* the Name has nothing in common with one or the other possibility opened by predication and nomination.

No doubt a final objection will be advanced: how, without resorting to a meaningless and even mad paradox, can the excess of giving intuition in the case of God be considered plausible, when the evidence attests that precisely and *par excellence* God is never given intuitively? Rigorously considered, this objection does not deserve a response, since it no longer concerns the formal possibility of a phenomenon corresponding to the third way, but is already concerned with its actuality. Nevertheless, I will address it, since it reflects a quite common point of view. It will be noted first of all that there is nothing mad about having recourse to paradox in this matter since this is precisely a case of a phenomenon that arises from the particular phenomenality of the paradox. For it is by no means self-evident that every phenomenon must be submitted to the conditions of possibility for experiencing objects and cannot sometimes contradict them. It could even be the case that this is a requirement proper to the phenomenality of God—supposing one admits its formal possibility, and what right does one have to exclude it? Next, one should keep in mind that even in the case when the positive form of the giving intuition would be missing, apparently or factually, this intuition is not wholly submerged beneath two of its undeniable figures, even if we can describe them only negatively. First, the excess of intuition is accomplished in the form of stupor, or even of the terror that the incomprehensibility resulting from excess imposes on us. "God is incomprehensible not only to the Cherubim and Seraphim but also to the Principalities and the Powers and to any other created power. This is what I wished to prove now, but my mind has grown weary. It is not so much the great number of arguments that tires me, but a holy terror at what I had to say. My soul shudders and becomes frightened since it has dwelt too long on speculations about heavenly matters."[22] Access to the divine phenomenality is not forbidden to us; in contrast, it is precisely when we become entirely open to it that we find ourselves forbidden from it—frozen, submerged, we are by ourselves forbidden from advancing and likewise from resting. In the mode of interdiction, terror attests the insistent and unbearable excess of the intuition of God. Next, it could also be that the excess of intuition is marked—strangely enough—by our obsession with evoking, discussing, and even denying that of which we all admit that we have no concept. For how could the question of God dwell within us so deeply—as much in our endeavoring to close it as in our daring to open it—if, having no concept that could help us reach it, an intuition did not fascinate us?

The question of the names of God is never about fixing a name to God or opposing a "non" to him. "Name" and "non," when heard [in French], sound the same sound, and nothing responds to the one any more than to the other. The "non"

---

[22] *On the Incomprehensible Nature of God*, III, *loc. cit.* p. 214 = PG 48, 725 [English trans., p. 108 (modified)]. I refer to the wise and well-argued suggestion made by Jean Daniélou, who interprets the theme of the "holy terror" (and all the conjoint terms) as attesting the excess of divine intuition, which subverts all our expectations and our capacity (*Introduction*, III, pp. 30–39).

of the so-called "negative theology" does not say the Name any more than do the "names" of the affirmative way. For if no one must say the Name, this is not simply because it surpasses all names, passes beyond all essence and all presence. In fact, not even not saying the Name would suffice for honoring it since a simple denegation would still belong to predication, would again inscribe the Name within the horizon of presence—and would even do so in the mode of blasphemy since it treats it parsimoniously. The Name must not be said, not because it is not given for the sake of our saying it, even negatively, but so that we might de-nominate all names of it and dwell in it.

The Name—it has to be dwelt in without saying it, but by letting it say, name, and call us. The Name is not said by us; it is the Name that calls us. And nothing terrifies us more than this call, "… because we hold it be a fearful task to name with our proper names He '… to whom God has bestowed the gift of the name above all names.'"

Index

independence 81, 82, 83
indetermination 81
infinitude of 80
as love 66
names for 83, 215–16
good, the 10, 35, 58, 96
Gregory of Nazianzus 62
Gregory of Nyssa 5, 52, 62, 64, 214

haecceitas 197, 198, 199
Harvey, David, on postmodernism 14, 45
Heidegger, Martin 5, 7, 9, 10, 20, 23, 30, 59, 62, 90
on being 37, 39, 42, 90–92, 95–96
on Descartes 37–38, 75–76, 77
on the *ego* 79
hammer example 42
on Husserl 39–40
on metaphysics 36–39
ontological difference 91–92
on *ousia* 18–19
on phenomenology 38–39
on Van Gogh 42–43
Hemming, Lawrence 92, 92n.11–13, 145n.69
Henry, Michel 8, 105, 110, 124, 127
hermeneutics 4, 18, 20, 56
Marion 117
and phenomenology 12
horizon, the 52n.2, 85, 92, 106, 109, 110, 113–14, 114n.33, 117, 118, 120, 121, 125, 127, 149, 205, 206, 212, 213, 216
Husserl, Edmund 7, 23, 26, 208
on constitution 27n.21
Derrida on 41–42
on the *ego* 32
Heidegger on 39–40
on intuition 28–29, 109, 110–11, 112
on phenomenology 24–25, 109–10
'principle of principles' 28, 29, 110–11

I, the 65, 114, 115, 125, 131, 138, 191, 198
icon, the 62, 63
and distance 64, 89
the face as 128–32
Marion on 63–65
as saturated phenomenon 131, 200
vs the idol 89, 125
iconography 4
idealism 29
ideation 26, 39
idol, the 61, 62

Marion on 126
vs the icon 89, 125
idolatry 50, 56, 61, 61–62, 63, 68, 90, 91, 93, 101
immanence 43, 138, 202, 208
immanent, vs transcendent 44
immensity 81, 83
incarnation 4, 62, 193
incomprehensibility
God 213
meaning 82
independence, God 81, 82, 83
indetermination, God 81
indifference, and the gift 99–102
infinite, the 78, 81, 38, 40, 43, 46, 50, 58, 58n.42, 59, 73, 82, 83, 84, 85, 86, 85n.52, 87, 89, 90, 91, 92, 93, 94, 106, 133, 134, 150
infinitude, of God 80, 81
Institut Catholique de Paris 7
intelligence, supreme 82, 83
intention 11, 53, 110, 11, 112, 113, 123, 124, 125, 134, 137, 191, 192, 195, 200n.5, 213, 214
intentional object *see* under object
intentionality 26, 27–28, 30, 109, 111
of love 70, 71, 200
meaning 25
reverse 7
see also counter-intentionality
intersubjectivity 33, 41n.31, 70
intuition 123
the given without 210–11
Husserl on 28–29, 109, 110–11, 112
Marion on 113
invisibility 128, 193
invisible, the 65, 128, 58, 62, 63, 64, 65, 68, 126, 128, 191, 192, 193, 196, 198, 199, 209, 214, 214n.20
invocation 20
ipseity 135, 140

Jameson, Frederic 15
John of the Cross 52
John of Damascus 58

Kant, Immanuel 20, 70
Kelly, Tony 98
kenosis 64, 73
Kerr, Fergus 9
Kierkegaard, Søren 85
knowing
and the *ego* 136
theological 66